The WAC Journal

Writing Across the Curriculum
Volume 35
2024

© 2025 Clemson University
Printed on acid-free paper in the USA
ISSN: 1544-4929

Editors

Cameron Bushnell, Clemson University
David Blakesley, Clemson University

Managing Editor

Allison Daniel, Clemson University

Copyeditors

Jessie Reynolds-Clay, Clemson University
Hana Liebman, University of Virginia
Allison Daniel, Clemson University

Editorial Board

Heather Bastian, UNC Charlotte
Kristine Blair, Duquesne U
Jacob S. Blumner, U of Michigan, Flint
Heather Falconer, U of Maine, Orono
Jeffrey Galin, Florida Atlantic U
Xiqiao Wang, U of Pittsburgh
Joanna Wolfe, Carnegie Mellon U
Terry Myers Zawacki, George Mason U

Review Board

William P. Banks, East Carolina University
Mairin Barney, Towson University
Christopher Basgier, Auburn University
Bhushan Aryal, Delaware State University
Allen Brizee, Saint Louis University

Jessica Jorgenson Borchert, Pittsburg State U
Lauren Brentnell, U of Northern Colorado
Amy Cicchino, Auburn U
Geoffrey Clegg, Midwestern State U
Anthony DeGenaro, U of Detroit Mercy
Rasha Diab, U of Texas at Austin
John Eliason, Gonzaga U
Crystal N. Fodrey, Moravian U
Traci Gardner, Virginia Tech U
Analeigh Horton, U of Arizona
Bradley Hughes, U of Wisconsin
Liz Hutter, U of Dayton
Anna Knutson, Duquesne U
Michelle LaFrance, George Mason U
Sean Morey, U of Tennessee, Knoxville
Savannah Paige Murray, Appalachian State U
Lee Nickoson, Bowling Green State U
Sarah Peterson Pittock, Stanford U
Rebecca Pope-Ruark, Elon U
Jenna Pack Sheffield, U of New Haven
Jennifer Ridgeway, Aims Community College
Michelle Stuckey, Arizona State U
Douglas Walls, North Carolina State U
Carrie Wastal, U of California, San Diego
Travis Webster, Virginia Tech U

Additional Reviewers for This Issue

Beth Davila
Mya Poe
Sarah Perrault

Subscription Information

The WAC Journal
Parlor Press
3015 Brackenberry Drive
Anderson SC 29621
wacjournal@parlorpress.com
parlorpress.com/products/wac-journal
Rates: 1 year: $25; 3 years: $65; 5 years: $95.

Submissions

The WAC Journal invites article submissions. The longest-running national peer-reviewed journal dedicated to writing across the curriculum, *The WAC Journal* seeks scholarly work at the intersection of writing with teaching, curriculum, learning, and research. Our review board welcomes inquiries, proposals, and articles from 3,000 to 6,000 words.

We are especially interested in contributions that creatively approach a diverse range of antiracist pedagogies, feminist rhetorics across the curriculum, intersectional contexts of feminism, and international WAC initiatives. Articles focusing on the ways WAC can be fostered in online courses are welcome as well. *The WAC Journal* supports a variety of diverse approaches to, and discussions of, writing across the curriculum. We publish submissions from all WAC scholars that focus on writing across the curriculum, including topics on WAC program strategies, techniques, and applications; emergent technologies and digital literacies across the curriculum; antiracist pedagogies; feminist rhetorics across the curriculum; intersectional contexts of feminism; international WAC initiatives; and writing in the disciplines at the college level.

The WAC Journal is an open-access journal published annually by Clemson University, Parlor Press, and the WAC Clearinghouse. It is available by subscription in print through Parlor Press at https://parlorpress.com/products/wac-journal and online in open-access format at the WAC Clearinghouse via https://wac.colostate.edu/journal/. Articles are accepted throughout the year on a rolling basis.

The peer review process is double-blind, which means all identifying information must be removed from the submission. Any submission notes must be included in the field provided for them, not in a separate cover letter or attachment. Submissions that aren't ready for double-blind review will be returned.

Subscriptions

The WAC Journal is published annually in print by Parlor Press and Clemson University. Digital copies of the journal are simultaneously published at The WAC Clearinghouse in PDF format for free download. Print subscriptions support the ongoing publication of the journal and make it possible to offer digital copies as open access. Subscription rates: One year: $25; Three years: $65; Five years: $95. You can subscribe to *The WAC Journal* and pay securely by credit card or PayPal at the Parlor Press website: https://parlorpress.com/products/wac-journal. Or you can send your name, email address, and mailing address along with a check (payable to Parlor Press) to Parlor Press, 3015 Brackenberry Drive, Anderson SC 29621. Email: sales@parlorpress.com.

Reproduction of material from this publication, with acknowledgement of the source, is hereby authorized for educational use in nonprofit organizations.

The WAC Journal
Volume 35, 2024

Contents

ARTICLES

Leveraging Institutional Circuits to Rethink Writing
Across the Curriculum at Two-Year Colleges   7
Tara Coleman and Dominique Zino

Reflections on Learning: Revision Reflections as Insight into the
Influences on Students' Revisions on a Writing-to-Learn Assignment   29
Solaire A. Finkenstaedt-Quinn, Isabella Sperry,
Alicia Romero, and Ginger V. Shultz

Surviving as Switzerland: WAC, SLW, and the Literacy Myth of
Linguistic Homogeneity   51
Analeigh E. Horton

Practicing Peer Feedback: How Task Repetition and Modeling Affect
Amount and Types of Feedback over a Series of Peer Reviews   74
Lucy Bryan, Dayna S. Henry, Sarah R. Blackstone,
Anna Maria Johnson, and Lacie Knight

STEM Faculty Focus Groups Respond to Student Writing and
Learning Goals: Entry Points and Barriers to Curricular Change   95
Megan Mericle, J. Patrick Coleman, and Julie Zilles

Cross-Disciplinary Solidarity Through Labor-Oriented Research in WAC   123
Lacey Wootton

SPECIAL FORUM: ADULTING WITH WAC

Introduction: Adult Learners in the Composition Classroom   143
Macy Dunklin

The Adult Learner in the Writing Classroom: Creating Value
through Experiential Education   146
JAMIE HUDSON

Resumers in and beyond a Writing-Intensive Preparatory Course:
Challenges, Assets, and Opportunities   165
KENDON KURZER, NATASHA J. LEE, AMY MACIAS-STOWE, MARY HER,
AND NIEVA MANALO

In Our Own Words: Adult Learners on Writing in College   181
COLLIE FULFORD, STEFANIE FRIGO, YASEEN ABDUL-MALIK, THOMAS KELLY,
ADRIENNE LONG, AND STUART PARRISH

Promoting Belonging among Adult Learners through
Sharing and Feedback   195
GABRIELLE ISABEL KELENYI

Contributors   211

Articles

Leveraging Institutional Circuits to Rethink Writing Across the Curriculum at Two-Year Colleges

TARA COLEMAN AND DOMINIQUE ZINO

Especially at large open-access institutions, WAC stakeholders face the challenge of understanding how particular writing skills are being reinforced (or overlooked) at various junctures during a student's career. For WAC to move beyond more isolated writing-to-learn scenarios and to shift how students engage in written communication during the two to three years most spend at a community college, WAC pedagogy needs to be coordinated with and built out of the existing institutional structures with which faculty members are already engaged. In this article, we use the concept of "institutional circuits" to identify networks of writing-related activity on our two-year college campus. Rather than presenting a specific set of recommendations for how to approach WAC at community colleges, this article offers a methodology for studying WAC work on campus that allows scholars and practitioners to think beyond the curriculum itself and attend to the forces that shape faculty choices within it.

Across all institution types, the first two years of higher education represent a crucial moment of exposure to critical literacy tasks, which present students with an opportunity to build on prior knowledge and establish productive habits. Given that nearly half of all recent baccalaureate graduates in the United States began their studies at community colleges, it is essential to develop our understanding of the role these institutions play in promoting writing across the curriculum (WAC).[1] Two-year institutions—sandwiched as they are between the K-12 system

---

1. The Community College Research Center (CCRC) has reported that among "graduates who completed a four-year degree in 2015-2016, 49 percent had been enrolled in a two-year college, and 63 percent of that group were enrolled in a two-year college for three or more terms." During the 2020-2021 academic year, 8.9 million students—41 percent of all undergraduates—were enrolled in community colleges.

and the four-year university, and between the opportunity for a liberal arts education and the demand for employable skills—are tasked with imagining an "elsewhere." As Howard B. Tinberg writes, "To teach at a community college is to be 'in translation' or between places. . . That complexity colors instruction at all times" (vii). Community college faculty are adept at working collaboratively across disciplines and job titles. For instance, faculty members may take on job duties that would be covered by student affairs staff in four-year colleges, and they sometimes work in departments comprising a range of disciplines. They are also often highly attuned to and accountable for intersecting and sometimes competing demands from various constituencies: college and university administrations, regional accrediting agencies, local government, the values and practices of their disciplines, their students, and the public that funds them. Moreover, because community colleges and other open-access institutions by definition do not select the students whom they accept at the outset—and yet have all the same requirements as any other higher education institution to teach students and assess their learning—they are under even more pressure to develop instruments and structures for producing, delivering, and ultimately assessing course content.

Writing across the curriculum efforts emerged in community colleges at the very start of the WAC movement in the 1970s. Scholarship documented these efforts and tracked their growth in the following decades, with some scholar practitioners highlighting an intrinsic alignment between community college missions and WAC principles. Linda Stanley and Joanna Ambron's 1991 book *Writing Across the Curriculum in Community Colleges* showcased a variety of curricular approaches, including the incorporation of WAC into learning communities, writing-intensive courses, and service-learning courses. In the 2010 special issue of *Across the Disciplines* devoted to community colleges, Mary McMullen-Light noted several areas of overlap between WAC ideals and community college values: "inclusiveness, diversity, provid[ing] support, [and placing an] emphasis on learning" (2). However, after three decades of scholarship that made a point of including two-year institutions in the scholarly conversation about WAC (see Blau; Pacht; Reiss; Rose and Theilheimer; Stanley and Ambron), a dearth of research sources from the 2010s onward suggests that more recent attention to the various manifestations of WAC in two-year college contexts has been limited. During this period, several other institutional forces at two-year colleges have shifted, including but not limited to new demands for assessment, the retooling of general education pathways, and the adoption of new learning management systems and other digital platforms. At present, community colleges face a range of challenges, from enrollment declines (caused by a combination of demographic shifts and the COVID-19 pandemic)[2] to growing pressure to increase retention and graduation rates, decrease time to degree, and justify the value of a two-year college education. What is the impact of today's institutional realities on the forms of engagement with WAC that we find at community colleges? And how can we adopt approaches to studying WAC efforts at these institutions that enable us to learn from and build on the forms of engagement that already exist?

In this article, our aim is not to measure the level of engagement with WAC at community colleges today—not to collect data on program size, the number of students taking writing-intensive courses, or the number of faculty certified to teach such courses—but to look more closely at the nature of that engagement. We examine the conditions in which faculty at our community college generate writing assignments; in particular, we are interested in the broader institutional forces that, from the perspective of faculty members, shape the culture of writing at the institution. As Mike Palmquist et al. have reminded us, the "use of writing to support disciplinary learning, a key tenet of WAC, is among the first pedagogical approaches identified by the Association of American Colleges and Universities as 'high-impact practices.'" Yet WAC can only be "high-impact" when an institution creates consistent pathways for faculty and other stakeholders to think and talk about how the writing happening in individual classrooms relates to what is happening across the entire curriculum. Especially at a large open-access institution, it is challenging, but necessary, for faculty to understand how particular writing skills are being reinforced (or overlooked) at various junctures during a student's career and adjust their pedagogy accordingly. For WAC to move beyond more isolated writing-to-learn scenarios and to shift how students engage in written communication during the two to three years most spend at a community college, WAC pedagogy needs to be coordinated with and built out of the existing institutional structures with which faculty members are already engaged.

We follow sociologists Alison I. Griffith and Dorothy E. Smith's use of the term *institutional circuits* to name how individuals coordinate their work with institutional expectations. Griffith and Smith define institutional circuits as "recognizable and traceable sequences of institutional action in which work is done to produce texts that select from actualities to build textual representations fitting an authoritative or 'boss' text" (12). As part of the methodology of institutional ethnography, following institutional circuits contextualizes the work taking place in classrooms within often invisible power relations at the local level, while also revealing how trends in the landscape of higher education play out in the particular contexts under examination. As

---

2. The CCRC reports that the pandemic "led to steep enrollment drops at community colleges but enrollment seems to be recovering. The National Student Clearinghouse Research Center estimates that enrollment in public two-year colleges in fall 2023 grew by 4.4% from fall 2022."

we will detail more fully below, we use the concept of institutional circuits to describe how we, as researchers and WAC proponents on our campus, identify networks of writing-related activity. WAC leaders can learn from the ways faculty members navigate institutional power dynamics and negotiate with textual representations of institutional priorities in order to promote writing amidst this ever-shifting landscape. In this article, rather than presenting a specific set of recommendations for how to approach WAC at community colleges, we offer a *methodology* for studying WAC work on campus that allows scholars and practitioners to think beyond the curriculum itself and attend to the forces that shape faculty choices within it.

Motive and Method for Our Study

This article reports on the results of a study of the factors that influence faculty decision-making around the incorporation of reading and writing assignments into courses at a large, urban community college. We both teach in the English department and currently serve as two of three codirectors of the writing program, which is notably separate from the college's writing in the disciplines (WID) initiative. As a result of significant changes to placement and developmental education in recent years, our writing program has been focused on how students arrive in our courses and how to prepare them for successfully completing our first-year composition sequence. In this research project, we wanted to shift the focus by learning more about the types of assignments being used outside our two one-hundred-level composition courses and how those assignments reflect faculty members' personal, programmatic, general education, and professional goals for their students.

Many larger-scale studies of faculty writing assignments across disciplines exist (e.g. Melzer; Soliday; Yancey, Robertson and Taczak). For example, while Dan Melzer and Mary Soliday focus primarily on analyzing features of writing assignments and the rhetorical situations students are asked to engage with, Kathleen Blake Yancey, Liane Robertson, and Kara Taczak discuss how to support students' transfer of writing knowledge and practices. We wanted to know not only what faculty do but *why*, and how faculty choices may be influenced by the multifaceted mission of our institution. Our study foregrounds the experiences of faculty who are experimenting with WAC and WID concepts, and contextualizes this work amidst the complex institutional forces that they encounter. Inspired in part by the systems approach developed by Michelle Cox, Jeffrey Galin, and Dan Melzer, which offers a way of identifying various "moving parts" in large networks to support more sustainable WAC program development, we have tried to understand how faculty design writing assignments within a system of institutional directives and material resources. To unpack the relationship between the individual experiences of teachers using writing in their courses and the institutional forces that influence their decisions, we turned to a methodology known as institutional ethnography.

Institutional ethnographers tie together "the local setting where life is lived and experienced by actual people and the extra-local that is outside the boundaries of one's everyday experience" (Campbell and Gregor 29). They analyze the discourse individuals use to describe their practices and pay particular attention to institutional texts and their role in coordinating work. Michelle LaFrance calls this a process of "looking up" to "tell a story about the ways personal experiences and work practices have been reflexively contoured by the material and discursive conditions" of the institution, while at the same time revealing "variations, disjunctions, disagreements or absences" in those conditions (31). In this study, we reveal how the range of decisions faculty members make around the implementation of writing-based pedagogies are "reflexively contoured"—but not fully determined—by existing approaches to curriculum design and assessment at our college. Institutional ethnography as a method uncovers the "ruling relations"—or hierarchical social relations—that coordinate an individual's activities, but it is equally interested in when and why the actualities of work fail to fully conform to the framework established by those ruling relations (Griffith and Smith 16). By tracing these realities which IE calls "problematics," the institutional ethnographer identifies potential sites for productive intervention.

At the outset of our study, we identified two key sets of documents that we assumed would coordinate the work of faculty members at our college: faculty syllabi and the degree maps provided to students as a suggested sequence of courses for their program. Taken together, these documents (syllabi and degree maps) are examples of "powerful institutional apparatus[es]" that are "authorized through institutional procedures" (LaFrance 82–83). To understand how reading and writing are approached in a cross section of disciplines, we focused on the seven most popular majors at the college: business administration, criminal justice, liberal arts: math and science, liberal arts: social sciences and humanities, nursing, computer science, and psychology. Using the degree maps designed for these majors, we identified courses at the early, mid- and late stages of each program (see Appendix 1). We presumed that writing tasks would increase in complexity as students moved through their programs. After identifying full-time and part-time faculty members who had recently taught these courses, we contacted a faculty member for each one, inviting them to share their syllabus in advance and participate in a one-hour interview. We also brought the relevant degree map for the program containing that course to the interview. Although adopting a departmental syllabus is a clear attempt to coordinate faculty choices regarding course design, we wanted to know if the degree map similarly impacts how faculty design writing assignments in the context of the sequence of courses students are expected to take.

Hour-long interviews with faculty members helped us to learn more about the role of particular assignments and courses in serving the learning goals of each degree program. Initially, we targeted approximately forty-five courses for our study to "map" the types of assignments students encountered in these seven programs. We began our study in the fall of 2019, but the onset of the COVID-19 pandemic in early 2020 disrupted both our funding and our ability to conduct interviews. The following analysis reflects the results of the nineteen interviews we were able to complete (see Appendix 2 for our list of questions). At the time of our interviews, two faculty were adjuncts, one was a full-time lecturer, five were assistant professors, nine were associate professors, and two were full professors. Ten faculty from across the assistant, associate, and full professor ranks were either program directors or course coordinators; while these administrative roles vary across departments, they generally include scheduling sections, hiring and/or communicating with adjunct faculty, and coordinating curriculum and assessment processes, among other tasks.

We noticed that particularly when it came to the use of writing, participants reported a lot more variation in the assignments and activities used by instructors teaching the same course than we had expected—even in cases where a standardized departmental syllabus was used. While faculty members' choices were still influenced by the ruling relations of the institution—particularly when it came to assessment—they were finding creative ways of working within, and sometimes around, the requirements in order to serve other learning goals, such as disciplinary or professional expectations for students. Our analysis below reveals the institutional and extra-institutional factors which influence a faculty member's decision to assign certain types of writing in their course, as well as the extent to which they consider the types of writing students do at other stages of their program when making those decisions. By using institutional ethnography, we traced how faculty members' participation in a variety of networks at the college, along with other professional experiences and/or disciplinary expertise, have led them to build writing into their courses. We followed how individual faculty members coordinate their work with writing in the course with what they understand to be the expectations and values of colleagues in the same department, at the college, at four-year institutions, or in their discipline or profession at large. Drawing on this methodology to identify and build on existing networks and values offers a prime opportunity for enhancing WAC in a community college setting, or at any institution where size, funding, or other institutional dynamics limit the potential for starting or expanding a formal WAC program.

Site of Study: Current Circumstances at our Community College

The WAC program at our college is limited in its scope and resources, primarily consisting of a semester-long writing in the disciplines professional development seminar that prepares faculty to teach writing-intensive courses. In the seminar, faculty discuss how to implement writing-to-learn techniques, guide students through reading difficult texts, evaluate student writing, and so on. They also develop high-stakes and low-stakes writing assignments, a grading rubric, and a writing intensive course syllabus. Originally a year-long program with up to fifty participants a year, due to a gradual erosion of funding and administrative support, participation in WID has dwindled (Pacht, "Email interview"). Our situation mirrors McMullen-Light's observation that although in the 1990s there was an emphasis on making sure WAC programs "institutionalized" rather than remaining at the level of an "initiative" or an "add-on," many community college programs have been unable to sustain that broader institutional investment over time (13). Outside of the semester-long WID seminar, faculty do not have a formalized way to continue their exploration of WAC pedagogy. In addition, neither the college's writing program nor its writing center have regular communication with the WAC program.

The current state of WAC at our institution is therefore in line with McMullen-Light's observation that rather than fostering independent WAC programs, community colleges organically seem to "promote the infusion of various new initiatives that emerge through various institutional agendas and don't require the same level of oversight [that] a WAC program does" (2). An example of such an initiative is general education outcomes assessment, which McMullen-Light notes became "a high priority of some accrediting agencies" in the 1990s (6). On our campus, general education assessment has indeed become an important site of faculty work with student writing across the curriculum. The college assesses courses across every program using three core competencies: integrative learning, inquiry and problem solving, and global learning. These competencies are demonstrated using three communication abilities: written, oral, and digital. Each program creates a curriculum map that specifies which courses are to be assessed for which competency and ability in the early, mid- and late stages of a student's degree. The college collects written, oral, and/or digital artifacts from students which are assessed annually by faculty across the college using rubrics derived from the AAC&U's VALUE rubrics. Annual benchmark readings, which include norming sessions and a post-scoring discussion, provide an opportunity for faculty across the college to discuss students' written work. In the first few years after the college adopted the competency and ability rubrics, assignment-design workshops were regularly held with the goal of designing assignment materials to target these goals, while the data from annual assessments is used (to varying degrees, depending on the program) to inform assignment revisions and additional support measures for students.

The college provides strong administrative and financial support for this work, which has led to year-on-year improvements in scores for written artifacts from when the rubric was adopted in 2015 through 2022. As we will discuss further below, many faculty have found creative ways to work both within and around this assessment framework at the college to promote writing within their programs and individual courses that meets their own pedagogical goals, while also helping the college meet its targets. At the same time, the intense focus on mapping assessment benchmarks onto the curriculum makes the existence of writing-focused assignment development outside assessment contexts nearly invisible at the college.

In the discussion of our results below, we will analyze the benefits and limitations of drawing on alternative networks for developing faculty engagement with student writing across the curriculum. McMullen-Light suggests that instead of mandates, such as a formal writing-intensive course requirement, a more effective way to grow a WAC program at a community college might be to "fold WAC into existing priorities and initiatives by demonstrating how it can assist with achieving their goals" (8). Our study identified several ways that writing work is happening outside the scope of formal curricular requirements. We argue that creating more opportunities for faculty to consider how their efforts connect to a student's other experiences with writing at the college would be more effective than a one-time, classroom-centered WID/WAC workshop model in truly building a student's writing skills over the course of their degree program. Learning from the most prominent of these efforts, such as reforms in assessment, can pave the way for identifying and building on a more diverse range of such opportunities.

Discussion of Results

Searching for "Boss Texts"

Through this study, we intended to trace how curricular frameworks may have impacted our participants' course design and pedagogy. Before turning to a discussion of institutional circuits, we want to acknowledge that we entered our investigation with certain assumptions about the impact of what institutional ethnographers call *boss texts*. Boss texts are documents that organize people's activities and "*transmit ruling relations between sites—carrying rhetorical influence, granting agency and authority, casting representations of people and their work, and sanctioning activities*" (LaFrance 42; original emphasis). In other words, boss texts represent individuals' work within the "objectified categories and concepts of the institution," making the actualities of the work "institutionally actionable" (339). Given our interest in understanding how and why faculty across the curriculum assign writing in their courses, we identified two types of boss texts we imagined might have influence on their decisions: degree maps and course syllabi. We focused on how our interviewees described these documents in order to explore the extent to which these texts structure the choices faculty members make about writing in their courses.

Degree maps, created for each major or program, recommend a course sequence, semester by semester, that enables students to graduate in two years. Students, faculty members, staff, and administrators all engage with them. We targeted faculty participants who frequently taught courses listed on the degree map; some also coordinated those courses, meaning they were responsible for determining the curricula and ensuring instructors followed it. We asked interviewees to discuss whether they thought students were generally following the sequence of recommended courses presented on the degree maps before and during the semester in which they took the target course, and then, what types of reading and writing experiences they thought their students had been exposed to previously. Despite the fact that administrators, department chairs, and program directors devoted significant time and effort to making these maps, and they are used regularly for advising purposes, we were surprised to discover that they did not guide faculty choices with regard to how they assigned writing in their courses. Even those faculty with experience as program directors or course coordinators tended to focus on program's core course sequences rather than the relationship between general education courses and their own programmatic requirements. The responses we received indicated to us that degree maps do less to aid faculty members in thinking about their course as part of a broader curriculum than one might expect given their widespread use for program development and advising purposes.

Participants pointed to two specific challenges that might indicate why degree maps organize behavior to a lesser extent than we anticipated: first, faculty recognize that a sizable number of students deviate from the suggested pathway, making it difficult to presume much about their prior learning experiences; students may put off courses they perceive to be most difficult, retake courses they previously failed, transfer in from another institution, or change programs midway through the course sequence. Secondly, faculty participants did not seem to view these recommended course sequences as prompts to inquire about their students' prior reading and writing experiences. Only seven of the nineteen faculty members we interviewed named a specific type of writing assignment or skill they expected students to have encountered previously. These participants mentioned either research papers or knowledge of citation formats, with only faculty members who had taught the previous courses themselves giving further details. Eleven of the nineteen participants mentioned English 101 (the only course required of all students at the college) as a prerequisite for work in later courses, but most faculty members simply discussed their general impressions of students' reading and/or writing abilities coming into their courses.

After asking faculty members about how their course relates to other courses students take, we asked them to discuss the assignments on their syllabus in more detail. We were especially interested in how they spoke about the role of writing in achieving course goals, as well as the various departmental, college, and professional expectations that impact course design. Some courses have a departmentally designated syllabus, but even in those that do not, an individual faculty member's syllabus needs to adhere to course requirements approved by departmental and college curriculum committees. We asked faculty members to discuss writing assignments on their syllabus as well as any other writing opportunities they provide in their classes. In some courses, where calculations, homework, and exams were the focus of the assignments on the syllabus, faculty members spoke about incorporating writing that is not a required part of the course. In some cases, this additional writing was low-stakes while in others, it involved replacing an exam with a term paper as in one accounting course. Several faculty spoke about personal or disciplinary motivations for these choices. For example, a natural sciences professor explained that he was working with a colleague to develop scientific literacy among students who were taking their one and only science class as a graduation requirement, inspired by a desire to make his course more like the liberal arts classes he took in college which "were more about thinking about the subject, not about . . . facts and figures." A social science professor, meanwhile, described how her expertise in developmental psychology informs her approach to teaching, where she tries to help students understand how learning happens. Rather than a lecture-based approach, she said that "the bigger thing is to try to engage them in the doing. And that's one of the big reasons for doing the writing because the more they write, the better they're going to get at what they're doing." In other cases, participants were influenced by what they had learned in a professional development seminar about the use of writing to achieve pedagogical goals, such as one mathematics faculty member, who learned about short, generally writing-based classroom assessment techniques in her new faculty seminar and still uses them in her class several years later. In all of these instances, participants expressed a sense that colleagues teaching the same course were likely not doing the same things with writing as they were, though these participants did not see themselves operating in a vacuum. Those who felt that their practice was not shared by colleagues in the same program aligned their choices with what they understood to be the expectations or practices of colleagues at other institutions, especially four-year colleges, or in the profession. At the same time, those in positions of leadership for their course or program expressed hesitation in pushing colleagues to change their approach too quickly, mentioning considerations of workload (for adjunct colleagues in particular) and academic freedom.

Like degree maps, syllabi also turned out not to be productive boss texts for learning about what happens with writing at the college. Tracking syllabi across programs was less effective than we thought it would be for learning about how writing is used in each academic program, and it proved to be an unreliable guide to what kinds of writing were actually happening in individual classrooms. Although deviations from the syllabus sometimes revealed exciting experiments with writing, they also reminded us that these innovations were far from being widespread enough to be considered part of the curriculum. At community colleges, a focus on "momentum" and degree completion has put strong pressure on faculty and staff to prioritize student movement through the defined pathway above all else (see Isserles). Yet our faculty interviews revealed a large degree of variation from the picture these standardized documents present of the curriculum. We assumed our public, two-year college was the kind of text-saturated and document-driven environment that would align with the operating procedures of the public sector workers that institutional ethnographers like Griffith, Smith, Marie Campbell, and Frances Gregor study. For example, Griffith and Smith's book *Under New Public Management* is a collection of institutional ethnographies that describe how institutional mandates and corresponding boss texts shape the work of public sector employees. Instead, we found that the boss texts rarely standardized faculty behavior to the extent they appeared to do. Faculty members' choices were clearly informed by these texts, but they were often actively negotiating with them rather than simply finding ways to serve their mandates. As Griffith and Smith write in their introduction to *Under New Public Management*, a collection of institutional ethnographies that describe how institutional mandates and corresponding boss texts shape the work of public sector employees, "when services provided directly to people are required to be performed in ways that are representable textually in a standardized and measurable form," and "[h]owever ingenious the technologies [for doing so], the disjuncture between textual realities produced to fit frames established in boss texts and the actualities of what is going on in people's lives remains as an obstinate presence" (18).

Leveraging Institutional Circuits to Strengthen WAC's Impact on Campus

Although our data revealed the limitations of boss texts in providing a map of how writing is used across the curriculum, our conversations with faculty members indicated that institutional ruling relations still impacted their decision-making around writing, only in more complex ways. When discussing their choices about assigning writing, the faculty members who spoke most comprehensively about the link between their course and writing taking place across the curriculum were those actively involved in initiatives at the college which gave them consistent opportunities to communicate with colleagues about their courses. In other words, these faculty members were participants in key institutional circuits—processes in which they coordinated their work with colleagues in alignment with institutional priorities. For institutional ethnographers, identifying the circuits is not the *product* of the research but the *method* through which the researcher comes to understand how the individuals under study produce texts to enable institutionally sanctioned action. Our interviews with faculty demonstrated that boss texts did not fully prescribe faculty choices, but they did often create the framework within which faculty could make their assignments institutionally legible and therefore actionable. In this context, the concept of institutional circuits highlights how texts must be activated within existing networks and pathways of meaning to have an impact. Understanding how faculty work within existing frameworks to achieve goals that meet, sometimes exceed, or evade the aims of the institution provides insight into how WAC work can be woven into preexisting efforts on campus. In the remainder of this article, we will focus on general education assessment and ePortfolio as two prime examples of institutional circuits.

Assessment as an Institutional Circuit

The most prominent example of how faculty worked together to build writing assignments that fit an existing institutional discourse was in relation to assessment. Faculty members who were (or had previously been) a program director or course coordinator expressed a sense of responsibility to show that their program had met the relevant benchmarks. Yet program directors also seemed to understand how to work within assessment requirements to achieve a range of goals for their course. A coordinator in the mathematics, engineering, and computer science department described doing research into how to design open-ended assignments for his general education mathematics course where students must "expound upon their thinking." As a professor in his tenth year at the college who previously worked in industry, he expressed a personal inclination to adopt writing-to-learn pedagogies, but used the college's general education assessment categories to institutionalize this approach:

> I would [teach this way] anyway . . . but the fact that there is an IPS core requirement [i.e., a general education assessment of inquiry and problem solving skills] allows me to find one high-stake or medium-stake assignment in there. In terms of the norms of the department there's no post-req, so I don't have that requirement. Systemically. It's more a question of, you know, my own conscience. . . . I'm the course coordinator and I do try to leave my faculty, my colleagues, with free reign.

He understands this assignment, which is assessed for both IPS and the written ability, as part of an important set of skills for "composition in general." To him, this means the "idea of trying to write about things that are inherently quantitative and trying to be clear," which he emphasizes over preparing students for future mathematics courses, because they are not likely to have any. Although he expressed frustration about seeing a faculty syllabus and assignment that presented the course he coordinates as something closer to a remedial algebra course, rather than one focused on quantitative reasoning and using written responses to explicate mathematical equations, he hoped that situating his assignment within the IPS requirement would make it more likely that colleagues will eventually adopt the approach.

In another case, a natural sciences course coordinator, who was making curricular changes in response to programmatic needs, strategically aligned these efforts with assessment targets to gain institutional support. This faculty member was working with his department chair to improve how their program teaches students to write lab reports. He explained that the assessment process provided an opportunity for his faculty to discuss student writing, but that it was difficult to use a college-wide written communication rubric to assess writing in lab reports, so his department was now developing its own rubric. Taking a scaffolded approach to building students' skills in writing lab reports, he helped to implement a series of ten lab reports over the course of the semester, with the first five providing an opportunity for students to become familiar with the genre of a lab report and the last five serving as parts to be compiled into a final, larger lab report. When we asked about the use of low-stakes writing to explain a scientific concept, however, he noted that in order to meet digital and oral communication requirements, the program asked students to verbalize a narrative of what they were doing in an experiment and post that on their ePortfolio. This example reveals one of the limitations of relying on the assessment process to help implement writing across the curriculum, because the separate assessment of the written, oral, and digital abilities leads to a segmented approach. Conceptualized from the perspective of WAC, this course could use writing to support these low-stakes assignments by asking students to script or, after the fact, to transcribe their recorded narratives. Instead, the potential role of writing in building analytical skills is less visible because assignments are treated as individual artifacts separate from the broader learning context.

By contrast, a faculty member who came to the college with experience at writing centers, and who coordinates the college's technical writing course, created what she calls a "global technical report," that is assessed as a global learning assignment while still reflecting her own expertise in writing-to-learn approaches. She told us that the assignment was influenced by both her humanities background and research into engineering pedagogy (the course is required primarily of engineering students). She said,

> If you follow the trends in engineering education, engineering scholars want to help engineering students develop a more global learning mindset because engineers do work a lot in places that they're not familiar with and cultures they're not familiar with. So this technical report asks them to identify some kind of global problem that happens in the world. . . . [T]hey find out what's causing the problem, what's the background, the cultural context, the political scenario around this problem. . . . Then they look at what solutions engineers can provide. . . . The goal of this is to get them to enlarge their understanding of what engineering is. . . . [I]t's about the people who use [a certain tool] and how it might help or hurt the local environment.

This faculty member pushed to get this course, previously overlooked both in the English department and at the college, put "on the map" as a global learning course. At the same time, her knowledge of writing pedagogy led her to approach this assignment with a focus on process: "I want [students] to understand that there's more to being an engineer than just devising the product." Not only did the faculty member revise the technical report assignment, but she adapted the entire course to "enlarge students' understanding" of the role of writing in professions like engineering. She emphasized "clear, concise writing" as integral to technical writing, as well as attention to the "rhetorical aspects of writing" on all assignments. In this case, rather than just bringing in writing to serve assessment targets, the faculty member leveraged assessment targets to incorporate writing-to-learn throughout the course.

While the frequency with which general education assessment came up in our interviews revealed that it was an important organizing framework coordinating the use of writing in a range of programs, presenting writing as only one of six competencies and abilities at the college has the potential to undermine WAC's guiding principle that writing is a tool for learning in all situations. In order for WAC to flourish on community college campuses (or any campuses where general education assessment reigns supreme), WAC coordinators can use examples of how faculty members successfully worked within assessment mandates to achieve writing-to-learn pedagogies; in this way, they can "flip" the assessment script and demonstrate for faculty across disciplines how writing is not a singular component but, rather, the backbone for the full body of competencies and abilities being assessed.

ePortfolio as an Institutional Circuit

Like general education assessment, an institutional circuit related to the use of ePortfolios at the college provides both a challenge and an opportunity for building writing across the curriculum. Every entering student creates an ePortfolio in a first-year seminar, using a template and a series of writing prompts that are customized to their major. They then return to these ePortfolios throughout their career at the college, to varying degrees depending on the program. In our interviews, multiple faculty referenced ePortfolios as a site of writing: the natural sciences course coordinator discussed above mentioned uploading labs to ePortfolio to create connections for students between general chemistry I and II; a lecturer in business and technology mentioned assigning an ePortfolio reflection for extra credit; and a nursing faculty member described ePortfolio reflections students wrote about their clinical experience as well as assignments like "data action responses," a description of patient symptoms and the resulting action taken. In programs like nursing, where ePortfolio prompts are the main vehicle for writing and assessing student writing, the college's promotion of ePortfolio has clearly enabled greater engagement with certain modes of and contexts for writing.

ePortfolio is a flexible tool to which the college devotes significant budgetary and administrative resources. In the prior examples, we see faculty members leveraging this institutional circuit to do work that meets their own learning goals. At the same time, this approach has its limits in terms of what it can provide for students: in the nursing program, for example, the pressures of an extensive course of study culminating in a stringent licensing exam leave faculty members little time to work with students on writing, so these reflections are graded pass/fail and do not allow time for drafting. Considering how the built-in ePortfolio writing prompts tend to be designed by the college's ePortfolio support team, we realized that they, too, can act as digital boss texts that structure how faculty assign, how students complete, and how the college assesses student writing. (In fact, one social science professor noted, "Maybe writing on ePortfolio makes [students] feel like they can write less.") As with assessment efforts, ePortfolio as a platform provides many opportunities for integrating writing across the curriculum both horizontally (across departments) and vertically (throughout the student's time at the college). To marshal the latent potential of this institutional circuit, WAC coordinators would need to give faculty the opportunity to reflect on how their use of writing in ePortfolios relates to students' broader writing development. Doing so might encourage both faculty and students to engage with ePortfolio as a space of exploration through writing that captures a student's holistic growth over time, rather than as a checklist of items to complete to meet certain course requirements.

As members of the institution ourselves, these interviews helped us to remember that even in the case of externally driven institutional priorities, the texts which coordinate faculty work within institutional circuits are often composed predominantly by faculty and, as such, are capable of being revised by faculty. As Griffith and Smith remind us, institutional circuits "impose an order of standardized representation on the tough recalcitrance of people-work actualities that *never quite fit* the frames established by the institutional boss texts" (16; emphasis added). Our interviews revealed the productive potential of thinking about curricular work, not in the binary terms of fealty versus resistance to administrative demands (communicated through boss texts), but in terms of coordinated efforts to negotiate within and respond to those demands over time. By observing how faculty work within these different institutional circuits, we can learn about effective approaches to developing writing-oriented initiatives from the inside out, rather than from the top down.

Conclusion

Rather than identify model pedagogical approaches that distinguish the work going on at our institution, we have sought to demonstrate a methodology that can enable both WAC leaders and faculty members to think more systematically about how their work in individual classes fits into larger initiatives related to writing. In our college, we found that although certain documents, like degree maps and course syllabi, were products of faculty members' collaborative curricular efforts, there was no sustained circuit of activity surrounding these documents after they had been created. By contrast, general education assessment and ePortfolio practices had significant administrative support, which provided regular opportunities for faculty members to communicate and coordinate their work in these areas. Faculty members looking to incorporate more writing into their courses had a variety of reasons for doing so, but several had strategically linked those efforts to these preexisting institutional circuits, providing a model for how to make WAC work more effective and sustainable in the long term.

Notably, the faculty members who were most successful in navigating institutional circuits were those with experience as program directors or course coordinators, roles that combine curricular responsibilities with a range of other administrative duties. Faculty members without this expertise may not be aware of how to enter into these circuits and/or produce the textual representations necessary to make their work legible within them. This study suggests that documents intending to coordinate individual work need to be made more visible and accessible to those who may wish to take them up. For example, while degree maps are often used in advising conversations with students, faculty members who are neither program directors nor mentors may not regularly consult these maps; as a result, they do not have the opportunity to reflect on both students' prior knowledge from past courses and how to prepare them for courses to come. Likewise, as part of this study we requested from assessment coordinators on our campus the list of which courses in our seven target degree programs submit student artifacts annually to be assessed using the college's written ability rubric. While faculty generally know when a course they are teaching requires an assignment to be deposited for assessment, and while those involved in programmatic decision-making are aware of which courses across the program are assessed for which competencies and abilities, only those involved in assessment leadership at the college typically review the full set of courses being assessed. We noted that none of our participants spoke about their assignments designated for assessment as part of a sequence in which students build writing skills over time, from their first semester up through their capstone course. This was unsurprising, given that none of them had access to the document listing the full set of courses being assessed for their program and that the document itself only included which courses deposit for which competencies and abilities, not the types of writing being done for each deposited assignment. Having access to information about the assignments being assessed in the courses on students' degree maps would help faculty begin to consider their writing assignments designated for assessment as part of a broader developmental sequence.

As the Statement on WAC Principles and Practices reminds us, "WAC is not a 'quick fix,' but an initiative that requires sustained conversations among faculty that extend beyond a single workshop or consultation" (Cox et al., "Statement" 1–2). Opportunities for sustained conversations are mostly lacking at our college, though our interviews showed that there is clearly an appetite for it among colleagues across the institution. In a time when ongoing budgetary constraints make initiating or expanding a formal, freestanding, and securely funded WAC program nearly impossible, our research reminds us that such an effort is neither necessary nor likely to be the most effective. Instead, community college faculty and administrators should consider how to adopt WAC principles to support existing goals and structures, such as general education assessment and other high-impact practices, in order to stitch WAC pedagogy more intentionally across and throughout the curriculum.

Looking ahead to the next steps for our college and other two-year, open-access institutions, we have sought to demonstrate that rather than envisioning a stand-alone "program" as the inception point for WAC work at community colleges, it may be more useful to study how WAC efforts correspond with other college initiatives and goals, to ask faculty across disciplines how they are engaging their students through writing and then to facilitate connections between people, processes, and goals in order to make this work legible within institutional priorities and therefore ensure its lasting support. This work may come more naturally to faculty members at two-year colleges who (as we have detailed above) are accustomed to working in interdisciplinary environments, are attuned to the range of transfer and career options their students may pursue, and are generally accepting of the reality that they are accountable to various constituencies at once. Regulatory frameworks and calls for compliance will persist, but institutional ethnography as a methodology can support two-year faculty members' professional authority by highlighting institutionally specific, actionable circuits and by helping faculty draw insights from them. Taking up institutional ethnography as a methodology requires us to ask not only what is happening with writing on our campuses but also *how* it happens.

Works Cited

Blau, Sheridan. "Academic Writing as Participation: Writing Your Way In." *What Is "College-Level" Writing? Volume 2: Assignments, Readings, and Student Writing Samples*, edited by Patrick Sullivan, Howard Tinberg, and Sheridan Blau, National Council of Teachers of English, 2010, pp. 29–56.

Campbell, Marie, and Frances Gregor. *Mapping Social Relations: A Primer in Doing Institutional Ethnography.* Garamond Press, 2004.

Community College Research Center. "Community College FAQs." *Community College Research Center*, https://ccrc.tc.columbia.edu/Community-College-FAQs.html. Accessed 16 Jan. 2024.

Cox, Michelle, et al. "Statement of WAC Principles and Practices." *WAC Clearinghouse*, Dec. 2014, https://wac.colostate.edu/docs/principles/statement.pdf.

Cox, Michelle, et al. *Sustainable WAC: A Whole Systems Approach to Launching and Developing Writing Across the Curriculum Programs.* National Council of Teachers of English, 2018.

Griffith, Alison I., and Dorothy E. Smith. *Under New Public Management: Institutional Ethnographies of Changing Front-Line Work*. University of Toronto Press, 2014.

Ihara, Rachel and Annie Del Principe. "What We Mean When We Talk About Reading." *Across the Disciplines*, vol. 15, no. 2, 2018, pp. 1-14, https://wac.colostate.edu/docs/atd/articles/ihara-delprincipe2018.pdf. Accessed 23 June 2025.

Isserles, Robin. "Make Community Colleges More Joyful." *Inside Higher Ed*, 28 Aug. 2022, https://www.insidehighered.com/views/2022/08/29/make-community-colleges-more-joyful-opinion.

LaFrance, Michelle. *Institutional Ethnography: A Theory of Practice for Writing Studies Researchers*. University Press of Colorado, 2019.

McMullen-Light, Mary. "Great Expectations: The Culture of WAC and the Community College Context." *Across the Disciplines*, special issue of *Writing Across the Curriculum at the Community Colleges*, vol 8, no. 3, 2010. *WAC Clearinghouse*, doi:10.37514/ATD-J.2010.7.2.02.

Melzer, Dan. *Assignments across the Curriculum: A National Study of College Writing*. Utah State University Press, 2014.

Pacht, Michelle. Email interview. 4 Oct. 2022.

Pacht, Michelle. "Overcoming Obstacles: How WID Benefits Community College Students and Faculty." *Across the Disciplines*, special issue of *Writing Across the Curriculum at the Community Colleges*, vol 8, no. 3, 2010. *WAC Clearinghouse*, doi:10.37514/ATD-J.2010.7.2.03.

Palmquist, Mike, et al. "Introduction: Fifty Years of WAC: Where Have We Been? Where Are We Going?" *Across the Disciplines*, vol. 17, 2020. *WAC Clearinghouse*, doi:10.37514/ATD-J.2020.17.3.0X.

Reiss, Donna. "From WAC to CCCAC: Writing Across the Curriculum Becomes Communication, Collaboration, and Critical Thinking (and Computers) Across the Curriculum at Tidewater Community College." *Education Resources Information Center*, 1996, https://files.eric.ed.gov/fulltext/ED412553.pdf.

Rose, Lisa, and Rachel Theilheimer. "You Write What You Know: Writing, Learning, and Student Construction of Knowledge." *The WAC Journal*, vol. 13, 2002, pp. 17–29. *WAC Clearinghouse*, doi:10.37514/WAC-J.2002.13.1.03.

Soliday, Mary. *Everyday Genres: Writing Assignments across the Disciplines*. Southern Illinois University Press, 2011.

Stanley, Linda, and Joanna Ambron, editors. *Writing Across the Curriculum in Community Colleges*. Jossey-Bass, 1991.

Tinberg, Howard B. *Border Talk: Writing and Knowing in the Two-Year College*. National Council of Teachers of English, 1997.

Yancey, Kathleen Blake, et al. *Writing across Contexts: Transfer, Composition, and Sites of Writing*. University Press of Colorado, 2014.

Appendix 1: Targeted Departments and Courses

Departments	Target Courses from Programmatic Degree Maps (Early-, Mid-, and Late-Stage)	Number of Faculty Participants (n = 19)
Business & Technology	BTF101 (First-Year Seminar for Business) BTM101 (Introduction to Business) BTM103 (Principles of Management) BTA111 (Principles of Accounting) BTC200 (Intro to Info Systems)	2
Health Sciences	HSF090 (First-Year Seminar for Health Science) SCR100 (Fundamentals of Nursing) and/or SCL101 (Fundamentals of Practical Nursing) SCL 103 (Concepts in Pharmacology and Nutrition) SCL114 (Parent-Child Nursing) and/or SCR270 (Parent-Child Health Nursing) SCB203 (Anatomy and Physiology) SCR 280 (Leadership and Delegation)	3

Departments	Target Courses from Programmatic Degree Maps (Early-, Mid-, and Late-Stage)	Number of Faculty Participants (n = 19)
Natural Sciences	SCB/C/P101 (Topics in Biological Sciences/Chemistry/Physics) SCC201 (General Chemistry I) SCP231 or SCP232 (General Physics I or II)	4
Social Sciences (Psychology, History, & Criminal Justice)	SYF101 (First-Year Seminar for Psychology) SSP101 (US Politics and Power) SSY101 (General Psychology) SSH102 (Themes in American History since 1865) SSA101 (Cultural Anthropology) SSS100 (Introduction to Sociology) SSN 187 (Urban Sociology) SSN204 (Crime and Justice in Urban Society) SSY230 (Abnormal Psychology)/SSY240 (Developmental Psychology I)/SSY250 (Social Psychology) CJF101 (First-Year Seminar for Criminal Justice) SSJ202 (Corrections and Sentencing) SSJ203 (Policing)	6
English	ENG101 (Composition I) ENG102 (Composition II) ENG103 (The Research Paper) ENG259 (Technical Writing)	1
Math, Engineering, & Computer Science	MAT107 (Mathematics and the Modern World) MAT115 (College Algebra and Trigonometry) MAT120 (Elementary Statistics) MAT201 (Calculus I) ECF090 (First-Year Seminar for Engineering) MAC102 (C/C++ Programming) MAE219 (Thermodynamics I)	2
English Language Acquisition	ELL101 (Introduction to Language)	1

Appendix 2: List of Interview Questions

1. What is your current title and department affiliation?
2. How long have you been teaching at [our college]?

3. Have you taught elsewhere prior to or in addition to teaching here? If so, where?
4. What courses do you usually teach?
5. Based on the degree map (provided for reference), is it your sense that students enter your course having completed the recommended courses listed prior to your course on the map? When they are in your course, is it your sense that they are simultaneously enrolled in the recommended four to five courses listed on the map?
6. What is your sense of the types of reading and writing students have done prior to your course?
7. What, if anything, do you do to assess the reading and writing ability of your students when they enter your course?
8. What is your sense of the change, if any, in students' reading and writing abilities from the beginning of the semester to the end?
9. Which of your high-stakes assignments on the syllabus involve writing? Could you describe what kind of writing students do?
10. What are your learning goals for those assignments? If the goal is not to improve writing skills specifically, how does writing help you achieve the objectives for the assignment?
11. How do you scaffold or otherwise prepare students for writing assignments?
12. Do you assign low-stakes writing or in-class writing?
13. Can you tell us a little about the reading you assign in your course? (Do you assign a textbook or other types of reading? About how many pages of reading do you assign for each class session/week? Is this reading mandated by your department?)
14. What are your goals in assigning reading for students to complete outside of class?
15. Do you assess students' reading compliance? If so, how?
16. How would you describe the connection, if any, between the reading assignments and writing assignments in your course? (Possible follow-up: do students write about the texts they read, and if so, how do you expect them to engage with those texts?)
17. What is your sense of the types of reading and writing they will go on to do after your course?
18. Do you see reading and writing instruction, or helping students with reading and writing, as part of your job? Why or why not?

19. To what extent are the reading and writing activities in your class assigned based on requirements from your department, the college, or professional standards?
20. Are there any projects you are engaged in outside of your class in which students are doing reading and writing activities related to your discipline(s)?[3]

---

3. Questions adapted from Ihara and Del Principe, "What We Mean When We Talk About Reading.

Reflections on Learning: Revision Reflections as Insight into the Influences on Students' Revisions on a Writing-to-Learn Assignment

SOLAIRE A. FINKENSTAEDT-QUINN, ISABELLA SPERRY, ALICIA ROMERO, AND GINGER V. SHULTZ

Peer review and revision have the potential to support the use of writing pedagogies across disciplines. The MWrite Program supports faculty across disciplines incorporate writing-to-learn (WTL) assignments in their classrooms. The WTL assignments incorporate peer review and revision to engage students in a collaborative co-construction of knowledge while alleviating the need for instructor feedback. Our study builds upon prior literature by examining how students view peer review as influencing their revisions in a WTL context. We analyzed the revision reflections students wrote as part of a WTL assignment in an introductory statistics course, characterizing the revisions students described and the sources to which they attributed their revisions. Students primarily described revising their arguments or adding missing content. They predominantly attributed revisions to receiving feedback, but they also valued reading their peers' drafts. This study adds to prior literature by demonstrating that students viewed peer review as a valuable and supportive exercise enabling them to make productive revisions.

Introduction

There have been calls for greater incorporation of writing in undergraduate STEM classrooms, and specifically for writing that supports learning (National Research Council, 2012). Accordingly, writing-to-learn (WTL) has been increasingly used in STEM to support conceptual learning and disciplinary thinking (Gere et al., 2019; Reynolds et al., 2012). Drawing on the benefits of WTL and in response to calls for increased writing in STEM, we developed the MWrite Program, which supports the use of an evidence-based design for WTL assignments in courses across the University of Michigan, with an emphasis on large introductory STEM courses.

The MWrite team supports instructors to develop and implement WTL through access to resources, such as writing fellows, and works with instructors to develop writing assignments for their course. Importantly, we guide instructors through a process of developing assignments that include the features found in effective WTL assignments—namely, meaning-making tasks, providing students with clear writing expectations, incorporating interactive writing processes, and supporting metacognitive reflection (Anderson et al., 2015; Gere et al., 2019; Klein, 2015).

Including peer review and revision stages into a writing assignment can incorporate the features of effective WTL assignments, namely, creating interactive writing as students interact with their peers; providing clear writing expectations in the form of a rubric that guides peer review; and supporting metacognitive reflection as students read their peers' writing, consider the feedback they receive, and revise their writing. Research on peer review for supporting revision is extensive and indicates that students benefit from the process (Chang, 2016; Huisman et al., 2019). Students can provide feedback to their peers that is similar to that of instructors and leads to higher-order revisions (Anson and Anson, 2017; Cho and MacArthur, 2010; Cho et al., 2006; Huisman et al., 2019; Patchan et al., 2009). Furthermore, research indicates that while both aspects of peer review (i.e., reading the work of peers and providing feedback and receiving feedback) inform students' revisions, reading the work of peers and providing feedback to them may be more impactful (Cho and Cho, 2011; Cho and MacArthur, 2011; Huisman et al., 2018; Lundstrom and Baker, 2009). This may be due to the fact that students engage in a reflective process as they read their peers' writing and draft feedback (Nicol and McCallum, 2022). However, students utilize peer review to different extents when they revise (Leijen and Leontjeva, 2012; Lu et al., 2023), and revision is tied to development in writing ability, where higher-order revisions lead to greater improvement (Cho and MacArthur, 2010; Wu and Schunn, 2020). In addition to variable engagement with peer review and revision, it can be difficult for students to transfer knowledge about writing across contexts, and incorporating stages for reflection can support them to do so (Adler-Kassner et al., 2016; Moore and Felten, 2019). While peer review and revision can support reflection, incorporating an explicit stage for reflection may more directly support students to engage in the practice. However, it is important to note that reflective writing can be prescriptive, and one must balance scaffolding student reflection with providing room for genuine reflection and not leading students to craft rote responses catering to the assessor (Scott, 2005). As part of our research program, we are interested in enhancing students' engagement with peer review and revision to ultimately enhance the benefits of WTL. In this article, we describe an exploratory study of how students described their peer-review and revision processes in revision reflections that were incorporated into the WTL process.

Investigations into MWrite WTL's Support of Learning

In alignment with the goals of the MWrite Program, we have undertaken a series of studies examining students' responses to MWrite WTL assignments to identify whether and how the assignments are supporting the intended learning goals (Finkenstaedt-Quinn et al., 2023). Our findings indicate that the assignments successfully support conceptual learning and disciplinary thinking due to the rhetorical features included in the assignment prompts (i.e., relevant context, genre, and audience) and, most pertinent to this work, the inclusion of peer review. Analyses of students' writing (i.e., feedback and revisions), survey responses, and interviews indicate that students can provide constructive, content-focused feedback to their peers that is related to content-focused revisions in biology, chemistry, and statistics contexts (Finkenstaedt-Quinn et al., 2020; Finkenstaedt-Quinn et al., 2019; Gupte et al., 2021; Halim et al., 2018; Moon et al., 2018; Petterson et al., 2022; Schmidt-McCormack et al., 2019; Watts et al., 2022). Furthermore, in alignment with other research on peer review and revision (e.g., Cho and Cho, 2011; Lundstrom and Baker, 2009), quantitative analyses comparing students' initial and revised drafts suggest that their revisions are also informed by reading their peers' draft and providing feedback, and that this aspect of peer review may have a greater impact than the feedback students receive (Finkenstaedt-Quinn et al., 2021; Watts et al., 2022); but the results have been mixed across studies (Watts et al., 2024). Additionally, in a case study analysis of students' writing artifacts from a WTL assignment focused on mechanistic reasoning in organic chemistry, we found a range in the extent to which students engaged with the processes of peer review and revision (Finkenstaedt-Quinn et al., 2024). Specifically, some students made meaningful revisions that related to both the feedback they received and the peers' drafts they read, while others made smaller-scale revisions tied only to feedback they received. As this study primarily drew from written artifacts, we were interested in exploring how students themselves described their revisions and the relationship to peer review. By better understanding both what students are doing and how they see themselves as doing it, we hope to gain insight into how to enhance students' engagement in the peer review and revision aspects of the MWrite Program's WTL assignments and thus increase the learning benefits of this pedagogy.

This study focuses on a MWrite WTL assignment in an introductory statistics course where the instructor recently incorporated student reflections into the revision stage of the assignments as a way to support student revisions. In the reflections, students are asked to write about how the revisions they made were informed by the peer-review process. This presented us with the opportunity to examine students' reflections as a representation of how students perceived aspects of the peer review process informing their revisions. Our thinking draws on the cognitive processes involved in revision as described by Flower et al. (1986) and Hayes et al. (1987). As the writer begins the revision process, they read their text to evaluate how it addresses their goals for the text and how it aligns with criteria related to the task. As they evaluate their text, they identify problems within it. They then consider what strategies to use in approaching revision—such as what problems they can ignore, if they need more information to address the problem, and the extent of revision that is needed—before actually beginning to revise their text. In our context, as students revise they consider how well their initial draft addresses the writing prompt and the peer review criteria, the feedback they received, and they also compare their peers' drafts to their own work. Based on these factors, they reflect on their initial draft, identify problems in their writing, and consider how they should address those problems. Students' revision reflections thus serve as external representations of their revision process that we, as researchers, can then examine to gain insight into their thinking.

We describe a focused examination of three students' final drafts and the corresponding revision reflections in response to one of the WTL assignments implemented in the statistics course. This is followed by an exploratory analysis across a subset of students' revision reflections. Our aim from this analysis was to develop a better understanding of how students revise in a WTL context, both what they revise on (e.g., content, reasoning, writing mechanics) and what informs their revisions (e.g., reading peers' drafts, receiving peer feedback, writing fellows, outside readings). This provides insight into the extent to which students are engaged with revision and utilizing their peers as resources, which can inform efforts to enhance the benefits of WTL through peer review and revision mechanisms. As such, the following research questions guided our analysis:

1. What types of revisions do students comment on making?
2. What sources do students identify as informing their revisions?

Methods

Study Overview

We qualitatively analyzed students' written reflections about their revision process, which formed one of the MWrite WTL assignments incorporated into an introductory statistics course. From this course, twenty students consented to participate in the study and allowed us to analyze their writing. We examined three students' final drafts and corresponding revision reflections as exemplar cases for how students performed and described their revisions. Additionally, we thematically analyzed the written revision reflections of all twenty students via an inductive coding process. This study is considered exempt by the institutional review board, and pseudonyms are used throughout when referring to specific students.

Course Context and Assignment Details

The introductory statistics course is primarily taken by sophomore and junior undergraduates across various disciplines and introduces basic statistical concepts. The course consists of a lecture session three times a week, as well as a lab once a week with a graduate-student instructor that focuses on the use of RStudio in the context of various data sets. Students are primarily assessed through exams supplemented by weekly homework, lab assignments, and two MWrite WTL assignments. Each WTL assignment consists of a supplemental assignment completed in the lab, an initial draft, peer review, and a final draft and revision reflection. Writing fellows assist with the WTL process—they are undergraduate students who previously performed well in the course and showed an advanced understanding of the topics covered by the assignments. Additionally, writing fellows are responsible for hosting office hours to answer questions and grading the initial drafts, peer reviews, and final drafts. When grading the initial drafts, the writing fellows provide students with feedback primarily focused on completion and deduct points if students' responses missed items asked for in the assignment description. They also typically provide a few directive comments for what students may want to focus on as they revise. Students receive the comments from the writing fellows after the peer review closes. Students also all receive a message describing common errors that the writing fellows identified in the first drafts.

The revision reflections examined herein were part of an assignment that appointed students as analysts for the American Hotel and Lodging Association (AHLA). They were given the larger goal of understanding the characteristics of a random sample of five hundred Airbnb listings in Chicago neighborhoods and asked to evaluate the characteristics in order to guide decisions in the hotel industry. Students were tasked with writing a five-to-seven-hundred-word memorandum that included a histogram, an analysis of two categorical variables in a grouped bar chart, an analysis of one quantitative variable versus one categorical variable, and recommendations to AHLA based on their findings. Finally, students were asked to close their memorandum with a summary of their findings and a response to the following query: "Your project manager suggests using the results from your analysis above to understand the characteristics of Airbnb's competitor, Vrbo. Do you agree with your manager that it is appropriate to do so? Why or why not?"

After writing an initial draft in response to the assignment, students read approximately three of their peers' drafts and offered feedback according to four content-focused criteria. They correspondingly received feedback from three peers, on average. Students were then tasked with revising their initial draft based on new or changed perspectives about the assignment. Lastly, they were asked to include a revision reflection in their final draft (see Figure 1).

> Include a reflection on the revise and resubmit process. This reflection should be between 100 and 150 words. The reflection should be placed at the end of your memorandum. A complete reflection will include the following 2 items:
> A. Now that you have received feedback from some of your peers read through their comments. Based on the comments received, identify the areas that you could improve. Summarize the edits you thought were appropriate to make to your writing piece based on the feedback from your peers, your writing fellow's comments, or feedback you've received during office hours. If you choose not to make a suggested change, provide a thorough and respectful rationale explaining why you declined to make the edit.
> - If you did not receive any peer review feedback, identify the areas you decided to change. Summarize the edits you thought were appropriate to make to your writing and explain why you made such changes.
> B. How did the three peer reviews you completed help improve your draft? Identify two areas in your revised memorandum that benefitted from reading submissions from your peers.

Figure 1. Prompt guiding students' revision reflections.

Data Analysis

We selected three students as cases for close analysis of their revision reflections and final drafts. Marcie, Yael, and Phillip were selected as they captured a range of experiences in their revision reflections. For each case, two researchers individually read through the student's revision reflection and final draft (in which the revisions were clearly marked) and wrote a memo noting how the student described their revision process and how their reflection corresponded to their revisions. Next, the two researchers read and discussed each other's memos. One of the researchers then wrote up a case profile for each of the three students, got feedback from the other researcher, and revised in order to incorporate the feedback.

We also thematically analyzed the revision reflections of all twenty students included in the study (Braun and Clarke, 2006). We individually read through each revision reflection to familiarize ourselves with the data and noted features of students' responses related to the peer review and revision processes. We then discussed what we had noted in the responses and through discussion inductively developed a coding scheme (Appendix, Table 1). We identified three groups of codes: type of change, source of revision, and evaluation. The type-of-change codes characterized the revisions students described making. The source-of-revision codes captured the resources students identified as influencing their revisions. The evaluation comment codes captured students' reflective and affective comments about the writing process. We iteratively applied the coding scheme to a subset of students' responses and discussed the coding to refine the coding scheme. We applied the final coding scheme to all of the revision reflections, comparing codes and discussing any differences to reach consensus on the applied codes. Finally, one researcher iteratively reviewed the reflections considering the applied codes and generated themes across the responses.

Results

To capture students' thinking about their revisions, we first present three student cases detailing the ties between the revisions they made and their revision reflections. This is followed by our analysis across students' revision reflections focused on the types of revisions they described making and the sources to which they attributed their revisions.

Table 1.
Codes applied to the revision reflections of the three cases.

Parent Code	Child Code	Marcie	Philip	Yael
Type of change	added missing content		x	x
	fixed incorrect content			x
	clarity	x	x	
	Explanation	x		x
	reasoning/argument	x	x	
	Grammar/structure			x
Source of revision	Peer feedback	x	x	x
	Reading and providing feedback	x	x	x
	Writing fellows/office hours		x	
Evaluation	Did not make a suggested change	x	x	
	Reflection/metacognition	x	x	
	mentions revisions for audience	x	x	
	Affective comment about peer review process			x
	Total applied	8	10	6

Student Cases

Marcie. Marcie's reflection demonstrated a deep understanding of the strengths and weaknesses of their initial draft, and they noted how their final draft was shaped by receiving and giving peer feedback. Marcie provided two examples of clarity-focused revisions they made: explaining an important term and expanding on their reasoning for using specific variables. Marcie noted, "[I]n my revision, I added explanations concerning the meaning of super host status and elaborated on my reason for using the variables I chose for the side-by-side boxplot." Marcie adjusted their definition of the term "Superhost" to clarify it for readers. When one peer suggested adjusting the boxplot variables, Marcie instead elaborated on their choice of variables. Marcie demonstrated metacognition when discussing this decision, which they connected to their primary argument: "I chose not to change the variables I used in boxplots (which was recommended by one of the peer reviewers) because I thought the comparison helped further evidence my main argument that customer satisfaction seems to depend more on service quality than price." Based on what they had observed in their peers' drafts, Marcie also added a discussion in their revised draft on the variables related to Superhost status. Overall, Marcie made a series of minor but effective revisions that enhanced their memorandum rather than changed it. These changes were largely attributed to advice from their peers and reflection after reading the work of others.

Phillip. In their reflection, Phillip described how the peer-review process (both reading their peers' drafts and receiving feedback) helped them better understand the assignment objectives and informed their revisions. Phillip positively reflected, "Aside from peer reviews, reading other students' memorandums helped me better understand the project and prompt. For example, after spending more time interpreting the prompt and goal of the assignment, I related the distribution of Airbnb prices to the lodging company." This last addition was a crucial change because the memorandum's purpose was to translate statistical findings into recommendations. Phillip further noted that they had not sufficiently connected their findings and corrected this in their revised draft by providing a reasonable suggestion to the intended audience. They also improved their argument by adding the specific reasons why further research into the topic is needed. Additionally, Phillip defined outliers and added justification for their use of means rather than medians, which demonstrated their understanding of the material, and noted a clarity-based revision regarding changing their decimals to percentages. They also decided not to follow a suggestion from one of their peers that they include more of their calculations, as they felt the audience would not have the appropriate statistical background to be able to interpret them. Per a comment left by a writing fellow, they also added an introduction, which helped structure their draft according to the correct format. Overall, informed by the peer review process, Phillip implemented significant changes that strengthened their piece considerably.

Yael. Yael's reflection largely focused on how, due to the feedback they received, they incorporated additional data and explanations that strengthened their arguments. Yael described their experience positively: "The reviewers overall also did a great job explaining what I should improve upon, while also telling me what I did a good job on and giving me positive feedback." Yael also identified areas to improve their argument and conclusion about the applicability of their statistical findings from reading their peers' drafts. Yael's most significant revision was to redo their description of conditional probabilities (i.e., the probability of one event occurring given the existence of another), which was in response to their peers identifying a computational error in Yael's draft. This revision resulted in a strong paragraph with numerical evidence supporting their overall argument. Furthermore, as with Phillip, Yael included a recommendation to the Lodging Association which was an essential aspect of the assignment. They also added further discussion of pricing data and sufficiently incorporated the findings from their graphs. Relatedly, they added text explaining key aspects of their first graph. Yael also improved their argument about whether Vrbo could use statistical analysis for their business model by pointing out other differences between the two data sets. Overall, they made both minor changes, such as adjusting their existing descriptions and explanations, and more considerable changes, such as switching out their incorrect analysis and tying their findings to the context given in the assignment.

Types of Revisions Students Describe Making

Similar to the three cases presented above, students described making a range of revisions that were primarily content focused. The content-focused revisions fell into three related categories: adding or revising content descriptions and analyses; adding or expanding on explanations of analysis; and enhancing arguments. Sixteen students described adding or revising content descriptions and explanations due to the peer review process. Of the sixteen, nine students attributed their additions to feedback they had received, two to information gleaned from reading their peers' drafts, and five to both receiving feedback and reading their peers' drafts. Students primarily described adding explanations describing their data or analyses. For example, Emily described how getting feedback led them to include more analyses in their revised draft:

> "After reading my peers' feedback, I began to pick more specific elements and comparisons to comment on in my analyses. The peer reviews definitely

helped me get started in the right direction as my initial submission honestly did not have much content."

Students also described adding numerical representations to support their analyses and revising numerical descriptions to address readability concerns. Lois said:

"I . . . unclearly used median and means in explaining why the presence of a pool doesn't affect the ratings. So instead of using means, I [provided] the quartiles for a meaningful conclusion."

Over half of the students discussed adding explanations or revising them. Students primarily added explanations that connected their data and analyses to the context given in the assignment. Some students also expanded existing descriptions of statistical concepts or the graphical representations of their data, explaining the choices they had made during data analysis (e.g., why they had used a certain data set) or describing the meaning and implications of their results.

Importantly, fourteen of the students described revising their reasoning or arguments. They almost entirely attributed this type of revision to receiving feedback, with one student stating that both aspects of the peer review process were helpful and two also recognizing the influence of writing fellows. Students primarily reflected on adding or revising the reasoning for their argument and final conclusion. As with the explanation-focused revisions, some students added contextual information to enhance and support their argument. Alternatively, some students described revising their analysis, or how it was posed, so as to better support their conclusions. Anne described this, as well as how they gained a better understanding of the significance of a specific statistical property:

"I feel I was able to edit and succinctly back up each of my claims with sufficient numerical evidence. The second part of my recommendations showed me that although I understood outliers, I did not understand the analytical importance of including them in my thought process and reasoning. After going back to where I was told I ignored the outliers, I was actually able to use them to create a more nuanced argument about the data I provided."

Two students described making larger revisions to their arguments due to a change in perspective resulting from feedback they received from their peers. Alexis described gaining a new perspective on the meaning of their analyses that they used to revise their argument, and Mahvesh gained a new perspective on how to present their argument. In both cases, this feedback led them to make substantial revisions to their argument. Lastly, two students made smaller, clarity-focused revisions.

About half of the students also commented on making revisions related to organization and style. Although this type of revision was not the focus of the assignment or the peer review, students primarily attributed these revisions to feedback received from their peers, with two students also relating these revisions to reading their peers' writing and one to the feedback from a writing fellow. The primary revisions falling into this category entailed making their responses more concise. Students also discussed revising their drafts so that they aligned more with the genre and criteria of the assignment (e.g., adding an introductory paragraph, employing the formatting of a memorandum) and resolved issues with grammar, sentence structure, and confusing language.

Sources Students Identify as Informing Their Revisions

Students described making revisions based on both aspects of the peer review process (i.e., from feedback they received from their peers, and due to reading and providing feedback to their peers) as well as from interacting with the writing fellows for the course. They also discussed positive perceptions of the peer review process and how it supported reflection on their responses that prompted revisions.

All eighteen of the students described peer feedback as informing their revisions, albeit to various extents. Four of the students did not provide specifics about the feedback they received but did describe how they revised their draft in response, or how feedback helped them recognize issues with their initial drafts. For example, Anne said:

> "Based on my peers' comments, I realize that I was doing two main things wrong: lacking specification about my points given the provided data, and ignoring outliers."

Three additional students broadly described the feedback they received, followed by a few specific examples and the revisions they made in response. The remaining eleven students detailed specific comments they got from their peers, followed by the revisions they made in response. They described receiving comments related to clarity, their explanations of the data they included, their analyses, and their final arguments. Students described two types of clarity-related suggestions: comments related to wording and sentence structure, and comments focused on the clarity of how they presented numerical and graphical information. Regarding their analyses, students primarily described receiving suggestions to add variables and quantitative evidence to their analysis, while some suggestions related to how they could interpret their findings. For example, Mahvesh said:

> "Reviews for Q1 said that I had great numerical summaries, but I should explain how this relates to hotels in Chicago. . . . Q4 reviews said my reasoning for Vrbo was a bit subjective so I gave more objective reasoning."

The comments on students' arguments related to how their argument could be expanded, clarified, or supported with evidence. All the students who described specific comments they got from their peers described receiving comments related to either their analysis or their crafted argument, or both, which indicates that students were overall providing feedback that could support their peers in achieving the goals of the assignment.

In their written reflections, eight students described how their revisions were influenced by reading their peers' drafts, with two students also mentioning that they benefited from providing their peers with feedback. Dave described the benefits of both reviewing their peers' drafts and getting feedback:

> "Overall, reading my reviews and reviewing others' memorandums helped me make my memorandum a lot more specific and professional, as I could take advice and inspiration from my peers."

Students described reviewing their peers' drafts as helping them identify missing content, content they should expand on in their drafts, and how they could better describe or summarize their data and analyses. Specifically, from reading their peers' drafts, students discussed how seeing their peers' writing helped them revise for clarity in their own writing. One student, Phillip, also talked about how reading their peers' responses helped them better understand the assignment itself, which led them to build additional connections that supported their final argument.

Five students also talked about making revisions due to feedback from the writing fellows affiliated with the MWrite WTL assignments. Four of them attributed revisions to both feedback from the writing fellows and feedback they received from their peers. The feedback primarily involved suggestions that students add data to their analyses and revise how they presented their data or analysis.

Interestingly, six students discussed feedback from their peers that they chose not to follow. Mahvesh received conflicting reviews about the understandability of their language and chose not to revise, whereas Tamsyn disagreed with the feedback they received as they felt that their response was already sufficient. Three of the students chose not to follow some of the suggestions from their peers since they felt the suggested revisions would negatively impact their response; these suggestions involved removing or changing portions of their response that students felt were important for interpreting their analyses or argument. For example, Claire did not follow the specific suggestion they received, though they still revised their draft in response to it:

> "For my analysis of a quantitative and categorical variable, someone said that my plot was confusing and I should get rid of the outliers, however, I ignored this because I believe that outliers are important to have and acknowledge. Instead, to try to make my analysis clearer I added numerical values to explain what I meant by 'nearly all' and 'most.'"

This shows that Claire recognized the importance of outliers to their response, but still took the feedback into consideration and made a productive revision.

Six students also considered the intended audience when revising. They primarily described revising their response to make it more understandable for an audience with limited statistical knowledge. Mohsin demonstrated the importance of considering the intended audience when writing when they said:

> "From the peer review of Q1 and the office hour, I add more information about the center and shape of the graph and list more data, such as Q1, Q3, and IQR. I think suggestions are really helpful because missing information can negatively impact the audience to understand the whole picture of price."

Comparatively, Phillip received a suggestion to add calculations to their memo but felt that the audience given in the assignment would not benefit from the addition and so chose to not revise. Interestingly, despite the lack of emphasis on the audience in the peer review rubric and from comments by the writing fellows, students seemed to place an importance on this aspect of the assignment.

Students also reflected on how they benefited from engaging in the peer review process, where both affect and reflection are important components of the revision process. Five students explicitly expressed positive experiences with the peer review process. Dave's description of the benefits captured the positive affect similarly expressed by their peers:

> "After reading my peer reviews I was definitely able to make some meaningful changes. . . . Overall, reading my reviews and reviewing others' memorandums helped me make my memorandum a lot more specific and professional, as I could take advice and inspiration from my peers."

All of the five students described finding the suggestions and feedback they received from their peers to be helpful for revising their drafts. Two of the students, Dave and Yael, additionally mentioned that reading their peers' draft was beneficial. Furthermore, six students explicitly engaged in metacognitive reflection on how the peer review process impacted their response to the assignment. Three of these focused on how they were able to improve their argument due to feedback they received from their peers. Anne said:

> "The second part of my recommendations showed me that although I understood outliers, I did not understand the analytical importance of including them in my thought process and reasoning. After going back to where I was told I ignored the outliers, I was actually able to use them to create a more nuanced argument about the data I provided."

As described above, Mohsin reflected on how they added content when they revised as they realized its importance for the audience to be able to understand their memo. Two students, Phillip and Marcie, demonstrated metacognition arising from reading their peers' drafts: Phillip described better understanding the assignment, and Marcie discussed adding reasoning to their draft due to seeing peers arguing counter to one of the analyses they had performed.

Discussion

Our results indicate that students thoughtfully engaged with peer review and revision during the WTL process situated in a STEM context. Students' revision reflections contained nuanced descriptions of the revisions they made and why, providing useful insight into students' revision process. As seen across the three cases, students described both specific revisions they made and what elements of the process informed the specific revisions. Our analysis furthers research on WTL by providing insight into how students use the information garnered from the peer review process to inform their revisions; it also aligns with the aims of WTL, which focuses on content rather than the ability to write (Gere et al., 2019).

Our findings also expand on the existing literature on benefits of peer review for writing by demonstrating the types of higher-order revisions students made when focusing on their argument and related concepts. Students described revising the arguments they presented in their responses, their statistical analyses and explanations thereof, and their responses in general to enhance clarity. Most of the students described revising their argument and reasoning in their revision reflections, which was a primary aim of the assignment as the ability to translate statistical findings within a data set to applicable recommendations for a client is an important aspect of the statistics discipline. This aligns with WTL research generally, which indicates that WTL can support students to engage in higher-order thinking and application of content that is known to be difficult for them (Gere et al., 2019; Nevid et al., 2017). It is promising that students identified revising their arguments and reasoning primarily due to receiving feedback from their peers and indicates that peer review can also support this skill in STEM disciplinary contexts.

Our findings indicate that students recognized that both aspects of peer review informed their revisions and that they viewed the experience in a positive light. The ubiquity of student revisions due to feedback, in conjunction with the complexity of the types of revisions they made (e.g., on the argumentation and analysis levels) indicates that students were constructively engaging with feedback from their peers. This contrasts with other studies focused on student revisions due to receiving feedback, which indicated that not all students use feedback to revise (Leijen and Leontjeva, 2012; Lu et al., 2023). Students also described how reading and providing feedback led them to engage in metacognitive reflection on their own writing. This aligns with prior peer review literature which indicates that students benefit from both receiving feedback and being the reviewer (Cho and Cho, 2011; Cho and MacArthur, 2011; Lundstrom and Baker, 2009; Zhang et al., 2017). However, our finding that students themselves recognized the benefits from both aspects of peer review is less common (Nicol et al., 2014). Thus, our findings may indicate that tasks such as the revision reflections support students to recognize the benefits of both aspects of the peer review process more fully when they revise.

Limitations and Implications

Our findings are bounded by the course and self-selected set of students from which we gathered data, which limits the claims we can make from this study. Additionally, students' responses to the revision reflection may have been shaped by the students' knowledge that they had agreed to participate in this study or by the prescribed nature of the reflections (i.e., students may have attempted to demonstrate that they engaged in the processes expected by the instructor). While the revision reflections were prescriptive, in this context it may further support the structure of the assignment as a whole: if directing students to comment on their revisions led students to consider and utilize information from the peer review process as they revised when they might not have otherwise, then the revision reflections played a useful role. In alignment with an interpretivist paradigm, we recognize that our analysis of students' reflections was informed by our positionality (i.e., our varying degrees of familiarity with the WTL process and the statistical concepts covered). However, our methodology, through which we engaged in reflexivity and discussion as a research team, allowed for an in-depth exploratory analysis that can inform future analyses.

This study provides an initial exploration of what students wrote about in revision reflections associated with a WTL assignment that incorporated peer review and revision. A key next step is to compare students' revisions when they do and do not write revision reflections in order to identify whether incorporating revision reflections enhances their engagement with and utilization of the peer review process. Furthermore, we found that some students engaged in explicit metacognitive reflection in their revision reflections. It is important to understand how metacognitive reflection was elicited by the revision reflections as opposed to arising naturally through the act of participating in the peer review process. Related, it is worth examining how modifications to the assignment or learning environment could support increased metacognitive reflection from students, as it is an important part of learning.

While we found that students only expressed positive views of peer review, prior research indicates that students have mixed perceptions (Huisman et al., 2018; Kaufman and Schunn, 2011; Nicol et al., 2014; Strijbos et al., 2010). This indicates research focused on how the assignment or feedback structure shapes students' affective experiences is needed. Furthermore, the alignment between feedback from writing fellows and peers seen here indicates a potential avenue for addressing students' negative perceptions of the peers' abilities (i.e., alignment between the two sets of feedback could reinforce peers' feedback and serve as an indicator of peers' abilities to provide meaningful feedback). Interestingly, students attributed some revisions to consideration of the rhetorical audience, even though it was not emphasized in the assignment or by the writing fellows. This finding aligns with prior MWrite research and indicates the importance of connecting the audience with the learning goals of the assignment (i.e., linking what we want students to be writing about to the depth of detail we want them to provide). Overall, students' revision reflections were a useful tool for capturing their thoughts and revision process, and our examination indicates the merit of using revision reflections to support students' engagement and reflection with peer review and revision.

Acknowledgments

We would like to acknowledge the students who consented to participate in the study. We would also like to acknowledge Larissa Sano, the writing fellows, and the graduate teaching assistants who play a key role in supporting the implementation of MWrite in Introductory Statistics. Funding for this study was provided by the NSF IUSE Grant No. 2121123.

References

Adler-Kassner, L., Clark, I., Roberston, L., Taczak, K., & Yancey, K. B. (2016). Chapter 1: Assembling knowledge: The role of threshold concepts in facilitating transfer.

Anderson, P., Anson, C. M., Gonyea, R. M., & Paine, C. (2015). The contributions of writing to learning and development: Results from a large-scale multi-institutional study. *Research in the Teaching of English*, *50*(2), 199–235. https://doi.org/https://doi.org/10.1002/tea.3660310910

Anson, I. G., & Anson, C. M. (2017). Assessing peer and instructor response to writing: A corpus analysis from an expert survey. *Assessing Writing*, *33*, 12–24. https://doi.org/https://doi.org/10.1016/j.asw.2017.03.001

Braun, V., & Clarke, V. (2006). Using thematic analysis in psychology. *Qualitative Research in Psychology*, *3*(2), 77–101. https://doi.org/10.1191/1478088706qp063oa

Chang, C. Y. (2016). Two decades of research in L2 peer review. *Journal of Writing Research*, *8*(1), 81–117. https://doi.org/10.17239/jowr-2016.08.01.03

Cho, Y. H., & Cho, K. (2011). Peer reviewers learn from giving comments. *Instructional Science*, *39*(5), 629–643. https://doi.org/10.1007/s11251-010-9146-1

Cho, K., & MacArthur, C. (2010). Student revision with peer and expert reviewing. *Learning and Instruction*, *20*(4), 328–338. https://doi.org/https://doi.org/10.1016/j.learninstruc.2009.08.006

Cho, K., & MacArthur, C. (2011). Learning by reviewing. *Journal of Educational Psychology*, *103*(1), 73–84. https://doi.org/10.1037/a0021950

Cho, K., Schunn, C. D., & Charney, D. (2006). Commenting on writing: Typology and perceived helpfulness of comments from novice peer reviewers and subject matter experts. *Written Communication*, *23*(3), 260–294.

Finkenstaedt-Quinn, S. A., Halim, A. S., Kasner, G., Wilhelm, C. A., Moon, A., Gere, A. R., & Shultz, G. V. (2020). Capturing student conceptions of thermodynamics and kinetics using writing. *Chemistry Education Research and Practice*, *21*(3), 922–939. https://doi.org/10.1039/C9RP00292H

Finkenstaedt-Quinn, S. A., Polakowski, N., Gunderson, B., Shultz, G. V., & Gere, A. R. (2021). Utilizing peer review and revision to support the development of conceptual knowledge through writing. *Written Communication*, *38*(3), 351–379. https://doi.org/https://doi.org/10.1177/07410883211006038

Finkenstaedt-Quinn, S. A., Snyder-White, E. P., Connor, M. C., Gere, A. R., & Shultz, G. V. (2019). Characterizing peer review comments and revision from a writing-to-learn assignment focused on Lewis structures. *Journal of Chemical Education*, *96*(2), 227–237. https://doi.org/10.1021/acs.jchemed.8b00711

Finkenstaedt-Quinn, S. A., Watts, F. M., Gere, A. R., & Shultz, G. V. (2023). A portrait of MWrite as a research program: A review of research on writing-to-learn in STEM through the MWrite Program. *International Journal for the Scholarship of Teaching and Learning*, *17*(1), Article 18. https://doi.org/10.20429/ijsotl.2023.17118

Finkenstaedt-Quinn, S. A., Watts, F. M., & Shultz, G. V. (2024). Reading, receiving, revising: A case study on the relationship between peer review and revision in writing-to-learn. *Assessing Writing*, *59*. https://doi.org/https://doi.org/10.1016/j.asw.2024.100808

Flower, L., Hayes, J. R., Carey, L., Schriver, K., & Stratman, J. (1986). Detection, diagnosis, and the strategies of revision. *College Composition and Communication*, *37*(1), 16–55. https://doi.org/10.2307/357381

Gere, A. R., Limlamai, N., Wilson, E., Saylor, K. M., & Pugh, R. (2019). Writing and conceptual learning in science: An analysis of assignments. *Written Communication*, *36*(1), 99–135. https://doi.org/10.1177/0741088318804820

Gupte, T., Watts, F. M., Schmidt-McCormack, J. A., Zaimi, I., Gere, A. R., & Shultz, G. V. (2021). Students' meaningful learning experiences from participating in organic chemistry writing-to-learn activities. *Chemistry Education Research and Practice*, *22*, 396–414. https://doi.org/10.1039/D0RP00266F

Halim, A. S., Finkenstaedt-Quinn, S. A., Olsen, L. J., Gere, A. R., & Shultz, G. V. (2018). Identifying and remediating student misconceptions in introductory biology via writing-to-learn assignments and peer review. *CBE - Life Sciences Education*, *17*(2), Article 28. https://doi.org/10.1187/cbe.17-10-0212

Hayes, J. R., Flower, L., Schriver, K. A., Stratman, J., & Carey, L. (1987). Cognitive processes in revision. *Advances in Applied Psycholinguistics*, *2*, 176–240.

Huisman, B., Saab, N., van den Broek, P., & van Driel, J. (2019). The impact of formative peer feedback on higher education students' academic writing: A meta-analysis. *Assessment & Evaluation in Higher Education*, *44*(6), 863–880. https://doi.org/10.1080/02602938.2018.1545896

Huisman, B., Saab, N., van Driel, J., & van den Broek, P. (2018). Peer feedback on academic writing: Undergraduate students' peer feedback role, peer feedback perceptions and essay performance. *Assessment & Evaluation in Higher Education*, *43*(6), 955–968. https://doi.org/10.1080/02602938.2018.1424318

Kaufman, J. H., & Schunn, C. D. (2011). Students' perceptions about peer assessment for writing: Their origin and impact on revision work. *Instructional Science*, *39*(3), 387–406. https://doi.org/10.1007/s11251-010-9133-6

Klein, P. D. (2015). Mediators and moderators in individual and collaborative writing to learn. *Journal of Writing Research*, *7*(1), 201–214. https://doi.org/10.17239/jowr-2015.07.01.08

Leijen, D. A. J., & Leontjeva, A. (2012). Linguistic and review features of peer feedback and their effect on implementation of changes in academic writing: A corpus based investigation. *Journal of Writing Research*, *4*(2), 177–202. https://doi.org/10.17239/jowr-2012.04.02.4

Lu, Q., Yao, Y., & Zhu, X. (2023). The relationship between peer feedback features and revision sources mediated by feedback acceptance: The effect on undergraduate students' writing performance. *Assessing Writing*, *56*. https://doi.org/https://doi.org/10.1016/j.asw.2023.100725

Lundstrom, K., & Baker, W. (2009). To give is better than to receive: The benefits of peer review to the reviewer's own writing. *Journal of Second Language Writing*, *18*(1), 30–43. https://doi.org/https://doi.org/10.1016/j.jslw.2008.06.002

Moon, A., Zotos, E., Finkenstaedt-Quinn, S. A., Gere, A. R., & Shultz, G. V. (2018). Investigation of the role of writing-to-learn in promoting student understanding of light-matter interactions. *Chemistry Education Research and Practice, 19*(3), 807–818. https://doi.org/10.1039/C8RP00090E

Moore, J. L., & Felten, P. (2019). Understanding writing transfer as a threshold concept across the disciplines. In J. A. Timmermans & R. Land (Eds.), *Threshold concepts on the edge* (pp. 341–352). Brill. https://doi.org/https://doi.org/10.1163/9789004419971_024

National Research Council. (2012). *Discipline-Based education research: Understanding and improving learning in undergraduate science and engineering.* The National Academies Press. https://doi.org/10.17226/13362

Nevid, J. S., Ambrose, M. A., & Pyun, Y. S. (2017). Effects of higher and lower level writing-to-learn assignments on higher and lower level examination questions. *Teaching of Psychology, 44*(4), 324–329. https://doi.org/10.1177/0098628317727645

Nicol, D., & McCallum, S. (2022). Making internal feedback explicit: Exploiting the multiple comparisons that occur during peer review. *Assessment & Evaluation in Higher Education, 47*(3), 424–443. https://doi.org/10.1080/02602938.2021.1924620

Nicol, D., Thomson, A., & Breslin, C. (2014). Rethinking feedback practices in higher education: A peer review perspective. *Assessment & Evaluation in Higher Education, 39*(1), 102–122. https://doi.org/10.1080/02602938.2013.795518

Patchan, M. M., Charney, D., & Schunn, C. D. (2009). A validation study of students' end comments: Comparing comments by students, a writing instructor, and a content instructor. *Journal of Writing Research, 1*(2), 124–152. http://www.jowr.org/abstracts/vol1_2/Patchan_et_al_2009_1_2_abstract.html

Petterson, M. N., Finkenstaedt-Quinn, S. A., Gere, A. R., & Shultz, G. V. (2022). The role of authentic contexts and social elements in supporting organic chemistry students' interactions with writing-to-learn assignments. *Chemistry Education Research and Practice, 23*, 189–205. https://doi.org/https://doi.org/10.1039/D1RP00181G

Reynolds, J. A., Thaiss, C., Katkin, W., & Thompson, R. J. (2012). Writing-to-learn in undergraduate science education: A community-based, conceptually driven approach. *CBE - Life Sciences Education, 11*(1), 17–25. https://doi.org/10.1187/cbe.11-08-0064

Schmidt-McCormack, J. A., Judge, J. A., Spahr, K., Yang, E., Pugh, R., Karlin, A., Sattar, A., Thompson, B. C., Gere, A. R., & Shultz, G. V. (2019). Analysis of the role of a writing-to-learn assignment in student understanding of organic acid-base concepts. *Chemistry Education Research and Practice, 20*(2), 383–398. https://doi.org/10.1039/C8RP00260F

Scott, T. (2005). Creating the subject of portfolios: Reflective writing and the conveyance of institutional prerogatives. *Written Communication, 22*(1), 3–35. https://doi.org/10.1177/0741088304271831

Strijbos, J.-W., Narciss, S., & Dünnebier, K. (2010). Peer feedback content and sender's competence level in academic writing revision tasks: Are they critical for feedback perceptions and efficiency? *Learning and Instruction, 20*(4), 291–303. https://doi.org/ https://doi.org/10.1016/j.learninstruc.2009.08.008

Watts, F. M., Finkenstaedt-Quinn, S. A., & Shultz, G. V. (2024). Examining the role of assignment design and peer review on student responses and revisions to an organic chemistry writing-to-learn assignment. *Chemistry Education Research and Practice, 25*, 721-741. https://doi.org/10.1039/D4RP00024B

Watts, F. M., Park, G. Y., Petterson, M. N., & Shultz, G. V. (2022). Considering alternative reaction mechanisms: Students' use of multiple representations to reason about mechanisms for a writing-to-learn assignment. *Chemistry Education Research and Practice, 23*, 486–507. https://doi.org/10.1039/D1RP00301A

Wu, Y., & Schunn, C. D. (2020). The effects of providing and receiving peer feedback on writing performance and learning of secondary school students. *American Educational Research Journal, 58*(3), 1–35. https://doi.org/10.3102/0002831220945266

Zhang, F., Schunn, C. D., & Baikadi, A. (2017). Charting the routes to revision: An interplay of writing goals, peer comments, and self-reflections from peer reviews. *Instructional Science, 45*(5), 679–707. https://doi.org/10.1007/s11251-017-9420-6

Appendix

Table 2.
Coding of revision reflections.

Parent Code	Child Code	Definition	Exemplar
Type of change	Added missing content	Student describes adding content descriptions or analyses.	"Finally, a recommendation was that I should give a couple more characteristics throughout my memorandum, so I tried including a couple I knew would relate to my conclusion." - Axie
	Fixed incorrect content	Student describes fixing incorrect content or analyses.	"Comments on the axis of the grouped bar chart pointed out my mistake." - Lois
	Explanation	Student describes adding or revising explanations (descriptive, lower-order).	"Doing peer reviews helped me see how others summarized their data. This helped me reword my statistical summaries." - Mahvesh
	Reasoning/ argument	Student describes making changes to their reasoning and/or final argument/ summary (causal, higher-order).	"My peers suggested [I] include some ratio or percentage . . . which can support my argument." - Sequoia
	Clarity	Student describes making clarity-related revisions.	"I . . . saw where I had trouble explaining my points in a concise but compelling manner." - Claire
	Grammar/ structure	Student describes making grammatical or structural (e.g., adding an intro, making text more concise) changes.	"I can learn from their sentence structure that analyzes the data." - Stephen
Source of revision	Peer feedback	Student mentions how feedback they received from their peer(s) influenced their revisions or revision process.	"My peers had suggested a change to take out a lot of heavy worded sentences and to provide more application to the hotels throughout the memorandum." - Tamsyn
	Reading and providing feedback	Student mentions how reading their peers' drafts and/or giving feedback influenced their revisions or revision process.	"I also think that giving out revisions was important because it gave me more ideas as to what to put in my paper." - Andy
	Writing fellows/ office hours	Student mentions writing fellows or attending office hours influencing their revisions or revision process.	"Based on the feedback from my peers and writing fellow . . ." - Nalo

Parent Code	Child Code	Definition	Exemplar
Evaluation	Did not make a suggested change	Student states that they did not make a change suggested to them.	"For the side-by-side box plot, I don't make any changes though it was mentioned in the comment." - Maia
	Reflection/ metacognition	Student reflects on their own writing/analysis from going through the peer review or revision processes (e.g., gains new perspective).	"I never thought of my analysis in this perspective." - Alexis
	Mentions revisions for audience	Student discusses making revisions with the prompt audience in mind.	"Also, I add explanations of Q3 and IQR for audiences with minimum statistical knowledge." - Mohsin
	Affective comment	Student makes a positive or negative affective comment about the peer review process.	"The peer reviews definitely helped me get started in the right direction." - Emily

Surviving as Switzerland: WAC, SLW, and the Literacy Myth of Linguistic Homogeneity

ANALEIGH E. HORTON

In this article, I call for increased collaboration across subfields of writing across the curriculum (WAC) to strengthen language awareness. I first recall Walvoord's (1996) message to not act like Switzerland, a metaphor she uses to describe neutrality. However, I recontextualize Switzerland as an aspiration for its attention to multilingualism. To position the need for this culture shift, I overview WAC's inattention to multilingualism in the United States, introducing the term *literacy myth of linguistic homogeneity* to describe the frequent default to standardized English and its users. Then, illustrating the contemporary linguistic diversity in US higher education, I affirm the need for revised conceptions of language. I use second language writing (SLW) studies as a touchstone for recent calls for language awareness that have gone mostly unanswered. Finally, I provide logistic, structural, and rhetorical possibilities with specific strategies to begin this work at the expert, field, and institutional levels. In closing, I seek to "walk the walk" by offering this text written in my second language (L2), Spanish. Available at https://bit.ly/horton-wac-suiza

Reclaiming Switzerland

"WAC cannot survive as Switzerland" (Walvoord, 1996, p. 69).

Barbara Walvoord, a WAC pioneer, poignantly wrote this statement at WAC's twenty-fifth anniversary in *College English*. Her metaphorical use of Switzerland drew on the Swiss' famous neutrality. Because of WAC's lack of connectedness, Walvoord speculated that it would not have enough funding or relationships with other fields and national organizations to be durable, and therefore WAC was going to "die" (p. 70).

But what if now, a half century later, we looked at Switzerland differently?

According to *Discover Switzerland*, the Swiss government's official site on Swiss society, politics, education, and more:

> Switzerland has four language regions: German, French, Italian, and Romansh.... Non-national languages are also gaining importance. The two most widely spoken non-national languages are English and Portuguese. *Multilingualism is an essential part of Switzerland's identity.* (Schweizerische Eidgenossenschaft, 2022, para. 1, emphasis added)

Walvoord's point was well-taken at the time. WAC as a field has since become more solidified through helpful resources like this journal, the Association of Writing Across the Curriculum (AWAC), and the biannual International Writing Across the Curriculum (IWAC) conference. However, now that WAC has made so much progress toward not dying as Switzerland, it's time to adapt to the Swiss' embrace of multilingualism and survive as Switzerland.

Surviving as Switzerland (i.e., multilingua-fying the field) is a complex endeavor of promoting diversity and inclusion across WAC's multiple dimensions (Perryman-Clark, 2023). Bouza (2023), also citing Walvoord's text, approaches linguistic justice at the departmental level. However, drawing from the whole-systems approach to WAC (Cox et al., 2018), our thinking about linguistically just WAC needs to be holistic. Multi-faceted. Strategic. I write this article with the positionality of a writing program administrator who knows institutional change necessitates external research to justify our requests for funding, status, course caps, and the like. The synthesis of WAC's monolingual tradition outlined in this paper illustrates how the kinds of scholarship departments might need to make their case is limited. There has been a delegation of us working at the WAC-SLW intersection. Still, the field overall has been slower to adopt a more linguistically nuanced epistemology, instead reinforcing what I term and define below, *the literacy myth of linguistic homogeneity,* that implies an archetypal university student who is a monocultural, monolingual English speaker.

WAC theorists might reflect on WAC's history to see where multilingualism has been excluded from the conversation and be encouraged to update our funds of knowledge in the age of globalism. WAC practitioners might consider local-level opportunities to embrace more sociocultural approaches to instruction and inclusion. Guided by Walvoord's (1996) metaphor of Switzerland, this discussion invites conversations about how the ubiquity of English in US higher education might be reconciled with the now-ubiquity of globalization. The logistic, structural, and rhetorical possibilities I present can be taken up to move us as a field so we can make moves within our own contexts. In doing so, we can maintain Walvoord's collaborative intentions and evolve them to fit a 2020s linguistic landscape, surviving as Switzerland with linguistic justice as an essential part of WAC's identity.

Monolingualism as Tradition

Between Walvoord's (1996) writing at WAC's twenty-fifth anniversary and Elder's (2023) Special Issue on its fiftieth, *College Writing and Beyond* (Beaufort, 2007) and *Undergraduates in a Second Language* (Leki, 2007) arose as two important texts for examining students' longitudinal development as writers across the curriculum. The former text (Beaufort, 2007) introduces Tim, whose story concluded that because "novice writers usually get little instruction on how to study and acquire the writing practices of different discourse communities," students struggle to navigate the "writing standards [that] are largely culturally and socially specific" (p. 11). This is a particularly salient finding because Tim identified as an L1 English, white male from the United States It begs the question that if Tim struggled to develop literacy in a sociolinguistic space that supported him, what kinds of challenges might students not matching his identity markers encounter? Leki (2007) responds by presenting international students from the People's Republic of China, Poland, and Japan: Ben, Jan, Yuko, and Yang, who regularly emoted exhaustion and powerlessness when working with instructors who "just want to keep misunderstanding" (Yang, in Leki, 2007, p. 273). Yang ultimately resolved to be "quite cautious in dealing with her instructors, managing her relationships carefully, deciding not to dispute her instructors' opinions about her, not to argue" (Leki, p. 274). Since these landmark publications of student experiences, writing experts have developed WAC methods to help smooth the kinds of bumps that Ben, Jan, Tim, Yang, and Yuko alike encountered.

However, extant literature (e.g., CCCC, 2020; Horner, 2023; Zhang-Wu, 2022) points to these programs potentially being designed more for students like Tim—who can serve as an archetype of a linguistically normative student in most US institutions—than students like Ben, Jan, Yang, and Yuko—examples of the many students who do not fit into the traditional sociolinguistic mold. If our threshold concepts of writing studies (Adler-Kassner & Wardle, 2016) affirm that literacy development is impacted by our social and rhetorical representations of the world, events, ideas, and feelings, it reasons that students whose worldviews are more closely aligned with their institution's might be more likely to succeed. Moreover, as our threshold concepts also affirm that writing involves the negotiation of language differences, students whose language is more closely aligned with their institution's language are probably also more likely to succeed. To further examine this idea of an archetypal student who thrives, let's turn to two pieces of writing studies lore: the literacy myth and the myth of linguistic homogeneity.

The Literacy Myth of Linguistic Homogeneity

We will begin by defining the literacy myth and the myth of linguistic homogeneity.

- The *literacy myth* is "the belief, articulated in educational, civic, religious, and other settings, contemporary and historical, that the acquisition of literacy is a necessary precursor to and inevitably results in economic development, democratic practice, cognitive enhancement, and upward social mobility" (Graff, 2010, p. 635).
- The *myth of linguistic homogeneity* is "the tacit and widespread acceptance of the dominant image of composition students as native speakers of a privileged variety of English" (Matsuda, 2006, p. 638).

If we consider them together, these beliefs might indicate that a student who can acquire expert-level academic English will earn prosperity. In turn, literacy education that upholds this belief (often zeroed in on the benefits of literacy knowledge), will prioritize functional literacy education, or the acquisition of a particular *"saying (writing)—doing—being—valuing—believing"* (Gee, 1989, p. 6, emphasis original) combination. Functional literacy education defaults to the rule-based pedagogy that only acknowledges specific linguistic and rhetorical forms as correct. However, this paradigm neglects that these are myths and, ergo, untrue. Gee goes on to explain how there are many ways in which people say, write, do, be, value, and believe. This perspective of multiplicity aligns with the sociocultural paradigm of literacy learning that affirms that there are many more methods of making meaning than just one. However, although many literacy scholars have turned toward the social approach, countless institutions still uphold more prescriptive traditions, which are challenging enough for L1 English, US-born students who are more enculturated into the social system, and even more difficult for students with divergent sociolinguistic backgrounds (Leki, 2007). Consequently, functional literacy pedagogies pursuant of what I call *the literacy myth of linguistic homogeneity* repeatedly limit, if not harm, multilingual students' literacy development.

Scholarship has portrayed the kinds of harm some multilingual students experience. For example, Inez, a Hispanic bilingual Spanish/English student, enjoyed writing in high school (Saidy, 2018). However, when she started college, she was placed into what she interpreted as a highly racialized, remedial writing course. She felt disconnected from other students on campus, sensing that the university had segregated her class of non-white students because it had little faith in these students' success. Over time, she lost confidence in her abilities because she perceived the university considered her a weak writer, and she lost her excitement for writing. Similarly, in "'We are a ghost in the class': First Year International Students' Experiences in the Global Contact Zone," six multilingual students evidenced little embedded language and literacy instruction in their courses across different disciplines (Freeman & Li, 2019). Each participant commented on feeling insecure in their intercultural competence and fearful to communicate with L1 English students, thus feeling isolated in their classes. Their expectations to form relationships and practice English went unmet, and they struggled consequently.

These studies are just two instances in the profusion of literature on multilingual writing in higher education. Overall, SLW research indicates that a) there is a significant population of multilingual writers, b) there are challenging questions about teaching multilingual students and encouraging their literacy and identity development, and c) that lacking support for multilingual writers is an ongoing issue. SLW praxis is capacious in its questions on

- How to accurately identify students and their language backgrounds (e.g., Nero, 1997; Ortmeier-Hooper, 2008; Riazantseva, 2012)
- Placement (e.g., Crusan, 2011; Ferris et al., 2017; Ruecker, 2011)
- Standards of academic writing (e.g., Canagarajah, 2015; De Costa, 2020; Horner et al., 2011)
- Supporting student identity development (e.g., Cox et al., 2010; Pavlenko & Blacklidge, 2004; Skerrett, 2013)
- Preparing and supporting students for writing beyond foundational writing courses (e.g., Pessoa & Mitchell, 2019; Zamel, 1995; Zawacki & Cox, 2014)

Across the literature are recurring issues of students not feeling comfortable with being labeled by certain terms (e.g., ESL, Generation 1.5), experiencing a sense of otherness, and encountering challenges navigating academic contexts and requirements. Adjacently, faculty struggle with supporting multilingual students: reactions range from frustration with underdeveloped language and literacy skills to self-disappointment in not knowing how to better serve multilingual writers and develop programs that support them (e.g., Fishman & McCarthy, 2001; Ives et al., 2014; Lindsey & Crusan, 2011; Patton, 2011; Zamel & Spack, 2003; Zawacki & Habib, 2014).

All of this suggests that deeply rooted challenges in supporting multilingual writers might be tied to institutional cultures that overlook the literacy myth of linguistic homogeneity. McLeod (2008) asks what North America can offer to WAC movements in other parts of the world. Donahue (2009) might answer that, as far as language goes, WAC in the United States is so far behind that we cannot even enter the global WAC conversation. Rather, we should be learning from movements like the European one that, like Switzerland, champions linguistic diversity. Hall (2009) writes that, as-is, higher education in the United States is so out of touch with modern language realities that the WAC movement requires transformation at its most foundational levels to begin including multilingual writers (and their rich cultural and linguistic knowledge). Below, I trace WAC's more monolingual epistemology.

WAC's Monolingual Traditions

WAC has been critiqued for not always being the most welcoming to users of non-standardized forms of English (Williamson, 1988). Arguments postulate that in WAC-based pedagogy, knowing English is not enough to be successful (Faigley, 1985). Rather, success relies on students' abilities to master prescriptive norms of academic English. Anson (1988) demonstrates the tendency in WAC towards this position, stating that "diversity within the academy—particularly of goals, methods, or characteristics—seems inimical to the perpetuation of cultural and intellectual traditions" (p. 2). Because it is well-established that a very particular brand of English is a hallmark of the US academy (Horner, 2001; Horner & Trimbur, 2002), it makes sense that if WAC fears losing certain traditions, which I will reword as normative ideologies, WAC has hesitated to welcome linguistic diversity, and, consequently, support linguistically diverse students.

WAC research has historically evaded multilingualism. For example, in their 1993 report, "Where Do We Go Next in Writing Across the Curriculum?" Jones and Comprone did not address linguistic diversity as an item on WAC's agenda. Then, when reporting on "The State of WAC/WID in 2010: Methods and Results of the U.S. Survey of International WAC/WID Mapping Project," Thaiss and Porter (2010) also sidestepped linguistic concerns. They stated that sixty-one percent of all 1,138 respondent colleges and universities reported "Standard Written English" as an emphasis of their program. However, they made no mention of how multilingual writers might fit into that ideal, even though the project was purportedly international. These reports bolster claims made around the same time that WAC was reinforcing monolingual ideas (Geller, 2011) and barring multilingual writers from success (Janopoulos, 1995).

Multilingual perspectives are similarly absent in more contemporary WAC literature. A recent example of the field not being guided towards a more linguistically diverse mindset is Thaiss' (2021) Plenary Address at the 2021 International Writing Across the Curriculum (IWAC) conference titled, "WAC Fearlessness: Sustainability and Adaptability: Part One." Thaiss has written elsewhere about multilingual writers in WAC (e.g., Ferris & Thaiss, 2011; Thaiss, 2014), but only in niche collections. At this broader IWAC scale, he failed to include multilingualism or respond to globalization as important steps toward WAC being sustainable and adaptable. His Part Two co-presenter, Rutz (2021), mentioned multilingual writers, but only to briefly recall that there was a growing concern about teaching these students at her institution in 1996. In Zawacki's (2021) interview with two Hong Kong scholars, Chen and Lai, she highlights WAC's growing curiosity about transnational approaches but joins Donahue (2009) and Hall (2009) to point out that this work is done "particularly in regions where English is an additional language and scholars often draw on different theoretical traditions" (Zawacki, 2021, p. 63). In other words, despite the recent increase in translingual and decolonial work informed by raciolinguistics (e.g., Benda et al. 2022; Cushman, 2021; Martinez, 2022), multilingual WAC work in the United States is largely lacking. This is perhaps because, as is demonstrated in "Fifty Years of WAC: Where Have We Been? Where Are We Going?" (Palmquist et al., 2020), SLW is only cursorily mentioned as a different area of writing studies, essentially positioning multilingual praxis on the periphery of WAC's agenda. Together, these documents indicate that many WAC models gloss over or entirely exclude multilingual writers, which is, as we will explore next, out of touch with the realities of globalization and its impact on higher education.

Multilingualism as the New Norm

Although considerations for multilingual writers were maybe less necessary in decades past, now, in the 2020s, rapid globalization is bringing users of different languages into contact more than ever before. Driven largely by technological advances and increased migration, contact between languages and cultures permeates society. The Migration Policy Institute recorded twenty-seven percent of the 2023 US population—90.8 million people—as immigrants and their US-born children (Batalova, 2024) and cites the Pew Research Center's prediction that this percentage will rise to approximately thirty-six percent by 2065 (Esterline & Batalova, 2022). The 2020 US census reported that 122,354,219 US households (21.6%) have limited English speaking skills, which is defined as "all members 14 years and over have at least some difficulty with English" (Census Bureau, 2020). The National Center for Education Statistics (2024), the primary federal entity for collecting education-related data, does not collect information about English use at the postsecondary level. However, their report of Fall 2021 students documented 5.3 million students classified as English language learners (ELLs) in K-12 public schools, where, across the fifty states, the state percentage of public school students designated as ELL was as high as 20.2% (Texas). Although the COVID-19 pandemic slowed physical migration, international internet traffic rose by forty-eight percent between mid-2019 and mid-2020 (Altman & Bastian, 2021). Responding to the correlation between COVID-19 and globalization, Altman and Bastian (2021), researchers leading the DHL Initiative on Globalization at New York University, posit that the pandemic "has not knocked globalization down to anywhere close to what would be required for strategists to narrow their focus to their home countries or regions" (para. 17). This data suggests that the sociolinguistic landscape continues to evolve across the globe.

US universities exemplify this shift. As of December 2023, there are 530,110 active Deferred Action for Childhood Arrivals (DACA) recipients, with as many as 1,160,000 people in the eligible population. There are thirty countries across Africa,

Asia, Europe, Oceania, North America, and South America represented by at least 450 active DACA participants as of December 2023 (Migration Policy Institute, 2024). First- and second-generation immigrant and international students accounted for one of every three students (thirty-eight percent) enrolled in US higher education in 2022 (Higher Ed Immigration Portal, 2024). In 2021, the United States hosted seventeen percent of 6.4 million globally mobile international students worldwide, more than any other country (Institute of International Education, 2023). International students accounted for approximately 4.6% of all US undergraduates in the 2019-2020 school year and contributed $39 billion to the US economy in the 2021-2022 school year (FWD.us, 2022). The President's Budget for Fiscal Year 2023 allocated over $1 billion in federal funding to Minority Serving Institutions (MSIs) (The White House, 2022).[1] The lucrative opportunities available in recruiting an international student body combined with increased domestic diversity have contributed to a greater focus on international and multicultural initiatives.

Institutionalized Monolingualism

Despite recognizing the material wealth of a diverse student body, institutions can devalue the sociolinguistic wealth that multilingual students offer by depositing them into monolingually-oriented systems. In other words, students who have different residency statuses or linguistic backgrounds are often normed into a standardized model of academic English discourse or else pushed to the boundaries of the academy. Instead of receiving support for their unique needs (Lee & Alvarez, 2020), students are stringently judged by their English proficiency in admissions practices (Andrade & Hartshorn, 2019), placement (Saenkhum, 2016), and assessments (Inoue, 2014). Horner (2001) comprehensively refers to these practices as English Only policies. Inoue (2015) might argue that this perpetuation of the literacy myth of linguistic homogeneity means that students must learn to "speak white." The Conference on College Composition and Communication (CCCC) *Statement on Globalization in Writing Studies Pedagogy and Research* (2017) describes the resulting paradox:

> At the heart of educational efforts is a conflict: On one hand, colleges and universities may recognize, respect, and respond to the complexities of globalization by reimagining administration, teaching, and research. On the other hand, they may use the pretext of globalization in a limited fashion to enhance institutional reputations, identify new sources of revenue, and entrench received standards. (para. 2)

---

1. There are seven types of MSIs. Not all MSIs are necessarily multilingual.

In settings where students are expected to have fully developed language skills, and support services (e.g., English institutes, intensive English programs, and writing centers) are short-term or maligned, literacy growth is stunted. These kinds of ideologies limit process-based writing teaching (Adler-Kassner, 2017; Driscoll & Cui, 2021; Melzer, 2022) and constrain world Englishes (Hankerson, 2022; Kubota, 2022; Milu, 2022). In turn, institutions further an idealized language or monolingual norm (Kynard, 2018; Lippi-Green, 2012).

Commentary on writing pedagogy unveils a spectrum of opinions about how institutions should respond to globalization and its impact on the linguistic landscape. Inoue (2019) compares language standardization to murder whereas Fish (2009) critiques descriptive language teaching as being "infected with the facile egalitarianism of soft multiculturalism" (para. 13). Delpit (2001) describes how many educators lie somewhere in the middle, facing "a certain sense of powerlessness and paralysis among well-meaning literacy educators who appear to be caught in the throes of a dilemma" as they try to "teach literate discourse styles to all of their students" but "question whether they are acting as agents of oppression by insisting that students who are not already a part of the 'mainstream' learn that discourse" (p. 545). This question is even more relevant as globalization continues to make classrooms more linguistically and culturally diverse than ever.

Institutions and institutional writing initiatives that engender more rigid notions of academic English and its users are likely investing more in the idealized archetypal student who excels within the literacy myth of linguistic homogeneity than creating a site where all students can work towards their unique literacy goals. Moreover, their stance presumably skirts the reality of a diverse student body, including:

> [M]ultilingual international visa students who come to the U.S. as short-term exchange students or to complete baccalaureate degrees or graduate degrees *and* multilingual U.S. residents—an amorphous group comprising students from linguistic enclaves in the US [sic], immigrant students who have spent part of their K-12 literacy education in U.S. secondary schools, and refugee students with interrupted literacy educations. (Zawacki & Cox, 2014, p. 2, emphasis original)

Critical awareness of these students' presence, needs, and goals situates language in social contexts and strengthens heteroglossic language ideologies (i.e., believing in the coexistence of distinct varieties within a language) instead of privileging monolingual norms (Bakhtin, 1986; García & Torres-Guevara, 2009). As we will discuss next, a cohort of SLW researchers have begun thinking through opportunities for WAC to become more malleable to dispersing power tied up in language, race, and nationality so as to dilute literacy ideologies that position privileged language varieties as essential for the acquisition of cultural, economic, or social capital.

Preliminary WAC-SLW Collaborations

A primary goal of WAC-SLW research is developing a system that acknowledges the literacy myth of linguistic homogeneity, transitioning institutional cultures from perceiving writers' *difference-as-deficit* to *difference-as-resource* (Canagarajah, 2002). Cox and Zawacki (2011) made the first major stride towards this paradigm shift through their landmark *Across the Disciplines* special issue, "WAC and Second Language Writing: Cross-field Research, Theory, and Program Development." Contributors analyzed how the curriculum might be better globalized by creating pathways for multilingual student success, strengthening interpersonal relationships between multilingual writers and other institutional members, and developing more integrated support for multilingual writers. These conversations continued in Zawacki and Cox's (2014) edited collection, *Second-Language Writers: Research Towards Linguistically and Culturally Inclusive Programs and Practices*, which again made history as the first book-length project to examine the SLW-WAC relationship explicitly within US contexts. Their introduction cited Leki's (1992) call for WAC to "embrace" (p. 133) multilingual writers. Horner and Hall (2018) responded to this instruction by developing another special issue of *Across the Disciplines*, "Rewriting Disciplines, Rewriting Boundaries: Transdisciplinary and Translingual Challenges for WAC/WID." Hall's (2018) introduction takes up the *trans-* prefix's etymology to show how an SLW-informed WAC program can meaningfully support multilingual students' transitions across disciplinary and linguistic boundaries. WAC-SLW research intends to help students feel less like foreigners in strange and perhaps harmful discoursal spaces and more like learners developing new sociolinguistic skills in a safe environment. This work is happening in other countries (see Hall & Horner, 2023)—for example, Canada (Gentil, 2023), China (Wu, 2013), Japan (Kwon, 2023), Korea (Jordan, 2022), Lebanon (Zenger et al., 2014), and Qatar (Hodges, 2023)—and can potentially act as a model for globalizing US-based WAC research and programming.

Globalizing academic writing initiatives has been a long time coming. Donahue (2023) reminds us how Silva et al. (1997) "predicted decades back that the absence of attention to writing in other languages, in our history, could have the huge effect of leading to 'inadequate theories of composition' (p. 400) overall" (p. 43-44):

> Such a theory could easily become hegemonic and exclusionary; that is, English/Western writing behaviors could be privileged as being "standard"

> [...] and such a theory could be seen as monolingual, monocultural, and ethnocentric. (Silva et al., 1997, p. 402)

Donahue argues that this then-hypothesis, now-reality has set US writing praxis completely out of touch with transnational dialogue. In reply, SLW experts are seeking to offer expertise to work toward infusing writing initiatives with a more globalized perspective and set of practices (e.g., Asaba, 2022; Burns, 2022). Globalizing academic writing initiatives does not mean that all boundaries of language are ignored (Matsuda, 2006). Rather, it means that academic writing initiatives recognize how many boundaries crisscross language as users introduce new dialects, modes, and cultures into ways of making meaning. Surviving as Switzerland looks like globalized academic writing initiatives designed not just for the Tims of the academy but for all students learning to write and writing to learn.

Rewriting the Literacy Myth of Linguistic Homogeneity

I was recently in a meeting with faculty and staff across the university convened by the provost, a committee called the Student Academic Success Team. We met to solidify a mission statement—a task that we had been assigned back in August (it was now late May). As weary teammates nodded along that our draft was fine, a colleague noted how the introduction promised to promote anti-racist, equitable, and culturally relevant practices, but the goals section outlined tasks that upheld standardized, Western, white, ableist norms, mostly embodied as top-down approaches to resolving students' barriers for them, without them. A respondent started typing in the shared document "equity-minded" and "inclusive" into each of the bulleted goals. "There! Problem solved!"

However, the problem was not solved. Just because you say it's anti-racist doesn't make it so. Bouza (2023) importantly encourages departmental intervention. However, this example showcases how the majority of our institutional populations are not equipped to actually intervene, akin to WAC's skirting of language awareness. For this reason, I, along with Shapiro (2023), argue for a more critical approach to the theoretical underpinnings of WAC. In my remaining space, I consider what linguistic justice looks like at the field level, guiding research and training that disciplinarians can draw from when they have to explain that debunking the literacy myth of linguistic homogeneity is more than just "talking the talk." Specifically, I propose possibilities at the logistic, structural, and rhetorical levels to usher in a more multilingual norm.

Logistic Change

The distance between WAC and SLW is complex, and an important facet is the lack of coalition building between fields. WAC is founded upon inter- and multidisciplinarity, but, at least within writing studies and applied linguistics, collaboration has been limited. In the CCCC SLW Standing Group, of which I am now the associate chair, we noticed that likeminded groups existed in isolation from each other. In 2023, we began by working with the TESOL SLW Interest Section by inviting the leadership from each group to speak at the conference meetings of the other. Then, in 2024, we expanded outreach beyond SLW by making inroads with the CCCC Linguistics, Language, and Writing Standing Group and the Progressive Approaches to Grammar Special Interest Group.[2] A noted issue, though, was that attending conferences was costly and, even at the same conference, our events often conflicted in time.

A logistic strategy for bringing together these funds of knowledge, then, is for a literacy broker like AWAC to host third-party meeting-of-the-minds events. Linguistic justice is a substantial endeavor. WAC should invest in uniting linguistic justice scholars from nearby areas like BIPOC research, international student and scholar affairs, and basic writing in conversations explicitly focused on WAC. Within these sites of expertise, scholars can learn from each other. For example, the aforementioned researchers who successfully conducted WAC research abroad can explain how they developed those sites of inquiry, or those skilled at creating safe spaces for marginalized voices to speak out can share their techniques. This approach could de-silo thought leadership by diversifying and developing theories and methodologies for recalibrating WAC's approaches to language. Carving out time and space for interdisciplinary discussions of linguistic justice in WAC mirrors the Swiss approach of valuing different voices.

Structural Change

Structural change concerns the ways we revise our ontology to WAC research and development. Restructuring first looks like asking questions about where linguistic diversity already exists. Young's (2018) call for proposals for the 2019 CCCC written in his vernacular and the CCCC Position Statement, "This ain't another statement! This is a DEMAND for Black linguistic justice!" (Baker-Bell et al., 2020, emphasis original) provide textual examples. CCCC has arguably been a stronger practitioner of linguistic diversity than some SLW spaces, offering, for example, American Sign Language and closed captioning at its annual conference. It has published texts like

---

2. These successful collaborations are largely ascribed to the leadership of Zhaozhe Wang, Shawna Shapiro, Estela Ene, Laura Aull, and Joseph Salvatore.

the above in non-standardized Englishes—progress compared to journals like the *Journal of Second Language Writing* that publish about second languages but only if written in (fairly formal) English.

A structural strategy for multilingua-fying our disciplinary artifacts is opening opportunities for different dialects and languages and destigmatizing their usage. An obvious approach is to invite multilingualism by allowing presentations and articles in other languages. Conferences might dedicate a room for presentations given in a specific L2, for example, or allow L2 presentations and ask presenters to provide transcripts in the meeting's lingua franca so that all can participate. Journals may respond similarly by accepting non-English languages or, at least, being more welcoming to Englishes that don't fit as precisely into prescriptivist norms by adopting a set of linguistic justice review guidelines. The "Anti-Racist Scholarly Reviewing Practices: A Heuristic for Editors, Reviewers, and Authors" (2021) exemplifies such a document. Lesser-cost possibilities include naming language diversity as a participant marker in studies' methodological designs. Or, instead of exclusively soliciting WAC-SLW research for niche collections, editors can encourage routine submissions of research that forefronts multiple languages and dialects. These internal changes can begin de-centering prescriptivist English so that our field no longer defaults, even if inadvertently, to the literacy myth of linguistic homogeneity.

Rhetorical Change

Beginning with logistic and structural changes is essential to carrying out rhetorical change, by which I mean academia's general tendency towards linguistic standardization. The past five or so years have seen an uptick in discussions on diversity, equity, inclusion, and accessibility in academia. In US states where this emphasis hasn't been straight under attack, academia has revised texts from institutional levels (e.g., naming *diversity* in strategic plans) to classroom levels (e.g., inserting *inclusion* in program outcomes). Some of these moves are likely attempts at relevancy, but even in more sincere instances, it has become a bit of a buzzword culture. Rhetorical change seeks to temper this trend by undergirding the words with wider-spread practical knowledge so that making universities more linguistically diverse, equitable, inclusive, and accessible is not just the domain of sociolinguists, but a collective effort across disciplines. This mirrors WAC's tenet of making the teaching of writing not the sole responsibility of writing program specialists, but all kinds of instructors.

A rhetorical change for empowering faculty, staff, and administrators to be agents of linguistic justice encompasses several strategies made possible by WAC's stronger investment in language awareness. Institutional WAC specialists can continue to lend and borrow case studies to examine instances of linguistic interventions. This collective development of WAC expertise can advance our understanding of issues at the WAC-SLW intersection, like how to make directed self-placement (DSP) protocols more effective for multilingual students (Horton, 2022). Producing this kind of scholarship enables alliance building between WAC leaders experiencing similar circumstances. Bolstering the community of practice strengthens camaraderie across WAC and produces scholarship and effective practices that WAC administrators can use to communicate with institutional stakeholders. These conversations can help administrators and instructors develop flexibility in institutional, programmatic, and pedagogic design. WAC programs might already be doing this kind of work with faculty fellows, preparing instructors with discoursal and pedagogical tools for linguistic justice works towards rhetorical change. Institutions that can recalibrate language ideologies will adapt to modern student populations, back their buzzwords with meaning, and model the Swiss' joy for prosperous multilingualism.

Surviving as Switzerland

In this article, sparked by the advent of WAC's fiftieth anniversary, I have reflected on the field's relationship with SLW as a touchstone for forwarding language awareness and linguistic justice. I have taken a bold step in dissenting from one of WAC's most influential founders in the United States, Barbara Walvoord, by repurposing her metaphor to describe the role of multilingualism in the 2020s and beyond. I still esteem her intention to strengthen our collaboration. Shapiro (2023) expertly articulates that promoting critical language awareness (CLA) in WAC "can build our own agency as teachers, administrators, scholars and advocates" (p. 94). Prioritizing linguistic justice in WAC work "can equip us for sustained dialogue and collaborative action that supports powerful languaging among student writers within and across academic disciplines" (Shapiro, 2023, p. 94-95). Surviving at Switzerland requires reflecting on our onto-epistemologies and taking appropriate action.

As the next generation of WAC emerges, we can strategize our logistic, structural, and rhetorical possibilities that can be defined communally. This work includes reflections such as:

- Where does the literacy myth of linguistic homogeneity prevail, and what are the implications of its assumptions?
- What potential collaborations exist, and how can they be meaningfully formed and sustained for linguistic justice?
- How can WAC scholarship pivot toward language awareness such that it becomes energy for productive change at local levels?

Engaging with these entry points hopefully points the path to Switzerland.

To bring myself to walk the walk of increasing linguistic diversity in WAC research, I have, imperfectly, translated this article into my L2, Spanish. Available at https://bit.ly/horton-wac-suiza

Acknowledgments

Many thanks to Aimee Mapes, Christine Tardy, and Shawna Shapiro for their support in writing this article, along with the anonymous reviewers.

References

Adler-Kassner, L. (2017). 2017 CCCC chair's address: Because writing is never just writing. *College Composition and Communication, 69*(2), 317–340.

Adler-Kassner, L., & Wardle, E. (Eds.). (2016). *Naming what we know: Threshold concepts of writing studies* (Classroom). Utah State University Press.

Altman, S. A., & Bastian, C. R. (2021, March 18). The state of globalization in 2021. *Harvard Business Review.* https://hbr.org/2021/03/the-state-of-globalization-in-2021

Andrade, M. S., & Hartshorn, K. J. (2019). *International student transitions: A framework for success.* Cambridge Scholars Publishing.

Anson, C. M. (1988). Toward a multidimensional model of writing in the academic disciplines. In D. A. Joliffe (Ed.), *Advances in writing research: Writing in academic disciplines* (Vol. 2, pp. 1–33). Ablex.

Anti-racist scholarly reviewing practices: A heuristic for editors, reviewers, and authors. (2021). https://tinyurl.com/reviewheuristic

Asaba, M. (2022). Pursuing expertise in L2 writing instruction research. *Journal of Second Language Writing, 58,* 100939. https://doi.org/10.1016/j.jslw.2022.100939

Baker-Bell, A., Williams-Farrier, B. J., Jackson, D., Johnson, L., Kynard, C., & McMurtry, T. (2020). *This ain't another statement! This is a DEMAND for Black linguistic justice!* Conference on College Composition and Communication. https://cccc.ncte.org/cccc/demand-for-black-linguistic-justice

Bakhtin, M. M. (1986). The problem of speech genres. In C. Emerson & M. Holquist (Eds.), *Speech genres and other late essays* (V. W. McGee, Trans.) (pp. 60–102). University of Texas Press.

Batalova, J. (2024, March 13). *Frequently requested statistics on immigrants and immigration in the United States.* Migration Policy Institute. https://www.migrationpolicy.org/article/frequently-requested-statistics-immigrants-and-immigration-united-states?gclid=Cj0KCQjwg_iTBhDrARIsAD3Ib5gHz53GxKh0Or5zsUlkDnCQ2-kc6GhQ-OT1LosSXSMCmYC8dreNC6QaAqfNEALw_wcB

Beaufort, A. (2007). *College writing and beyond: A new framework for university writing instruction.* Utah State University Press.

Benda, J., Jones, C. E., Poe, M., & Stephens, A. Y. L. (2022). Confronting superdiversity again: A multidimensional approach to teaching and researching at a global university. In J. R. Daniel, K. Malcolm, & C. Rai (Eds.), *Writing across difference: Theory and intervention* (pp. 218–238). Utah State University Press.

Bouza, E. (2023). (Re)Defining WAC to guide linguistic justice ideological changes across campuses. *The WAC Journal, 34,* 64–82. https://doi.org/10.37514/WAC-J.2023.34.1.05

Burns, A. (2022). Emergence in teacher writing expertise: Teachers be(com)ing expert. *Journal of Second Language Writing, 58,* 100938. https://doi.org/10.1016/j.jslw.2022.100938

Canagarajah, A. S. (2002). *Critical academic writing and multilingual students.* University of Michigan Press.

Canagarajah, A. S. (2015). The place of world Englishes in composition: Pluralization continued. In S. Perryman-Clark, D. E. Kirkland, & A. Jackson (Eds.), *Students' right to their own language: A critical sourcebook* (pp. 279–304). National Council of Teachers of English.

Conference on College Composition and Communication. (2017). *CCCC statement on globalization in writing studies pedagogy and research.* https://cccc.ncte.org/cccc/resources/positions/globalization

Conference on College Composition and Communication. (2020). *CCCC statement on second language writing and multilingual writers.* https://cccc-ncte-org.ezproxy2.library.arizona.edu/cccc/resources/positions/secondlangwriting

Cox, M., Galin, J. R., & Melzer, D. (2018). *Sustainable WAC: A whole systems approach to launching and developing writing across the curriculum programs.* National Council of Teachers of English.

Cox, M., Jordan, J., Ortmeier-Hooper, C., & Schwartz, G. G. (Eds.). (2010). *Reinventing identities in second language writing.* National Council of Teachers of English.

Cox, M., & Zawacki, T. M. (2014). Introduction. In T. M. Zawacki & M. Cox (Eds.), *WAC and second-language writers: Research towards linguistically and culturally inclusive programs and practices* (pp. 15–40). The WAC Clearinghouse; Parlor Press. https://doi.org/10.37514/PER-B.2014.0551.1.3

Crusan, D. (2010). *Assessment in the second language writing classroom.* University of Michigan Press.

Crusan, D. (2011). The promise of directed self-placement for second language writers. *TESOL Quarterly, 45*(4), 774–780. https://doi.org/10.5054/tq.2010.272524

Cushman, E. (2021). Decolonial translation as methodology for learning to unlearn. In C. Donahue, K. Blewett, & C. Monrow (Eds.), *The expanding universe of writing studies: Higher education writing research* (pp. 199–213). Peter Lang.

De Costa, P. I. (2020). Linguistic racism: Its negative effects and why we need to contest it. *International Journal of Bilingual Education and Bilingualism, 23*(7), 833–837. https://doi.org/10.1080/13670050.2020.1783638

Delpit, L. (2001). The politics of teaching literate discourse. In E. Cushman, E. R. Kintgen, B. M. Kroll, & M. Rose (Eds.), *Literacy: A critical sourcebook* (pp. 545–554). Bedford/St. Martin's.

Donahue, C. (2009). "Internationalization" and composition studies: Reorienting the discourse. *College Composition and Communication, 61*(2), 212–243.

Donahue, C. (2023). "We are the 'Other'": The future of exchanges between writing and language studies. In J. Hall & B. Horner (Eds.), *Toward a transnational university: WAC/WID across borders of language, nation, and discipline* (pp. 35–58). The WAC Clearinghouse; University Press of Colorado.

Driscoll, D. L., & Cui, W. (2021). Visible and invisible transfer: A longitudinal investigation of learning to write and transfer across five years. *College Composition and Communication, 73*(2), 229–260.

Elder, C. L. (Ed.). (2023). Special issue: Transforming WAC at 50: What, how, and for whom? *The WAC Journal, 34*. https://wac.colostate.edu/docs/journal/vol34/vol34.pdf

Esterline, C., & Batalova, J. (2022, March 17). Frequently requested statistics on immigrants and immigration in the United States. *The Online Journal of the Migration Policy Institute.* https://www.migrationpolicy.org/article/frequently-requested-statistics-immigrants-and-immigration-united-states

Faigley, L. (1985). Nonacademic writing: The social perspective. In L. Odell & D. Goswami (Eds.), *Writing in nonacademic settings* (pp. 231–248). Guilford.

Ferris, D. R., Evans, K., & Kurzer, K. (2017). Placement of multilingual writers: Is there a role for student voices? *Assessing Writing, 32*, 1–11. https://doi.org/10.1016/j.asw.2016.10.001

Ferris, D., & Thaiss, C. (2011). Writing at UC Davis: Addressing the needs of second language writers. *Across the Disciplines, 8*(4), 1–25. https://doi.org/10.37514/ATD-J.2011.8.4.27

Fish, S. (2009, September 7). What should colleges teach? Part 3. *The New York Times.* https://archive.nytimes.com/opinionator.blogs.nytimes.com/2009/09/07/what-should-colleges-teach-part-3/

Fishman, S. M., & McCarthy, L. (2001). An ESL writer and her discipline-based professor: Making progress even when goals don't match. *Written Communication, 18*(2), 180–228. https://doi.org/10.1177/0741088301018002002

Freeman, K., & Li, M. (2019). "We are a ghost in the class." First year international students' experiences in the global contact zone. *Journal of International Students, 9*(1), 19–38. https://doi.org/10.32674/jis.v9i1.270

FWD.us. (2022, September 14). *International students and graduates in the United States: 5 things to know*. https://www.fwd.us/news/international-students/#:~:text=During%20 the%202019%2D2020%20school,are%20from%20China%20and%20India

García, O., & Torres-Guevara, R. (2009). Monoglossic ideologies and language policies in the education of U.S. Latinas/os. In J. Sánchez Muñoz, M. Machado-Casas, E. G. Murillo Jr., & C. Martínez (Eds.), *Handbook of Latinos and education: Theory, research, and practice* (pp. 182–193). Taylor & Francis Group.

Gee, J. P. (1989). Literacy, discourse, and linguistics: An introduction. *The Journal of Education, 171*(1), 5–176.

Geller, A. E. (2011). Teaching and learning with multilingual faculty. *Across the Disciplines, 8*(4), 1–20. https://doi.org/10.37514/ATD-J.2011.8.4.06

Gentil, G. (2023). Remapping writing instruction at the borders of modern languages, bilingual education, and translation studies: A Canadian proposal for a transnational conversation. In J. Hall & B. Horner (Eds.), *Toward a transnational university: WAC/WID across borders of language, nation, and discipline* (pp. 59–83). The WAC Clearinghouse; University Press of Colorado.

Graff, H. J. (2010). The literacy myth at 30. *Journal of Social History, 43*(3), 635–661.

Hall, J. (2009). WAC/WID in the next America: Redefining professional identity in the age of the multilingual majority. *The WAC Journal, 20*(1), 33–49. https://doi.org/10.37514/WAC-J.2009.20.1.03

Hall, J. (2014). Multilinguality is the mainstream. In B. Horner & K. Kopelson (Eds.), *Reworking English in rhetoric and composition* (pp. 31–48). Southern Illinois University Press.

Hall, J. (2018). Introduction to the special issue: Rewriting disciplines, rewriting boundaries. *Across the Disciplines, 15*(3), 1–10. https://doi.org/10.37514/ATD-J.2018.15.3.08

Hall, J., & Horner, B. (Eds.). (2023). *Toward a transnational university: WAC/WID across borders of language, nation, and discipline*. The WAC Clearinghouse; University Press of Colorado.

Hankerson, S. (2022). "Why can't writing courses be taught like this fo real": Leveraging critical language awareness to promote African American Language speakers' writing skills. *Journal of Second Language Writing, 58*, 100919. https://doi.org/10.1016/j.jslw.2022.100919

Higher Ed Immigration Portal. (n.d.). *Immigrant and international students in higher education*. Retrieved June 4, 2024, from https://www.higheredimmigrationportal.org/national/national-data/#:~:text=Immigrant%2Dorigin%20students%20represent%20 a,all%20students%2C%20in%20higher%20education

Hodges, A. (2023). Mapping transnational institutions: Connecting between WAC/WID and Qatar's engineering industry. In J. Hall & B. Horner (Eds.), *Toward a transnational university: WAC/WID across borders of language, nation, and discipline* (pp. 167–188). The WAC Clearinghouse; University Press of Colorado.

Horner, B. (2001). "Students' right," English only, and re-imagining the politics of language. *College English*, *63*(6), 741–758. https://doi.org/10.2307/1350100

Horner, B. (2023). Introduction. The transnational translingual university: Teaching academic writing across borders and between languages. In J. Hall & B. Horner (Eds.), *Toward a transnational university: WAC/WID across borders of language, nation, and discipline* (pp. 3–10). The WAC Clearinghouse; University Press of Colorado. https://doi.org/10.37514/ATD-B.2023.1527.1.3

Horner, B., & Hall, J. (Eds.). (2018). Special issue: Rewriting disciplines, rewriting boundaries: Transdisciplinary and translingual challenges for WAC/WID. *Across the Disciplines*, *15*(3).

Horner, B., NeCamp, S., & Donahue, C. (2011). Toward a multilingual composition scholarship: From English only to a translingual norm. *College Composition and Communication*, *63*(2), 269–300.

Horner, B., & Trimbur, J. (2002). English only and U.S. college composition. *College Composition and Communication*, *53*(4), 594–630. https://doi.org/10.2307/1512118

Horton, A. E. (2022). Two sisters and a heuristic for listening to multilingual, international students' directed self-placement stories. *Journal of Writing Assessment*, *15*(1), 1–19. https://doi.org/10.5070/W4JWA.222

Inoue, A. B. (2014). Theorizing failure in US writing assessments. *Research in the Teaching of English*, *48*(3), 330–352.

Inoue, A. B. (2015). *Antiracist writing assessment ecologies*. The WAC Clearinghouse; Parlor Press.

Inoue, A. B. (2019). 2019 CCCC chair's address: How do we language so people stop killing each other, or what do we do about white language supremacy? *College Composition and Communication*, *71*(2), 352–369.

Institute of International Education. (2023). *2023 Project Atlas infographic*. https://www.iie.org/wp-content/uploads/2024/01/Project-Atlas_Infographic_2023_2.pdf

Ives, L., Leahy, E., Leming, A., Pierce, T., & Schwartz, M. (2014). Chapter 8. "I don't know if that was the right thing to do": Cross-Disciplinary/cross-institutional faculty response to L2 writing. In T. M. Zawacki & M. Cox (Eds.), *WAC and second-language writers: Research towards linguistically and culturally inclusive programs and practices* (pp. 211–232). The WAC Clearinghouse; Parlor Press. https://doi.org/10.37514/PER-B.2014.0551.2.08

Janopoulos, M. (1995). Writing across the curriculum, writing proficiency exams, and the NNS college student. *Journal of Second Language Writing*, *4*(1), 43–50. https://doi.org/10.1016/1060-3743(95)90022-5

Jones, R., & Comprone, J. J. (1993). Where do we go next in writing across the curriculum? *College Composition and Communication*, *44*(1), 59–68. https://doi.org/10.2307/358895

Jordan, J. (2022). *Grounded literacies in a transnational WAC/WID ecology: A Korean-U.S. study*. The WAC Clearinghouse; University Press of Colorado. https://wac.colostate.edu/books/international/grounded/

Kubota, R. (2022). Decolonizing second language writing: Possibilities and challenges. *Journal of Second Language Writing, 58*, 100946. https://doi.org/10.1016/j.jslw.2022.100946

Kwon, M. H. (2023). Challenges in positioning WAC/WID in international contexts: Perspectives from a Japanese engineering undergraduate program. In J. Hall & B. Horner (Eds.), *Toward a transnational university: WAC/WID across borders of language, nation, and discipline* (pp. 189–204). The WAC Clearinghouse; University Press of Colorado.

Kynard, C. (2018). Stayin woke: Race-Radical literacies in the makings of a higher education. *College Composition and Communication, 69*(3), 519–529.

Lee, E., & Alvarez, S. P. (2020). World Englishes, translingualism, and racialization in the US college composition classroom. *World Englishes, 39*(2), 263–274. https://doi.org/10.1111/weng.12459

Leki, I. (1992). *Understanding ESL writers: A guide for teachers*. Boynton/Cook.

Leki, I. (2007). *Undergraduates in a second language: Challenges and complexities of academic literacy development*. Lawrence Erlbaum Associates.

Lindsey, P., & Crusan, D. (2011). How faculty attitudes and expectations toward student nationality affect writing assessment. *Across the Disciplines, 8*(4), 1–19. https://doi.org/10.37514/ATD-J.2011.8.4.23

Lippi-Green, R. (2012). *English with an accent: Language, ideology, and discrimination in the United States*. Routledge.

Martinez, A. (2022). English as past and present imperialism: A translingual narrative on Chicanx language and identity in the US-Mexico borderlands. In T. Do & K. Rowan (Eds.), *Racing translingualism in composition: Toward a race-conscious translingualism* (pp. 56–66). Utah State University Press.

Matsuda, P. K. (2006). The myth of linguistic homogeneity in U.S. college composition. *College English, 68*(6), 637–651. https://doi.org/10.2307/25472180

McLeod, S. H. (2008). The future of WAC—plenary address, ninth international writing across the curriculum conference, May 2008 (Austin, Texas). *Across the Disciplines, 5*(1), 1–6. https://doi.org/10.37514/ATD-J.2008.5.1.03

Melzer, D. (2022). Responding for transfer. *Composition Forum, 50*. https://compositionforum.com/issue/50/responding-transfer.php

Migration Policy Institute. (n.d.). *Deferred action for childhood arrivals (DACA) data tools*. Retrieved June 4, 2024, from https://www.migrationpolicy.org/programs/data-hub/deferred-action-childhood-arrivals-daca-profiles

Milu, E. (2022). Hip-Hop and the decolonial possibilities of translingualism. *College Composition and Communication, 73*(3), 376–409.

National Center for Education Statistics. (2024). *English learners in public schools*. https://nces.ed.gov/programs/coe/indicator/cgf

Nero, S. J. (1997). English is my native language . . . or so I believe. *TESOL Quarterly*, *31*(3), 585–593. https://doi.org/10.2307/3587842

Ortmeier-Hooper, C. (2008). English may be my second language, but I'm not "ESL." *College Composition and Communication*, *59*(3), 389–419.

Palmquist, M., Childers, P., Maimon, E., Mullin, J., Rice, R., Russell, A., & Russell, D. R. (2020). Fifty years of WAC: Where have we been? Where are we going? *Across the Disciplines*, *17*(3), 5–45. https://doi.org/10.37514/ATD-J.2020.17.3.01

Patton, M. D. (2011). Mapping the gaps in services for L2 writers. *Across the Disciplines*, *8*(4), 1–19. https://doi.org/10.37514/ATD-J.2011.8.4.26

Pavlenko, A., & Blackledge, A. (Eds.). (2004). *Negotiation of identities in multilingual contexts*. Channel View Publications.

Perryman-Clark, S. M. (2023). *The new work of writing across the curriculum: Diversity and inclusion, collaborative partnerships, and faculty development*. Utah State University Press.

Pessoa, S., & Mitchell, T. D. (2019). Preparing students to write in the disciplines. In N. A. Caplan & A. M. Johns (Eds.), *Changing practices for the L2 writing classroom: Moving beyond the five-paragraph essay* (pp. 150–177). University of Michigan Press.

Riazantseva, A. (2012). "I ain't changing anything": A case-study of successful generation 1.5 immigrant college students' writing. *Journal of English for Academic Purposes*, *11*(3), 184–193. https://doi.org/10.1016/j.jeap.2012.04.007

Ruecker, T. (2011). Improving the placement of L2 writers: The students' perspective. *WPA: Writing Program Administration*, *35*(1), 91–117.

Rutz, C. (2021). Fearlessness, sustainability, and adaptability via WAC in a small school. *The WAC Journal*, *32*(1), 16–22. https://doi.org/10.37514/WAC-J.2022.32.1.03

Saenkhum, T. (2016). *Decisions, agency, and advising: Key issues in the placement of multilingual writers into first-year composition courses*. Utah State University Press.

Saidy, C. (2018). Inez in transition: Using case study to explore the experiences of underrepresented students in first-year composition. *WPA: Writing Program Administration*, *41*(2), 17–34.

Schweizerische eidgenossenschaft. (2020, May 11). *Language*. Retrieved June 18, 2022, from https://www.eda.admin.ch/aboutswitzerland/en/home/gesellschaft/sprachen.html

Shapiro, S. (2023). Languaging across the curriculum: Why WAC needs CLA (and vice versa). *The WAC Journal*, *34*, 83–100. https://doi.org/10.37514/WAC-J.2023.34.1.06

Silva, T., Leki, I., & Carson, J. (1997). Broadening the perspective of mainstream composition studies: Some thoughts from the disciplinary margins. *Written Communication*, *14*(3), 398–429.

Skerrett, A. (2013). Building multiliterate and multilingual writing practices and identities. *English Education*, *45*(4), 322–360.

Thaiss, C. (2014). Afterword: Writing globally, right here, right now. In T. M. Zawacki & M. Cox (Eds.), *WAC and second-language writers: Research towards linguistically and culturally inclusive programs and practices* (pp. 465–476). The WAC Clearinghouse; Parlor Press. https://doi.org/10.37514/PER-B.2014.0551.3.2

Thaiss, C. (2021). WAC fearlessness, sustainability, and adaptability: Part one. *The WAC Journal, 32*(1), 8–15. https://doi.org/10.37514/WAC-J.2022.32.1.02

Thaiss, C., & Porter, T. (2010). The state of WAC/WID in 2010:Methods and results of the U.S. survey of the international WAC/WID mapping project. *College Composition and Communication, 61*(3), 534–570.

United States Census Bureau. (2020). *Limited English speaking households* (S1602) [Table]. https://data.census.gov/cedsci/table?q=language%20spoken%20at%20home&tid=ACSST5Y2020.S1602

Walvoord, B. E. (1996). The future of WAC. *College English, 58*(1), 58–79.

The White House. (2022, March 30). *President Biden's FY 2023 budget advances equity.* https://www.whitehouse.gov/omb/briefing-room/2022/03/30/president-bidens-fy-2023-budget-advances-equity/

Williamson, M. M. (1988). A model for investigating the functions of written language in different disciplines. In D. A. Joliffe (Ed.), *Advances in writing research: Writing in academic disciplines* (Vol. 2, pp. 89–132). Ablex.

Wu, D. (2013). *Introducing writing across the curriculum into China: Feasibility and adaptation.* Springer.

Young, V. A. (2018). *Call for program proposals.* Conference on College Composition and Communication. https://cccc.ncte.org/cccc/conv/call-2019

Zamel, V. (1995). Strangers in academia: The experiences of faculty and ESL students across the curriculum. *College Composition and Communication, 46*(4), 506–521.

Zamel, V., & Spack, R. (Eds.). (2003). *Crossing the curriculum.* Taylor & Francis Group.

Zawacki, T. Myers. (2021). Conversations in process: Two dynamic program builders talk about adapting WAC for trilingual Hong Kong. *The WAC Journal, 32*(1), 63–71. https://doi.org/10.37514/WAC-J.2022.32.1.06

Zawacki, T. M., & Cox, M. (2011). Introduction to WAC and second language writing. *Across the Disciplines, 8*(4), 1–11. https://doi.org/10.37514/ATD-J.2011.8.4.19

Zawacki, T. M., & Cox, M. (Eds.). (2014). *WAC and second-language writers: Research towards linguistically and culturally inclusive programs and practices.* The WAC Clearinghouse; Parlor Press. https://doi.org/10.37514/PER-B.2014.0551

Zawacki, T. M., & Habib, A. S. (2014). Chapter 7. Negotiating "errors" in L2 writing: Faculty dispositions and language difference. In T. M. Zawacki & M. Cox (Eds.), *WAC and second-language writers: Research towards linguistically and culturally inclusive programs and practices* (pp. 183–210). The WAC Clearinghouse; Parlor Press. https://doi.org/10.37514/PER-B.2014.0551.2.07

Zenger, A., Mullin, J., & Haviland, C. P. (2014). Chapter 17. Reconstructing teacher roles through a transnational lens: Learning with/in the American University of Beirut. In T. M. Zawacki & M. Cox (Eds.), *WAC and second-language writers: Research towards linguistically and culturally inclusive programs and practices* (pp. 415–437). The WAC Clearinghouse; Parlor Press. https://doi.org/10.37514/PER-B.2014.0551.2.17

Zhang-Wu, Q. (2022). Rethinking translingualism in college composition classrooms: A digital ethnographic study of multilingual students' written communication across contexts. *Written Communication, 40*(1), 145–174. https://doi.org/10.1177/07410883221127208

Practicing Peer Feedback: How Task Repetition and Modeling Affect Amount and Types of Feedback over a Series of Peer Reviews

LUCY BRYAN, DAYNA S. HENRY, SARAH R. BLACKSTONE, ANNA MARIA JOHNSON, AND LACIE KNIGHT

Providing feedback on peers' writing is a complex endeavor that engages several higher-order cognitive processes. While some evidence suggests that practice improves peer-review skills, more research is needed to understand how peer feedback changes with practice. The present study aims to (1) explore the impact of practice on the amount and types of feedback that students give in peer review and (2) investigate whether providing model feedback in addition to practice enhances students' development as peer reviewers. The researchers analyzed 3,761 comments provided by eighty students over the course of four peer-review sessions. Quantitative analysis of feedback quantity and qualitative analysis of feedback content revealed changes over time, including differences in the feedback of students who did and did not have access to model feedback, and differences in feedback from minimal, moderate, and heavy commenters. Practicing providing feedback throughout several rounds of peer review may help students generate more and higher-quality feedback, especially when paired with training in the form of reviewing model feedback.

Across many disciplines in higher education, instructors require students to provide feedback on their peers' coursework. In contrast with peer assessment, which asks students to rate or grade the work of their peers, peer feedback is generally understood to be process-oriented and formative (Elizondo-Garcia et al., 2019; Kasch et al., 2022). As an instructional method, peer feedback can facilitate learning for both the giver and the receiver, improving critical-thinking and problem-solving skills, enhancing knowledge of the subject matter, and deepening understanding of a task or creation process (Baker, 2016; Cho and Cho, 2011; Cho and MacArthur, 2011; Nicol et al., 2014; Patchan and Schunn, 2015; Vickerman,

2009). Peer feedback also offers a practical way to ensure that students receive personalized responses to their works-in-progress, a task that may not always be feasible for instructors, particularly those with heavy teaching loads and large class sizes (Elizondo-Garcia et al., 2019; Zong et al., 2021).

Much of the literature on peer feedback in higher education focuses on its use with writing assignments, including literature reviews, concept-application papers, term papers, research reports, and evaluation essays in a range of disciplines (Baker, 2016; Gao et al., 2019; Kelly, 2015; Huisman et al., 2018; Simpson and Clifton, 2015; Zong et al., 2021). In the context of undergraduate- and graduate-level writing assignments, peer feedback is often called peer review (Baker, 2016; Min, 2016; Reddy et al., 2021; Simpson and Clifton, 2015). The present study adds to this body of literature by investigating the impact of practice on the amount and types of feedback that undergraduate students give over the course of four writing assignments. Furthermore, this study investigates whether, in addition to practice, providing peer reviewers with model feedback from a teaching assistant enhances their development as peer reviewers.

Previous studies of peer review have produced typologies for classifying peer-review comments and investigating their effects and efficacy (Cho and Cho, 2011; Cho and MacArthur, 2011; Cho et al., 2006; Kelly, 2015; Nelson and Schunn, 2009; Patchan et al., 2016). Scholars have analyzed both quantitative and qualitative features of peer feedback, including number, length, focus, scope, and function of comments (Elizondo-Garcia et al., 2019; Huisman et al., 2018; Patchan and Schunn, 2015; Patchan et al., 2016; Zong et al., 2021). The findings of these investigations have important implications for how peer review is taught and delivered. For example, comment length appears to be positively associated with helpfulness (Zong et al., 2021). Additionally, feedback that identifies the location of a problem seems to improve the writer's understanding of the comment (Nelson and Schunn, 2009). Moreover, the presence of a solution in a review comment, particularly when paired with a description of the problem, appears to increase the likelihood that the writer will implement that feedback—though some research suggests that explanations of problems can interfere with understanding (Elizondo-Garcia et al., 2019; Nelson and Schunn, 2009; Patchan et al., 2016).

The literature of peer review has also offered insights into how instructors should implement peer-feedback processes in their classrooms (Min, 2016; Reddy et al., 2021; Topping, 2009; van den Berg et al., 2006). For example, research has shown that instructors can help their students develop peer-review skills by modeling how to give feedback on sample papers (Min, 2016; Topping, 2009). Research also supports the use of feedback groups in which writers receive commentary from multiple peers, a practice that gives writers "an opportunity to compare their fellow students' remarks, and to determine their relevance" (van den Berg et al., 2006, p. 34–35).

A number of researchers have acknowledged that providing peer feedback is a cognitively demanding task (Carless and Boud, 2018; Deiglmayr, 2018; Gielen and De Wever, 2015; Min, 2016; Reddy et al., 2021). Particularly when student peer reviewers are unfamiliar with the conventions of academic or disciplinary writing, they struggle to identify the issues that are most worthy of a writer's attention (Kelly, 2015). Student peer reviewers may have difficulty detecting higher-order concerns, such as problems with organization, counter-arguments, audience awareness, and evidence (Baker, 2016; Crossman and Kite, 2012; Gao et al., 2019; Kelly, 2015). Instead of devoting their attention to those important issues, they may focus on "polishing" or "fixing" surface-level problems, such as typos or errors in grammar, spelling, and punctuation (Baker, 2016; Crossman and Kite, 2012; Gao et al., 2019; Kelly, 2015). As Krishneel Reddy et al. (2021) have pointed out, student peer reviewers are likely to require practice in order to realize "the full benefits of peer review" (p. 826). However, the vast majority of studies of peer feedback analyze a single instance of peer review. That said, the few studies that do explore the effects of practicing peer review indicate that task repetition improves students' ability to provide helpful feedback, particularly when paired with training or guidance from an instructor (Gielen and De Wever, 2015; Reddy et al., 2021; Zong et al., 2021). Research from Zheng Zong et al. (2021) reveals some of the mechanisms through which students improve as reviewers over the course of multiple rounds of peer review. Their study found that over the course of six rounds of peer review, students "were more likely to provide helpful feedback after they received helpful feedback" themselves (p. 981). However, the strongest predictor of feedback helpfulness was, in fact, the total length of commentary that the peer reviewer provided in the previous round. In other words, the more feedback a student provided in one round of peer review, the more likely they were to provide helpful feedback in the next round.

While these studies show the promise of practice in developing students' peer-review skills, more research is needed to understand how peer feedback changes over the course of multiple rounds of practice, as well as how additional variables, such as feedback models, influence students' evolution as peer reviewers. The present study investigated how peer-review comments changed over the course of four peer-feedback assignments that took place in the span of five weeks. We also imposed an experimental condition that offered insights into the effects of modeling feedback: students in the experimental condition were able to view feedback offered by a teaching assistant (TA) before providing their own commentary, while students in the control condition were not. We advanced four research questions:

1. Is there a relationship between practice and the amount of feedback peer reviewers provide?
2. Is there a relationship between practice and the types of feedback peer reviewers provide?
3. Are minimal, moderate, and heavy commenters more or less likely to offer certain types of feedback?
4. Does the availability of model feedback from a TA influence the amounts and types of feedback peer reviewers provide?

Method

Course Setting and Participants

Participants were undergraduate health sciences majors enrolled in an upper-division course on health-behavior change at a regional university in the southern United States. We collected data from three sections of this course in the same academic year, one in the fall semester and two in the spring semester. All sections were taught by the same instructor, covered the same content, and included the same assignments. IRB approval (no. 18-0254) was obtained prior to the course ending, and consent procedures were handled by a member of the research team who was not the instructor of the course. Of the 115 students enrolled in the three sections of the course, 70% (n = 80) participated in this study. Students who did not provide informed consent and students whose group members did not provide informed consent were excluded from the study.

Procedures

Group Selection. In this course, students worked in groups of five throughout the semester on a series of assignments that concluded with a group paper and presentation on a health intervention. Prior to assigning groups, the instructor administered a survey and gathered information about students' academic performance and habits. The instructor then matched students with similar GPAs and work styles. This approach was intended to limit conflict and social loafing. A total of sixteen groups (eight from each semester) were included in this study.

Article-Summary Assignment. To prepare for the high-stakes group assignments at the end of the semester, each student individually completed a two-to-three-page summary of a scholarly article relevant to their group's topic and to a particular theory of health-behavior change. For this assignment, students had to cite and summarize the content of the article, identify how it employed the theory, and reflect on their own learning. Along with the assignment instructions, students were provided with a copy of the instructor's grading rubric. Students submitted drafts of their article summaries according to staggered deadlines—one student per group per week. Each week, the writers submitting the assignment were instructed to post their summaries and a copy of the original article in a group discussion board, where they received feedback from their fellow group members. After receiving feedback, the writers had four days to revise and resubmit their article summaries, at which time the instructor graded them. This cycle was repeated five times over five weeks.

Peer-Review Instructions. Students were required to provide feedback on each of their group members' article summaries, so they provided four peer reviews over the course of five weeks. Peer reviews had to be submitted within three days of the submission of the article summary. For each peer review, students had to read both the article summary and the scholarly article it summarized. They were then instructed to provide feedback, questions, and comments on their peer's writing using the comment function in Microsoft Word. Peer reviewers were explicitly told to focus on the effectiveness of the writer's paraphrasing, their accuracy in interpreting the article, and the correctness of their citation. After reviewing the article summary, students were required to upload the document with their commentary to the discussion board, along with a reflection on what they had learned in the peer-review process. Their feedback and reflections were visible to the writer and to the other group members.

Evaluation and Grading of Peer Reviews. As a way to hold reviewers accountable for providing high-quality feedback and writers accountable for implementing it, writers were asked to evaluate the depth and utility of the feedback they received. Along with their revised article summaries, writers had to submit a list ranking their peer reviewers from most helpful to least helpful, supported by descriptions of why each peer's feedback was or was not useful. In addition to the peer reviewers' comments themselves, the course instructor used these evaluations to inform the grades for the peer reviews. The instructor assigned grades according to the number of comments, the quality of comments, and evidence that the peer reviewer had thoroughly read the original article. If the reviewer lost any points, the instructor provided summative feedback.

Experimental Manipulation

In the two sections of the course that ran in the spring, a key change was made to the procedures outlined above. Unlike the fall section of the course, each spring section had an undergraduate teaching assistant (TA) who had previously taken the course with the instructor. These TAs were required to provide comments on each article summary within twenty-four hours of its submission and to post their review to the relevant discussion board. The goal was to provide reviewers in the group with model feedback before they had to submit their own feedback.

Materials

After grades were submitted at the end of the semester, the instructor examined the signed consent forms, removed identifications from the peer-reviewed article summaries of those who had consented, and supplied them as PDF files to the research team. The vast majority of the eighty participants submitted all four of the required peer reviews. However, six of them submitted only three, and one submitted only two. Hence, a total of 312 article summaries with peer-review comments were provided for analysis.

Coding Process

All documents were imported into NVivo12 for qualitative coding. A total of four coders performed the coding process. Participants were randomly assigned to coders so that all peer-review comments provided by a given participant were coded by two different coders. Although interrater reliability (calculated using Cohen's kappa) was very high in all categories, a third "master coder" reviewed the codes assigned by the two initial coders and resolved any discrepancies in order to generate a final dataset to be used for analysis.

Because peer reviewers provided the vast majority of comments via the comment function in Microsoft Word, comments were already broken into discrete units. Coders were instructed to code each comment as a single unit and to select all codes applicable to the material in that comment. Thus, it was possible for a single comment to be coded according to multiple classifications, or "nodes," within a single category. In the rare case that a peer reviewer provided a comment using the track-changes function, the coder was instructed to highlight the entire sentence and code it as a single unit. Similarly, in the rare case that a peer reviewer provided end comments within the document, the coder was instructed to code the entire block of commentary as a single unit. This approach resulted in a total of 3,761 discrete comment units.

Coding Categories

The coding approach involved classifying the mode, scope, and topic of each peer-review comment. This coding scheme drew upon the work of previous scholars, in particular Cho and Cho (2011), Cho and MacArthur (2011), Cho et al. (2006),

Kelly (2015), Nelson and Schunn (2009), and Patchan et al. (2016). The coding categories are briefly described below and elaborated in Appendix A.

Feedback Mode. Feedback mode describes the function of the peer feedback. Every comment unit coded met at least one of these five mode classifications: problem-detecting, advising, editing, justifying, and praising. The feedback mode category had near perfect interrater reliability, with percentage agreement between pairs ranging from 98.12% (κ = .94) to 99.67% (κ = .99).

Feedback Scope. Feedback scope describes a comment's degree of focus, indicating whether it addresses a specific instance of a problem or achievement, a holistic trend, or something in between. Every comment unit coded met at least one of these three scope classifications: local, mid-range, and global. The feedback scope category had near perfect interrater reliability, with percentage agreement between pairs ranging from 97.75% (κ = .93) to 99.56% (κ = .98).

Feedback Topic. Feedback topic describes the subject matter of a comment. Every comment unit coded met at least one of these nine topic classifications: accuracy; citations; clarity, precision, and wording; grammar, mechanics, formatting, spelling, and typos; idea development; paraphrasing; purpose; structure, organization, and flow; and wordiness and concision. The feedback topic category had near perfect interrater reliability, with percentage agreement between pairs ranging from 97.85% (κ = .93) to 99.46% (κ = .97).

Descriptive and Quantitative Measures

The following descriptive and quantitative measures were also included in the dataset.

Round of Feedback. Each document in the dataset was labeled with a review number designating whether it was from the first, second, third, or fourth round of feedback provided by the peer reviewer. This made it possible to view the data as a time series.

Paper Number. Each document in the dataset was labeled with a number designating when it had been submitted and received comments. Any given document, for example, could have been the first, second, third, fourth, or fifth article summary within the group to receive a peer review.

Group Number. Each document in the dataset was labeled with a number designating the group to which its writer and reviewer belonged. This made it possible to explore group effects.

Semester. Each document in the dataset was labeled with an *F* or *S* designating whether it came from the fall or spring semester. This made it possible to compare the feedback from participants in the experimental condition (spring) with the feedback from those in the control group (fall).

Comment Count. Each document in the dataset was assigned a number designating how many discrete comment units were present in the document.

Word Count. Each document in the dataset was assigned a number designating the aggregate word count of all of the comments in the document. Because there was more variability and a greater range in word count than in comment count, we referenced this measure when we wanted to analyze the amount of feedback provided.

Commenter Designation. Each participant in the study was labeled as a minimal, moderate, or heavy commenter based on the average number of words they provided per review. Their designation was determined using percentiles: participants in the 1st–32nd percentile were labeled as minimal commenters, those in the 33rd–65th percentile as moderate commenters, and those in the 66th percentile and above as heavy commenters.

Data Analyses

Research Question 1: The Relationship between Practice and Amount of Feedback Provided. In order to determine if there was a relationship between practice and the amount of feedback peer reviewers provided, we calculated average word counts for each round of feedback and ran a linear regression, controlling for round of feedback and semester, with word count as the dependent variable.

Research Question 2: The Relationship between Practice and Types of Feedback Provided. To explore any changes in feedback mode, scope, and topic over the course of the peer-reviews, we calculated the total number of comments coded at each node for each of the four rounds of feedback. We then ran an analysis of variance (ANOVA) to determine whether the number of comments coded at any of the feedback mode, scope, and topic nodes changed according to round of feedback.

Research Question 3: The Relationship between Commenter Designation and Types of Feedback Provided. Because the total number of comments varied by round, comment counts were not used as the basis for comparing the types of comments made by minimal, moderate, and heavy commenters. Instead, each reviewer received a *Y* (yes) or *N* (no) for each feedback type, indicating whether they had given any commentary that fell into each of the seventeen available feedback classifications under mode, scope, and topic. Then, we used a chi-squared test to determine whether minimal, moderate, or heavy commenters were more or less likely than the others to provide feedback of each type.

Research Question 4: The Influence of Model Feedback on Amount and Types of Feedback Provided. We investigated whether the experimental condition—presenting students with model feedback, provided by a TA during every round of peer review—influenced the amount of feedback peer reviewers provided. We used a T-test to compare the average word counts given by reviewers during each semester. We also explored the influence of the experimental condition on feedback mode, scope, and topic. Looking at the proportion of reviewers who had or had not given any commentary within each of the seventeen available feedback classifications, we used a chi-squared test to determine whether participants in the spring semester were more or less likely than those in the fall semester to provide particular types of feedback.

Results

Research Question 1: The Relationship between Practice and Amount of Feedback Provided

Students saw a statistically significant increase ($p = 0.005$) in average word count per comment set between their first ($n = 171$) and second ($n = 237$) rounds of peer review (see Table 1).

Table 1.
Changes in average word count over four rounds of feedback.

Round of peer review	Average word count	Degree of change (β)	95% confidence interval	p-value
Round 1	171			
Round 2	237	66	17, 95	0.005
Round 3	203	26	-13, 66	0.2
Round 4	186	11	-28, 51	0.6

Research Question 2: The Relationship between Practice and Types of Feedback Provided

Peer reviewers also shifted their commenting strategies and the foci of their feedback over the four rounds of peer review (see Table 2). Changes occurred in each of the major coding categories, though not at every node. In terms of feedback mode, peer reviewers were more likely to offer praise in later rounds of feedback ($F = 7.646$,

$p < 0.001$), particularly in the last two rounds. While a greater proportion of comments contained editing during the first round and justifying during the second round, these differences were not statistically significant. Additionally, peer reviewers increased the scope of their comments over time. Students were more likely to offer mid-range comments after the first round of feedback ($F = 9.33$, $p < 0.001$) and global comments in the latter two rounds of feedback ($F = 3.17$, $p = 0.025$). Finally, peer reviewers were more likely to focus on idea development after the first round of feedback ($F = 5.09$, $p = 0.002$).

Table 2.
Number of comments, per person mean, coded at feedback mode, scope, and topic over four rounds of feedback.

	Round 1		Round 2		Round 3		Round 4	
	Number	Mean	Number	Mean	Number	Mean	Number	Mean
	Feedback mode							
Advising	310	4.01	422	5.29	388	4.85	354	4.75
Editing	425	5.54	431	5.32	403	5.13	388	5.2
Justifying	118	1.56	175	2.15	131	1.66	125	1.69
Praising	88	1.14	149	1.87	180	2.23	167	2.25
Problem-detecting	188	2.48	256	3.19	188	2.39	189	2.55
	Feedback scope							
Local	681	8.87	742	9.2	682	8.66	658	8.83
Mid-range	143	1.87	261	3.29	272	3.46	248	3.32
Global	32	0.41	33	0.43	53	0.61	49	0.67
	Feedback topic							
Accuracy	39	0.51	50	0.62	35	0.44	38	0.51
Citations	63	0.84	73	0.9	71	0.9	61	0.81
Clarity, precision, wording	256	3.34	287	3.57	258	3.22	229	3.08
Grammar, mechanics...	215	2.81	192	2.35	205	2.53	235	3.15
Idea development	187	2.43	293	3.67	287	3.57	266	3.56
Paraphrasing	61	0.77	93	1.18	76	0.96	66	0.89
Purpose	79	1.01	107	1.35	125	1.59	102	1.39
Structure, organization, flow	52	0.7	86	1.08	82	1.04	72	0.97
Wordiness, concision	72	0.92	113	1.42	87	1.11	80	1.08

Research Question 3: The Relationship between Commenter Designation and Types of Feedback Provided

The percentages of comment units coded at each node were remarkably similar among minimal, moderate, and heavy commenters, but there were a few notable trends within these designations (see Table 3). The more comments peer reviewers provided, the more likely they were to advise ($x^2 = 10.58$, $p = 0.005$), to justify (x^2 = 25.78, p < 0.001), and to offer comments that were mid-range in scope (x^2 = 8.08, p < 0.018). Additionally, reviewers who wrote more commentary were more likely to comment on wordiness and concision (x^2 = 23.3, p < 0.001). Finally, heavy commenters were more likely than minimal or moderate commenters to comment on structure, organization, and flow (x^2 = 20.8, p < 0.001).

Table 3.
Number and proportion of comments, by commenter designation, coded at feedback mode, scope, and topic.

	Minimal		Moderate		Heavy	
	Number	Proportion	Number	Proportion	Number	Proportion
Feedback mode						
Advising	280	32.4%	478	39.6%	716	42.3%
Editing	365	42.3%	525	43.5%	763	45.1%
Justifying	77	8.9%	161	13.3%	313	18.5%
Praising	170	19.7%	182	15.1%	231	13.6%
Problem-detecting	176	20.4%	267	22.1%	385	22.8%
Feedback scope						
Local	648	75.1%	891	73.8%	1235	73.0%
Mid-range	197	22.8%	291	24.1%	442	26.1%
Global	44	5.1%	59	4.9%	61	3.6%
Feedback topic						
Accuracy	28	3.2%	49	4.1%	85	5.0%
Citations	82	9.5%	94	7.8%	93	5.5%
Clarity, precision, wording	220	25.5%	323	26.8%	488	28.9%
Grammar, mechanics...	224	26.0%	250	20.7%	370	21.9%
Idea development	230	26.7%	356	29.5%	445	26.3%
Paraphrasing	60	7.0%	107	8.9%	130	7.7%
Purpose	94	10.9%	123	10.2%	200	11.8%
Structure, organization, flow	59	6.8%	66	5.5%	170	10.1%
Wordiness, concision	51	5.9%	108	8.9%	195	11.5%

Research Question 4: The Influence of Model Feedback on Amount and Types of Feedback Provided

Amount of Feedback. This study imposed an experimental condition in which half of the peer reviewers in the study (those who took the course during the spring semester) had the opportunity to view model feedback from a TA before submitting their own peer-review comments. On average, peer reviewers in the experimental condition generated about fifty more words per comment set than peer reviewers in the control condition. Reviewers in the fall cohort wrote an average of 175.4 words per round of feedback, while reviewers in the spring cohort wrote an average of 225.3 words per round of feedback (t = -3.492, df = 309.42, p = 0.0005). In fact, in every round of feedback, reviewers in the spring semester produced average word counts that were higher than those produced by reviewers in the fall semester (see Figure 1). That said, after the boost in average word count that occurred in the second round of feedback, word counts in the experimental condition dropped in the subsequent two rounds, even dipping beneath the word count of round one in the final round. On the other hand, students in the control group only saw a dip in word count after the second round of feedback.

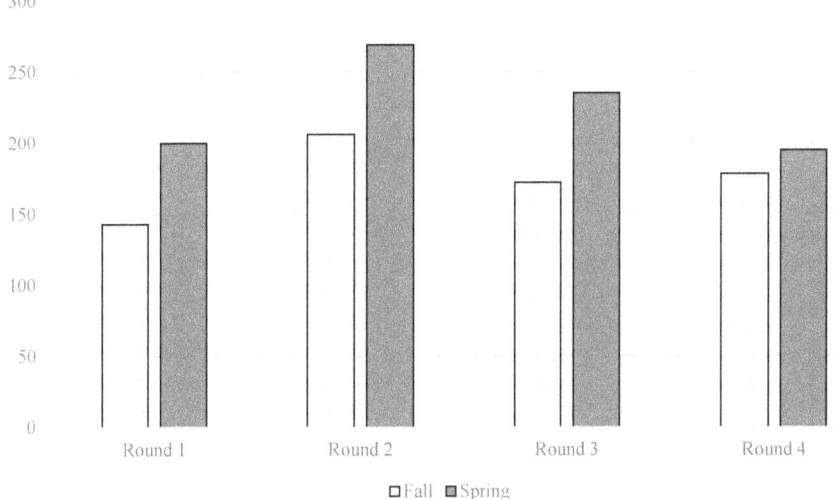

Figure 1. Average word count per participant, per round of feedback, and by semester.

Types of Feedback. Additionally, peer reviewers in the control and experimental conditions appeared to favor different types of feedback (see Table 4). Comments from reviewers in the spring semester were more likely to include problem-detecting (x^2 = 6.74, $p < 0.001$) and to focus on mid-range concerns (x^2 = 12.92, $p < 0.001$). Additionally, idea development (x^2 = 7.03, $p = 0.008$), paraphrasing (x^2 = 19.49, $p < 0.001$), purpose (x^2 = 9.38, $p = 0.002$), and wordiness and concision (x^2 = 14.83, $p < 0.001$) were more likely to be topics of commentary for reviewers in the experimental condition. There were also some trends in the control condition that were marginally significant. For example, peer reviewers who took the course in the fall semester appeared more likely to address citations (x^2 = 2.73, $p = 0.063$) and surface-level concerns, such as grammar and spelling (x^2 = 2.21, $p = 0.087$), in their comments.

Table 4.
Number and proportion of comments, by semester, coded at feedback mode, scope, and topic.

	Fall semester (control group)		Spring semester (experimental group)	
	Number	Proportion	Number	Proportion
Feedback mode				
Advising	686	36.5%	788	41.8%
Editing	878	46.7%	775	41.1%
Justifying	271	14.4%	280	14.9%
Praising	285	15.2%	298	15.8%
Problem-detecting	373	19.9%	455	24.2%
Feedback scope				
Local	1456	77.6%	1318	70.0%
Mid-range	408	21.7%	522	27.7%
Global	76	4.0%	88	4.7%
Feedback topic				
Accuracy	71	37.8%	91	48.3%
Citations	140	7.5%	129	6.8%
Clarity, precision, wording	549	29.2%	482	25.6%
Grammar, mechanics ...	508	27.1%	336	17.8%
Idea development	473	25.2%	558	29.6%
Paraphrasing	109	5.8%	188	10.0%
Purpose	183	9.7%	234	12.4%
Structure, organization, flow	128	6.8%	167	8.9%
Wordiness, concision	139	7.4%	215	11.4%

Discussion and Conclusion

The present study had two aims: (1) to explore the impact of practice on the amount and types of feedback that peer reviewers give and (2) to investigate whether providing peer reviewers with model feedback in addition to practice promotes their development as peer reviewers. Here, we discuss how the findings of our study advanced those aims.

Amount of Feedback

Our data revealed two important trends regarding the amount of feedback (measured in word count) that peer reviewers provided over the sequence of four peer-review sessions. First, the peer reviewers in our study wrote significantly more commentary in their second round of feedback than in their first. Next, peer reviewers in the experimental condition—that is, those who had the opportunity to view a model set of comments written by a TA before submitting their own feedback—wrote an average of 22% more words per peer review than those in the control group.

While it is impossible to separate task repetition from other influences, it seems likely that the learning gains enabled by practice played some role in the increase in word count that occurred during the second round of feedback. A single round of peer review may have been sufficient to allow reviewers to "automate" familiar aspects of the task—for example, using the comment function in Microsoft Word, toggling between a peer's article summary and the scholarly article, or revisiting the assignment description to review criteria. As a result, peer reviewers may have been able to dedicate more cognitive resources to generating feedback in the second round. This explanation aligns with educational psychologists' current understanding of the relationship between practice and learning as informed by cognitive load theory (Sweller et al., 2019).

It is worth considering these findings in conjunction with studies that have explored the effects of practice on feedback quality. Zong et al. (2021) have found that the amount of commentary a peer reviewer provides is a powerful predictor of feedback helpfulness in the subsequent round of peer review. This finding suggests that many reviewers in our study provided their most helpful commentary in their third round of feedback, as reviewers generally wrote the most feedback in round two. Zong et al.'s findings also lead us to believe that, at least in the latter three feedback rounds, peer reviewers in the experimental condition provided more helpful commentary than those in the control group, who by comparison wrote fewer words in every round of peer review. This inference is bolstered by the findings of Gielen and De Wever's (2015) study, which indicates that the more guidance students receive about how to provide feedback, the higher quality their reviews become. We think it likely that having access to model feedback gave peer reviewers an enriched task representation; that is, reviewing model feedback improved their understanding of the expectations regarding peer-review comments and therefore their ability to fulfill those expectations.

Types of Feedback

As peer reviewers in the present study gained more practice giving peer feedback, numerous shifts occurred in the types of feedback they provided. We think it is helpful to view these findings through the lens of previous research, which indicates that student reviewers often favor "fixing" superficial problems that are local in scope at the expense of addressing recurring problems and higher-order concerns that more broadly and profoundly affect the paper (Crossman and Kite, 2012; Gao et al., 2019; Kelly, 2015). This tendency, which may be a result of the cognitive demands of peer review, demonstrates students' inclination to focus on simpler or more familiar problems with clear solutions as opposed to issues of greater complexity.

Our results did document a strong focus on local concerns. In all of the feedback rounds, the majority of comments (78.3%) given by peer reviewers were local in scope. However, as peer reviewers got more practice, they tended to expand the scope of their comments to include problems (or successes) that affected multiple sentences, whole sections, or even the entire paper. Additionally, the proportion of comments focused on the clarity and precision of wording dropped in each successive round, while the proportion of comments focused on idea development increased. This trend suggests that practice facilitated movement from lower-order concerns toward higher-order concerns, presumably reflecting increased motivation or ability to engage in the cognitively demanding aspects of peer review. A possible explanation for this shift is that the more participants practiced providing feedback, the better they understood the aims and expectations of the assignments, enabling them to identify larger-scale problems in their peers' writing. It is also possible that the drafts submitted in later rounds were more clearly and precisely written than those in earlier rounds—potentially because the writers had benefited from the process of reviewing peers' drafts in previous rounds (Cho and MacArthur, 2011). That said, a significant portion of comments in all rounds, including the last one, devoted attention to grammar, mechanics, formatting, spelling, and typos. Additionally, some higher-order concerns, such as purpose and structure, only received slightly more attention in later rounds of feedback.

In our study, the example set by model feedback from a TA appeared to increase the likelihood that peer reviewers would comment on higher-order concerns. Peer reviewers in the control group were more likely than those in the experimental condition to comment on grammatical concerns and citations. Meanwhile, those in the experimental condition were more likely to focus on mid-range concerns and to comment on accuracy, idea development, purpose and structure, organization, and flow. Similarly, peer reviewers who were designated heavy commenters (those in the 66th percentile and above for aggregate word count) were more likely to offer mid-range commentary and feedback on structure, organization, and flow than peers who were minimal or moderate commenters. Furthermore, peer reviewers of higher commenter designations were more likely to advise and to justify in their feedback—suggesting that they moved beyond "fixing" to offering more complex forms of commentary, such as instructions and explanations. These findings align with our understanding that higher word counts correspond with higher-quality commentary (Zong et al., 2021).

We wish to highlight a final finding regarding types of commentary: peer reviewers were most likely to offer praise in the third and fourth rounds of feedback. There are a number of possible explanations for this trend. First, it seems likely that the article summaries reviewed in these rounds were objectively better because their writers had applied insights gleaned from earlier rounds of peer review. Second, peer reviewers in the later rounds may have been more sensitive to writers' desire for praise, having recently received peer feedback on their own article summaries. A third possibility is that practice improved peer reviewers' ability to perceive and articulate what was working well in their peers' papers. Whether or not this finding is the direct result of practice, it has interesting implications. Patchan and Schunn (2015) have proposed that the process of *giving* praise may help peer reviewers better understand or discover successful writing strategies. Thus, the presence of praise is a desirable trait in peer review, but our results indicate that it is less likely to happen without practice.

Practical Implications, Limitations, and Directions for Future Research

Our study's findings suggest that giving students the opportunity to practice providing feedback throughout several rounds of peer review may help them generate more and higher-quality feedback, especially when paired with training in the form of reviewing model feedback. While one round of practice produced some significant changes in the amount and types of commentary given, three or more rounds may further increase the likelihood that peer reviewers offer feedback related to higher-order and global concerns.

As is often the case with studies conducted in real-word educational settings, it is impossible to isolate the impact of practice and of feedback modeling from other potential influences. For example, peer reviewers in this study may have been motivated to change their feedback practices after receiving their professor's summative feedback and grade or after seeing commentary written by other group members. Additionally, this study did not account for students' dispositions and academic behaviors, which could have influenced their feedback practices. Despite these limitations, as Huisman et al. (2018) have pointed out, "the authenticity of the learning context" is vital "in determining the practical value of the research findings" (p. 964).

It is worth noting that our study did not assess feedback helpfulness; instead, we used word count as a corollary for helpfulness in subsequent feedback rounds, relying on previous research from Zong et al. (2021). Similarly, we did not explore the uptake of feedback or how the experience of peer review affected students' writing, as this would have involved qualitative analysis of student's writing, which we chose not to pursue.

One potential downside of the peer-review structure employed in this study is that students whose work was reviewed in earlier rounds had more opportunity to integrate what they had learned into their own commentary, while students whose work was reviewed in the final round were deprived of this opportunity. This inequitable distribution of learning opportunities could be mitigated by having students assume the role of writer multiple times (for example, by also submitting a revision for peer review) in addition to acting as reviewer multiple times over the course of the peer-review sequence.

Because our study took place in a specific context—namely, an upper-division health sciences course—its findings may not be generalizable to other contexts. More research is needed to determine whether similar patterns emerge when students engage in a series of peer reviews in other disciplines and for other assignments. Future research might explore whether there are differences in feedback uptake following successive rounds of peer review. Additionally, researchers might explore the effects of peer-review series with structures different from the one we studied—for example, a series of three peer reviews in which students serve as both writers and reviewers in every round. Because research has underscored the important role that providing feedback can play in developing students as writers, it would be worthwhile to study whether students' growth as peer reviewers over a sequence of peer reviews correlates with their growth as writers over a sequence of writing assignments.

References

Baker, K. M. (2016). Peer review as a strategy for improving students' writing process. *Active Learning in Higher Education, 17*(3), 179–192. https://doi.org/10.1177/1469787416654794

Carless, D., & Boud, D. (2018). The development of student feedback literacy: Enabling uptake of feedback. *Assessment & Evaluation in Higher Education, 43*(8), 1315–1325. https://doi.org/10.1080/02602938.2018.1463354

Cho, Y. H., & Cho, K. (2011). Peer reviewers learn from giving comments. *Instructional Science, 39*(5), 629–643. https://doi.org/10.1007/s11251-010-9146-1

Cho, K., & MacArthur, C. (2011). Learning by reviewing. *Journal of Educational Psychology, 103*(1), 73–84. https://doi.org/10.1037/a0021950

Cho, K., Schunn, C. D., & Charney, D. (2006). Commenting on writing: Typology and Perceived helpfulness of comments from novice peer reviewers and subject matter experts. *Written Communication, 23*(3), 260-294. https://doi.org/10.1177/0741088306289261

Crossman, J. M., & Kite, S. L. (2012). Facilitating improved writing among students through directed peer review. *Active Learning in Higher Education, 13*(3), 219–229. https://doi.org/10.1177/1469787412452980

Deiglmayr, A. (2018). Instructional scaffolds for learning from formative peer assessment: Effects of core task, peer feedback, and dialogue. *European Journal of Psychology of Education, 33*(1), 185–198. https://doi.org/10.1007/s10212-017-0355-8

Elizondo-Garcia, J., Schunn, C., & Gallardo, K. (2019). Quality of peer feedback in relation to instructional design: A comparative study in energy and sustainability

MOOCs. *International Journal of Instruction*, *12*(1), 1025–1140. https://doi.org/10.29333/iji.2019.12166a

Gao, Y., Schunn, C. D. D., & Yu, Q. (2019). The alignment of written peer feedback with draft problems and its impact on revision in peer assessment. *Assessment & Evaluation in Higher Education*, *44*(2), 294–308. https://doi.org/10.1080/02602938.2018.1499075

Gielen, M., & De Wever, B. (2015). Structuring the peer assessment process: A multilevel approach for the impact on product improvement and peer feedback quality. *Journal of Computer Assisted Learning*, *31*(5), 435–449. https://doi.org/10.1111/jcal.12096

Huisman, B., Saab, N., van Driel, J., & van den Broek, P. (2018). Peer feedback on academic writing: Undergraduate students' peer feedback role, peer feedback perceptions and essay performance. *Assessment & Evaluation in Higher Education*, *43*(6), 955–968. https://doi.org/10.1080/02602938.2018.1424318

Kasch, J., Van Rosmalen, P., Henderikx, M., & Kalz, M. (2022). The factor structure of the peer-feedback orientation scale (PFOS): Toward a measure for assessing students' peer-feedback dispositions. *Assessment & Evaluation in Higher Education*, *47*(1), 15–28. https://doi.org/10.1080/02602938.2021.1893650

Kelly, L. (2015). Effectiveness of guided peer review of student essays in a large undergraduate biology course. *International Journal of Teaching and Learning in Higher Education*, *27*(1), 56–68.

Min, H. (2016). Effect of teacher modeling and feedback on EFL students' peer review skills in peer review training. *Journal of Second Language Writing*, *31*, 43–57. https://doi.org/10.1016/j.jslw.2016.01.004

Nelson, M. M., & Schunn, C. D. (2009). The nature of feedback: How different types of peer feedback affect writing performance. *Instructional Science*, *37*(4), 375–401. https://doi.org//10.1007/s11251-008-9053-x

Nicol, D., Thomson, A., & Breslin, C. (2014). Rethinking feedback practices in higher education: A peer review perspective. *Assessment & Evaluation in Higher Education*, *39*(1), 102–122. https://doi.org/10.1080/02602938.2013.795518

Patchan, M. M., & Schunn, C. D. (2015). Understanding the benefits of providing peer feedback: How students respond to peers' texts of varying quality. *Instructional Science*, *43*(5), 591–614. https://doi.org/10.1007/s11251-015-9353-x

Patchan, M. M., Schunn, C. D., & Correnti, R. J. (2016). The nature of feedback: How peer feedback features affect students' implementation rate and quality of revisions. *Journal of Educational Psychology*, *108*(8), 1098–1120. https://doi.org/10.1037/edu0000103

Reddy, K., Harland, T., Wass, R., & Wald, N. (2021). Student peer review as a process of knowledge creation through dialogue. *Higher Education Research & Development*, *40*(4), 825–837. https://doi.org/10.1080/07294360.2020.1781797

Simpson, G., & Clifton, J. (2015). Assessing postgraduate student perceptions and measures of learning in a peer review feedback process. *Assessment & Evaluation in Higher Education, 41*(4), 501–514. https://doi.org/10.1080/02602938.2015.1026874

Sweller, J., van Merriënboer, J. J. G., & Paas, F. (2019). Cognitive architecture and instructional design: 20 years later. *Educational Psychology Review, 31*, 261–292. https://doi.org/10.1007/s10648-019-09465-5

Topping, K. J. (2009). Peer assessment. *Theory Into Practice, 48*(1), 20–27. https://doi.org/10.1080/00405840802577569

van den Berg, I., Admiraal, W., & Pilot, A. (2006). Peer assessment in university teaching: Evaluating seven course designs. *Assessment & Evaluation in Higher Education, 31*(1), 19–36. https://doi.org/10.1080/02602930500262346

Vickerman, P. (2009). Student perspectives on formative peer assessment: An attempt to deepen learning? *Assessment & Evaluation in Higher Education, 34*(2), 221–230. https://doi.org/10.1080/02602930801955986

Zong, Z., Schunn, C. D., & Wang, Y. (2021). Learning to improve the quality peer feedback through experience with peer feedback. *Assessment & Evaluation in Higher Education, 46*(6), 973–992. https://doi.org/10.1080/02602938.2020.1833179

Appendix A

Table 5.
Coding categories with definitions and examples.

Classification	Definition	Example
Feedback mode		
Advising	Gives general direction or options for revision in response to a problem, concern, or error	"Add in some of the findings of the experiment here."
Editing	Supplies the actual deletion, punctuation, or language needed to resolve a problem	"Comma instead of semicolon"
Justifying	Justifies advice or an edit by describing the reviewer's reasoning or the intended outcome	"Consider including a brief definition of meaning. . . . What is a longitudinal cohort study? It would help in readers' comprehension."
Praising	Highlights something the author is doing well	"I agree with this statement, and I think it is an important take away from this journal article."
Problem-detecting	Indicates a problem, concern, or error	"The sentence is a little wordy."
Feedback scope		
Local	Narrowly focuses on a specific problem or achievement, typically a word or something sentence-level	"Use a different word here."
Mid-range	Discusses a problem or achievement that occurs multiple times or encompasses multiple variables, sentences, or paragraphs but does not apply to the entire composition	"I couldn't really find the main results and findings of this study within your paper. Maybe reference the Results section in the article and expand more on what was concluded."
Global	Holistically describes the product, highlighting problems or achievements that affect most or all of the paper	"Overall, I think your draft is really well put organized and has very few grammatical errors. I think you did a great job at paraphrasing and not taking too much detail from the article. It was easy for me to read the paper (meaning it had good flow)."
Feedback topic		
Accuracy	Makes comments and/or suggestions regarding the accuracy of the writer's interpretation of the article's purpose, methods, results, theories, etc.	"Although this might be true, I did not read any supporting information from the study for this claim."
Citations	Makes comments or suggestions regarding whether or not the citation follows APA guidelines	"Other than missing the page numbers, the citation looks good."
Clarity, precision, wording	Identifies content that generates confusion and/or suggests additions, substitutions, or changes that will increase clarity, precision, or effectiveness of language; alternatively, praises writer for clear, precise, or direct writing	"This part of the sentence sounds a bit off. I would maybe change it to 'the individuals were chosen purely based on geographical location.'"
Grammar, mechanics, formatting, spelling, typos	Makes comments or suggestions related to the rules of written language and the presentation of textual and visual elements	"Good sentence but watch your tense. You start in past tense, switch to present, and then switch back to past tense."

Idea development	Makes comments or suggestions regarding the ideas in the article summary; typically, identifies a need to add information, explanation, detail, or examples, but may offer praise for insights	"Great point! Maybe here you can elaborate on how the TPB was used in this study and why it was the most appropriate and accurate theory to use!"
Paraphrasing	Comments on the writer's success or failure in paraphrasing content from the original article by employing different wording and sentence structures	"This sentence appears to be quite similar to the sentence on page 879. Maybe try and paraphrase it using a few more of your own words!"
Purpose	Gives feedback regarding the purpose of the assignment, paragraph, or type of writing (in this case, an article summary); may comment on how well or poorly the writer conformed to conventions, expectations, or instructions; may also comment on the general efficacy of the prose	"She was very critical on my conclusion when it was written like this. Specify exactly what you learned about this theory."
Structure, organization, flow	Makes comments or suggestions about the order of ideas, flow of information, or paragraphing	"I would try to find a way to combine these paragraphs."
Wordiness, concision	Identifies wordiness and/or suggests deletions or changes that will result in more concise phrases or sentences; alternatively, praises writer for concision	"To remain concise, you can eliminate these sentences."

STEM Faculty Focus Groups Respond to Student Writing and Learning Goals: Entry Points and Barriers to Curricular Change

MEGAN MERICLE, J. PATRICK COLEMAN, AND JULIE ZILLES

Collaboration between WAC practitioners and disciplinary faculty on the development of writing goals helps center field-specific expertise and build long-term investment. However, the tacit nature of writing knowledge in STEM presents challenges. We provide a snapshot of such challenges through faculty focus groups conducted in three departments (civil and environmental engineering, crop sciences, and physics) that aimed to surface tacit knowledge, gain insight into disciplinary writing values, and promote conversations about the integration of writing across a curriculum. Faculty responded to student writing by evaluating students' scientific becoming and occasionally co-constructing process narratives. In contrast to the specificity and variety of their expectations regarding student writing, faculty largely expressed agreement on a preliminary set of writing goals. We found that (1) faculty experiences integrally shape curricular conversations, (2) instructional barriers (e.g., time, labor) can lead to the persistence of generalized conceptions of writing, and (3) the focus groups revealed the difficulty of translating writing expectations into concrete curricular changes.

Introduction

Building long-term pedagogical investment in writing requires surfacing the rich literate[1] histories and tacit knowledge of disciplinary faculty while differentiating that knowledge from limiting assumptions about writing and student writers (e.g., Anson & Dannels, 2009; Bohr & Rhoades, 2014; Flash, 2016; Hughes, 2020). Curricular

---

1. We use the term "literate" in reference to our use of Paul Prior's (1998) framework of "literate activity," an approach that moves beyond material texts to view writing as situated, mediated and dispersed. According to Prior, literate activity "is not located *in* acts of reading and writing, but *as* cultural forms of life saturated with textuality, that is strongly motivated and mediated by texts" (p. 138).

change requires faculty to adopt a process orientation to writing (Kovanen et al., 2020), recognizing that disciplinary writing cannot be fully addressed in a single class but requires continuous, situated practice within students' fields (e.g., Crowley, 1998; Jamieson, 2009; Kerri, 2017; Melzer, 2014; Rhoades & Carroll, 2012). As a six-year transdisciplinary, writing-across-the-curriculum (WAC) team with members from engineering, the sciences, and writing studies, we aim to build writing goals situated within STEM departmental expectations, interrogating faculty ideologies around writing and identifying barriers to curricular change.

Our work as a team began with a needs analysis of engineering curricula at our institution, the University of Illinois Urbana-Champaign. We found that students in engineering departments frequently place out of first-year writing courses (60 percent in Fall 2016) and, aside from fulfilling an upper-division composition requirement, primarily encounter writing instruction in laboratory or design classes toward the end of their curricula (Yoritomo et al., 2018). Engineering curricula at our institution are heavily influenced by criteria set by ABET, including "an ability to communicate effectively with a range of audiences" (Accreditation Board for Engineering and Technology, 2023), but this wording is sufficiently vague that it cannot really guide instruction. To address these gaps, one of our ongoing initiatives is to vertically integrate writing instruction across all four years of undergraduate STEM curricula.

In this paper, we focus on one stage of this work: faculty focus groups conducted in three departments (civil and environmental engineering, crop sciences, and physics) with the aim of building learning goals around writing in STEM. Through these focus groups, we sought to surface faculty knowledge around disciplinary communication and build investment in shared writing values. We reflect on the disciplinary expectations and challenges in developing writing goals that these focus groups revealed, offering implications for other WAC stakeholders.

WAC/WEC Models for Constructing Writing Learning Goals

To inform our approach, we looked to other WAC programs that construct writing learning goals with faculty. Such programs emphasize the importance of centering faculty knowledge, maintaining departmental pedagogical agency, and situating writing studies researchers as catalysts for change. These principles were recently united by Chris Anson and Pamela Flash (2021) in a writing-enriched curricula (WEC) model. WEC programs position writing as central to learning, implement "ongoing, partnered support," view tacit understandings of writing as hugely influential in writing instruction, and seek to build meaningful integration of writing into curricula through sustained questioning of "assumptions and expectations" (p. 20). WEC literature reinforces the time and resource investment necessary to build change. In this paper, we respond to the need for more discussion of the initial stages of this long-term, resource-intensive process.

For example, the communication-across-the-curriculum (CAC) program at North Carolina State exemplifies WEC values by giving departments complete control over their response to formative reports profiling the placement of writing in department curricula, and by centering faculty voices throughout these conversations (Anson & Dannels, 2009). Similarly, a WAC offering at the University of Wisconsin–Madison, integrated as a unit within a year-long faculty professional development program, emphasizes articulating "discipline-specific rhetorical knowledge" over "converting uninitiated colleagues" (Hughes, 2020, p. 54). Faculty self-select to join the program and, as Bradley Hughes (2020) noted, articulate a rich range of pedagogical writing goals. At Wisconsin–Madison, taking up a WEC approach means accounting for these goals while also acknowledging possible limitations in faculty's conceptions of writing.

The University of Minnesota's WEC program provides another example of challenging writing ideologies through ongoing conversations in which faculty are empowered to make change in their departments (Flash, 2016). Pamela Flash (2016) outlines the role that writing studies researchers and WAC stakeholders can play in questioning and challenging the "long-held and socially reinforced characterizations" of writing that faculty hold in their fields (p. 229). We likewise work to build "active, dialogical reflection . . . [that] effectively mak[es] the familiar strange," a process Flash (2016) argues "can catalyze a dismantling of entrenched and unproductive pedagogical thinking" (p. 231). Notably, both the NC State and Minnesota programs exist in the context of a university mandate for the articulation and assessment of communication or writing-related curricular goals; our work takes place in the absence of such a driver. However, we share a recognition of the time and iteration sponsoring these conversations require, as well as the need for situated strategies to draw out disciplinary knowledge and surface assumptions.

STEM Programs Pursuing Curricular Change around Writing

While WEC programs provide crucial models for initiating curricular change, STEM curricula in which writing goals are integrated across all four years of an undergraduate program seem to be relatively scarce, likely due to barriers posed by institutional structures. Vertical integration requires sustained support from key faculty campus units, financial commitment, and community buy-in. However, one notable example is the materials science and engineering (MSE) department at Virginia Tech, which instituted a comprehensive writing and communication program led by a director from the English department. The program includes eight required courses taught by MSE faculty with team-teaching support from the director (Hendricks and Pappas,

1996). At the University of New Haven, engineering faculty were trained to develop course materials as part of the Project to Integrate Technical Communication Habits (PITCH), in which instruction on technical communication genres and habits was scaffolded across all four years in seven STEM majors (Harichandran et al., 2014). In examples like these of vertical integration of writing instruction in STEM, curricular change was typically guided by learning goals and supported by individuals with expertise in technical communication and/or WAC, illustrating the efficacy of collaborative goal development (Ford, 2012; Mathison, 2019; Patton, 2008).

Faculty views of writing are instrumental in building toward curricular change. When developing curricular goals for writing, both WEC and STEM literature demonstrate the importance of centering student writing and leveraging points of tension as "pivot points of change" rather than attempting to reduce these points to "resistance" (Flash, 2016, p. 230). As Michelle Cox, Jeffrey Galin, and Dan Melzer (2018) write, "there is a complex and codependent relationship between the structure of campus writing programs and faculty ideologies regarding writing" (p. 98). Regarding our own team, we have found that narratives of student writers, or "backstage" teacher-to-teacher talk (Goffman, 1956; Vaughan, 2007), play a key role in writing instruction. Because of genesis amnesia—the phenomenon whereby we forget how we acquired knowledge and skills (Bourdieu, 1977)—along with the tendency for memory to become increasingly conventionalized over time, these narratives of student writers can become typified and allegorical, obscuring the complexity of literacy development.

In the sections that follow, we investigate one of the central principles of the WEC approach: "unchallenged, tacit-level conceptions of writing and writing instruction inform the ways writing is taught and the degree to which writing is meaningfully incorporated into diverse undergraduate curricula" (Flash, 2016, p. 20). As Stacey Sheriff (2021) points out, WAC and writing-in-the-disciplines (WID) research has yet to fully explore "the dynamics of how groups of faculty come to articulate their tacit knowledge and disciplinary expectations for writing" (p. 147). Our contribution addresses these dynamics in the initial stages of curricular goal development across departments to better understand and respond to the "fits and starts" (Ware et al., 2022) of curricular change.

Our Context and Approach

Begun in 2016, the Writing Across Science and Engineering (WAES) program is a transdisciplinary WAC initiative centered in the Grainger College of Engineering at the University of Illinois Urbana-Champaign. At the time the focus groups were conducted, our team included six faculty members and six graduate students from engineering, the sciences, and writing studies. We follow a transdisciplinary action research (TDAR) model (Stokols, 2006) in which assessment and research are interconnected in an iterative cycle. Our primary interventions include a semester-long faculty learning community (FLC) that meets weekly, followed by individualized mentoring of faculty by teams of writing studies and STEM mentors (Gallagher et al., 2020; Kovanen et al., 2022; Ware et al., 2019; Yoritomo et al., 2019).

Seeking to integrate the efforts of course- and department-level interventions and to promote a more distributed model of writing instruction, we began in the summer of 2018 to develop departmental learning goals for writing that could be used to guide curricular assessment and change. During a FLC for physics that fall, we facilitated conversations about the kinds of texts faculty expected students to produce in their careers and which learning objectives might be relevant for their curriculum. Those conversations informed what we came to call the Learning Goals and Shared Values for Writing in STEM (hereafter referred to as "Learning Goals"), which were discussed and revised across several WAES team meetings. We provide an excerpt of the Learning Goals in Table 1, which highlights the disciplinary values coded most frequently in our analysis of the focus-group discussions. The Learning Goals were designed as a tool for working with faculty to assess and implement writing across curricula and individual courses, not as a student resource or a one-size-fits-all set of writing objectives.

Table 1.
Example excerpt of the Learning Goals and Shared Values for Writing in STEM.

Disciplinary Value	Goals Surrounding Value
Precision	• Employ specific language • Learn and adhere to conventions • Describe methods so they can be repeated
Clarity	• Favor simple sentence structures • Recognize and follow audience's expected organization • Organize ideas so old information leads into new
Evidence	• Interpret results and explain their significance • Identify and evaluate relevant data • Design experiments and models

To further develop the Learning Goals, we decided to hold faculty focus groups. Although "focus groups," "faculty learning communities," and "WAC workshops" are descriptors sometimes used interchangeably to refer to groups of faculty learning together about writing pedagogy, in this paper, the term "focus groups" refers to the research method we used to elicit feedback on the Learning Goals. This approach builds on prior WAC work in which focus groups were used as a step toward curricular revision (e.g., Peters, 2009). We identified three primary objectives for the focus groups: (1) surface tacit knowledge about writing pedagogy and development while exposing assumptions, (2) elicit feedback on the Learning Goals and ways to adapt them for different departments, and (3) foster conversations about vertically integrating writing across engineering curricula.

In our team meetings and interventions, we are privileged to observe the nonlinear, affective, and bumpy process through which faculty reevaluate their ideologies of writing and revise their writing instruction. Ryan M. Ware and Julie L. Zilles (2024) recently described this phenomena as "discursive turbulence" (p. 140). The framework of discursive turbulence reminds us that uncertainty and "affective struggle" are core components of instructional change, and it compels us to pay attention to the ways in which pedagogical change is intertwined with "professional identities and foundational conceptions of writing" (Ware et al., 2022, p. 4). In the faculty focus groups, we observed how this process surfaced tensions between faculty instructional contexts, responses to student writing, and visions for writing across the curriculum. Discursive turbulence was particularly evident in the persistence of generalized conceptions of writing and challenges in envisioning integration.

Methods

Description of Focus Groups

In Fall 2019, members of our team organized and facilitated focus groups in three departments: civil and environmental engineering (CEE), crop sciences, and physics. These departments were selected based on prior interventions and team connections. We hoped to hear from faculty who had participated in the physics FLC whether they felt the Learning Goals reflected their input; meanwhile, the CEE and crop sciences focus groups provided an opportunity to explore how well the Learning Goals represented a range of engineering and science disciplines. The CEE focus group was hosted by the department's curriculum committee. The composition of the focus groups, organized by faculty rank and history with WAES, is provided in Table 2.

Table 2.
Focus group composition.

	CEE	Crop Sciences	Physics
Rank			
Nontenure track	2	2	1
Asst. Prof.	0	0	2

	CEE	Crop Sciences	Physics
Assoc. Prof.	3	3	0
Prof. (Admin. Role)	1 (1)	2 (2)	4 (2)
History with WAES			
None	2	7	3
FLC participant	2	0	1
Mentee	1	0	1
FLC & Mentee	1	0	1
WAES team member	0	0	1

The majority of the focus-group members were tenured faculty, and five total held administrative roles such as department head or director of undergraduate studies. Crop sciences focus-group members had no prior history with WAES aside from being colleagues of Julie Zilles, our principal investigator. CEE and physics participants had about the same level of prior engagement with WAES, as faculty were present who had participated in both past FLCs and WAES mentoring. A WAES team member was also in attendance as a physics focus-group participant.

The focus groups were facilitated by a WAES graduate-student research assistant in writing studies, Megan Mericle, and the WAES principal investigator and crop sciences faculty member, Julie Zilles. The focus groups ranged from just under an hour (CEE) to around one hour and twenty minutes (physics and crop sciences) in length. To ground the conversation in what faculty valued in student writing as well as where they saw room for development, we began the focus groups with a discussion of student writing, using Patricia Carini's (2001) process of descriptive review. According to Rob Simon (2013), "the goal of the process [is] to remain descriptive rather than evaluative," "situating our readings in 'what is' rather than focusing attention on what isn't working" (p. 124). This process aligns with our own goal of unearthing tacit knowledge rather than centering established feedback practices. By approaching student writing at a slower pace, descriptive review allows faculty to attend to what they value about student texts. When possible, two contrasting writing samples were chosen—one written by a student early in their program, and the other from a student in an upper-division course (Appendix 1). Due to a lack of available student samples approved for use, the CEE samples came from two different assignments from the same advanced composition course. In accordance with the descriptive-review process, each sentence was read by a different faculty member, who then added an observation. Each sentence was read three times as turns proceeded around the table to ensure full participation. Faculty members were asked to be descriptive rather than evaluative and were given prompting questions to guide their observations (Appendix 1). After reading and responding to both samples, faculty members were asked to identify the broader themes appearing in their observations. We then shared the Learning Goals and prompted the faculty members to identify connections and gaps based on their knowledge of writing in their discipline.

Data Analysis

The focus groups were video- and audio-recorded with participants' informed consent (IRB #18471). Julie Zilles took field notes along with another WAES team member, Patrick Coleman, who was a graduate-student research assistant in physics at the time. According to our IRB protocol, participants chose whether to be referred to using a pseudonym or their real name.[2] We transcribed the conversations utilizing a partial verbatim approach, including false starts and repetition as potential markers of interruption, changes in word choice, or uncertainty. However, as we are not engaging in detailed linguistic analysis, we removed back-channel talk (e.g., "um") in order to save space and focus on points of analysis (see Appendix 2).

Following transcription, we composed research memos for each focus group. Drawing on grounded theory methods (Strauss & Corbin, 2015), we identified initial resonances across focus groups in a secondary memo. We then segmented the faculty responses from the slow group reading by conversational turns (Geisler & Swarts, 2019), conducting open coding to get a more holistic view of trends in the observations. Following open coding, we analyzed the slow group reading responses again using the Learning Goals as a coding scheme. For the turn-based practice of slow group reading, the combination of open coding and coding according to an existing scheme allowed us to gain insight into both how faculty responses aligned with the writing values identified in the Learning Goals, and how faculty co-constructed narratives and values around student writing that were not entirely captured by the Learning Goals. The remainder of each focus group was analyzed through an iterative process informed by themes emerging from the memos and conversations with the WAES team.

Findings

Theme 1: Moving from Observation to Evaluation

Despite grounding the focus groups in Carini's (2001) descriptive-review process, which centers observation over evaluation, we found that the faculty responses to the student samples were largely evaluative. In the open-coding process, 61 percent of faculty turns were labeled as evaluations (48 percent negative and 13 percent positive), while only 39 percent of turns were labeled as observations—that is, defined as descriptors or questions posed in relation to the text absent of assessment

---

2. Faculty pseudonyms are labeled using an asterisk (*).

or evaluative language (i.e., "good," "bad," "ineffective") (Table 3). Faculty participants tended to focus on textual features, frequently sharing judgments in which they voiced preferences for alternative constructions.

Table 3.
Descriptive-review faculty turns coded by observation and evaluation.

Dept.	Code	Turns (#)	Turns (%)[a]	Example Faculty Responses
CEE	Observation	6	17	I am not quite sure what they mean by notched, and I don't know what PMMA is.
	Negative Evaluation	18	51	Verb tense here is incorrect. It's either plural "tests" or "bending test was performed."
	Positive Evaluation	11	31	I already like this author better. . . . I find this to be an informative sentence.
Physics	Observation	48	45	So what I notice is that this sentence is written in the passive voice.
	Negative Evaluation	51	48	Long sentence. . . . Oh, too too many problems with this sentence.
	Positive Evaluation	8	7	Especially after reading the last excerpt, it just stands out how much more succinct this one is.
Crop Sciences	Observation	23	42	So my observation there is it's relatively informal with the "sorry home owners."
	Negative Evaluation	25	45	Yeah, it's . . . forty-some words. . . . Just feels like a forever sentence. . . . I don't think it's a very effective sentence.
	Positive Evaluation	7	13	[I]t's pretty clear in terms of giving some specific data, which is I think- which is good.
Total	Turns	197		
	Observation	77	39	
	Negative Evaluation	94	48	
	Positive Evaluation	26	13	

[a]Percentage of turns classified into this code in either the specified department or the complete dataset (total).

The evaluations of students' writing were frequently hedged. Faculty framed evaluations as their own preferences and perspectives, using phrases like "in my opinion," "I don't like that," and "it bothers me" (Conrad, 2017; Hyland, 1998). Hedges were used to mitigate uncertainty around error and as invitations to other faculty to collaboratively investigate issues of clarity. The persistence of hedging in faculty's writing evaluations likely derives from their enculturation in disciplines where hedging is expected in cases where the data provide insufficient proof, along with the social dynamics of the focus groups and potentially a lack of confidence in evaluating writing. Reevaluating characterizations of faculty "resistance" to WAC interventions, Judith Halasz and Maria Brincker (2006) found that faculty sometimes avoid WAC approaches due to a lack of confidence in teaching and responding to writing, leading them to treat writing instruction as the responsibility of English departments. While hedging was possibly a result of the focus-group faculty's unfamiliarity with WAC, the hedged evaluations also created space to co-construct values around textual features in student writing.

In the CEE focus group, these hedged evaluations frequently centered on passive voice. One faculty member, Ashlynn Stillwell, initiated the conversation. Hedging her evaluation as a preference, she noted a sentence was "passive voice, and knowing that this is a lab report *I would prefer* to see it phrased as taking ownership over one's performance of this bending test" (emphasis added). Kelly Mixon* added that passive voice made it more difficult to determine what the student had done in the lab. In response to a different sentence, Ashlynn connected passive voice directly to a question about students' roles in conducting class laboratory tests: "because of the use [of] passive voice, I'm not clear whether the students did this test, or it was done for them." Remaining observations of passive voice were bundled with other remarks about textual features; since the problematic nature of passive voice was already established, faculty spent less time hedging and rationalizing their evaluations.

Negative evaluations of passive voice were backed by several different rationales. At certain times, passive voice was said to obscure clarity in methodological descriptions; at others, it prevented students from taking responsibility for their actions; and in yet other cases, it allowed students to take credit for aspects of the experiment that were completed for them. Faculty's expectations regarding passive voice were grounded in classroom contexts and did not necessarily accord with professional engineering conventions, which, as Ashlynn noted toward the end of the focus group, are still contested:

> [W]e as an industry . . . have lagged behind in innovation sometimes, such that our primary professional organization, American Society of Civil Engineers, in their journals still do not allow first-person active voice. . . . I think we could move forward as a discipline with more conventions around

writing like that. . . . [E]ntire generations of civil engineers . . . stressed that you never use "I," "we," "my," "us" in technical writing, which I think is perhaps several decades ago, of a convention.

As evidenced by Ashlynn's comment about changes in engineering conventions, different disciplinary values, classroom contexts, and professional standards are all implicated in faculty members' evaluations of passive voice. In a corpus linguistic study of civil engineering writing, Susan Conrad (2018) describes the wide range of rationales in engineering communication guides for and against passive voice. Her own study revealed complex uses of passive voice in nonacademic civil engineering writing to place old information before new concepts and relay information more concisely. The conversation around passive voice in the CEE focus group illustrates how systems of values and tacit knowledge impact the consensus on writing features. Across the focus groups, the conversations around and evaluations of student writing reveal deeply held beliefs concerning sentence-level choices that, we argue, should be surfaced and interrogated.

Theme 2: Constructing Student Writers' Scientific Becoming and Processes

In keeping with critiques of current-traditional rhetoric (Crowley, 1998), and in part due to the nature of responding to decontextualized student work, the focus groups largely analyzed the texts as products rather than the students' processes in creating them. As products, the writing samples were seen as a direct lens into students' scientific thinking. This approach was prompted, at least in part, by one of the guiding questions of the descriptive-review process: "What does this sentence communicate about the author?"

For example, in the CEE focus group, Sotiria Koloutsou-Vakakis made the following comment on a writing sample: "[T]he last two sentences actually changed [the] opinion I had from the first sentences that the writer is somebody who has very clear thinking . . . now it gets cloudy." Similarly, during a discussion in the physics focus group about how an equation was integrated into a sentence, Brian DeMarco claimed that the student's use of the equation "shows the way they're thinking about physics at this point, right? They just need an equation to plug numbers into, that's the thing that's important." The faculty frequently used the writing samples to identify room for growth in students' scientific practices and thinking.

In the physics focus group, a conversation around word choice evoked reflections reminiscent of David Bartholomae's (1986) "Inventing the University." Mats Selen argued that one student was "trying to make it sound kind of fancy . . . big words and, and, you know, I think . . . they're writing in a way that they think sounds, like, professional." While Mats observed limitations in students' understanding of effective scientific communication, in the crop sciences focus group, Reid Christianson felt that a lack of clarity around methods demonstrated that "the student lacks the format of how to set up an experiment. And so they're showing that they're not trained yet in terms of how to put the pieces together."

In their conversations, faculty constructed writers who lacked training, were confused about methods, and were unfamiliar with the expectations around scientific communication. These responses evoke genesis amnesia (Bourdieu, 1977) by conflating writing ability with scientific knowledge and privileging conventionalized accounts that flatten the diversity of student writing experiences. Faculty sometimes tied their evaluations to speculations about students' processes, especially in terms of time management. For example, David Ceperley, a physics professor, remarked that a student defining terms in a conclusion was "trying to pad the report, because presumably, this has all been defined several times before." David's comment imagines a student composing a last-minute report, trying to find the fastest way to meet length expectations. However, Keya Vig* recontextualized this construction as indicative of physicists in the field rather than amateur error: "I do that sometimes. In writing grant proposals."

Time management came up in the crop sciences focus group as well, suggesting it is both a common concern and a possible entry point for shifting faculty's perceptions. This topic marked a key moment in the CEE focus group and our team's subsequent discussions, as it encouraged a shift from a deficit-based, product-oriented view of a student's ability as a writer to a process-oriented perspective allowing for pedagogical change. Following a series of critiques, Omar Faris* observed,

> I have seen students . . . get to the body of the narrative of the report and they . . . delay the abstract part, and that's typically the last task . . . and it is typically rushed, so they grab sentences from the report. . . . [T]o me, it doesn't necessarily reflect . . . whether he has a mastery of the words, but more in terms of time management. . . . [T]his problem with language may be reflected in the other parts of the course.

Omar's comment encouraged the other faculty members to consider the writing process, as evidenced by Sotiria Koloutsou-Vakakis's next observation: "I would agree with [Omar], this sentence shows somebody who was either very rushed, or is very confused about what they actually observed and what they did in the lab." Sotiria moved from interpreting writing as a direct reflection of students' thinking to considering the contexts in which students compose texts.

Theme 3: Discrepancy between Descriptive-Review Evaluations and Learning Goals Assessment

Although our aim was to use the descriptive review of student writing to ground the discussion of the Learning Goals, we observed a discrepancy between these two parts of the focus groups. While the descriptive-review process elicited an animated discussion around textual features, student becoming, and audience expectations, faculty largely accepted the Learning Goals. They expressed a few discipline-specific concerns and identified potential missing elements before moving to a discussion of how they might apply the Learning Goals in their department, as summarized in Table 4.

Table 4.
Summary of departmental responses to the Learning Goals.

	CEE	Crop Sciences	Physics
Accepted?	Yes: "you could find and replace physicists with engineers"	Yes: "you could find and replace physicists [with] crop scientists"	Implicit yes: discussion focused on what was missing
Discipline-Specific Concerns	CEE-specific audiences (clients, lawyers), field conventions	None raised	Differences between theorists & experimentalists
Missing Elements	More emphasis on audience	Storytelling, professionalism	Storytelling, more emphasis on interpretation
Comments on Application	Interest in resources to give directly to students, concerns about motivating students to care about writing	Time as a major barrier	Concerns around being too general for integration, course content and time constraints, lack of TA training in giving writing feedback

In all three groups, there appeared to be widespread acceptance of the content of the Learning Goals. Although the Learning Goals had been originally developed based on physics faculty input and were framed as physics writing goals and values, both CEE and crop sciences faculty stated that we could "find and replace physicists" with members of their respective fields and the Learning Goals would still be accurate. In physics, the acceptance of the Learning Goals was more implicit, perhaps because they were already framed in terms of the field's disciplinary values. Discussion moved quickly in the physics focus group to what faculty felt was missing, and no points were raised about revisions to existing content.

The faculty involved in the focus groups raised a few discipline-specific concerns when asked about ways to ensure that the Learning Goals represented their field. In CEE, faculty felt that the Learning Goals focused primarily on academic audiences, while in their field and its associated career paths, writers navigated a wide range of audiences beyond academia, including city council members, clients, and lawyers. To better reflect the writing values of CEE, faculty expressed that the Learning Goals could better emphasize a wider range of engineering audiences and genres. In crop sciences, however, no discipline-specific concerns were raised. Faculty instead agreed that the Learning Goals applied to "general science." When asked about the applicability of the Learning Goals to nonacademic careers in crop sciences, Reid Christianson responded, "[W]riting is kind of universal, and a good writer is going to be a good writer in every setting."

In contrast, faculty in the physics focus group considered the potential universality of the Learning Goals to be problematic. Yonatan Kahn asked, "Is it possible that writing in physics is actually qualitatively different than writing in other branches of science?", adding that he saw the Learning Goals as limited in utility because he could replace "physicists" with "biologists" and the values would still hold. Yonatan argued, "[A] set of principles for writing in physics should acknowledge that distinction [between the way theorists and experimentalists tell stories] and figure out how to work within it." However, the physics focus group did not identify any specific principles or conventions associated with experimental or theoretical physics writing, aside from using the document-preparation software LaTeX. Outside of the select disciplinary concerns raised, faculty relied on generic accounts of writing in the Learning Goals discussion.

Faculty suggested a few possible additions or changes to the Learning Goals, aside from the suggestion from CEE to emphasize writing for different kinds of audiences. For example, the importance of storytelling emerged in both the crop sciences and physics focus groups. One of the physics faculty members commented that effective storytelling is "how you get proposals funded." Since faculty expressed broad agreement on this feature, we incorporated it in later versions of the Learning Goals. In the physics focus group, Brian DeMarco also called for more emphasis on interpretation. He observed that the Learning Goals included "interpret[ing] results," but the importance of "the meaning of what you've done" and tying it to the "storytelling aspect" of scientific writing was not captured by the Learning Goals.

In all three focus groups, faculty moved of their own accord to discussing possible applications of the Learning Goals; however, many expressed feeling overwhelmed. In CEE, one faculty member noted, "[I]f you gave that to the student, they would just throw it away." While not our intended purpose, this perception of the Learning Goals as a resource to be shared directly with students appeared in all three groups.

This faculty response likely indicates familiarity with scalable, transposable writing resources that can be added to curricula without pedagogical restructuring, along with a lack of curricular space or faculty bandwidth to envision applications of the Learning Goals beyond direct transmission to students. Faced with these obstacles, faculty discussed solutions in the form of outside writing-instruction support, such as writing software (i.e., Grammarly), the campus writing center, the required first-year writing course, and high-school writing preparation.

It was in the physics focus group that the most debate around vertical integration and the placement of writing in curricula arose, centering on the motivation for and purpose of the Learning Goals rather than on specific content. When Lance Cooper, a member of the WAES team, noted that the focus group was a starting point for conversations about integrating writing across the physics curriculum, Keya Vig* responded, "Are we going to talk about why you'd want to do this at all?" Keya raised concerns about adding writing to her upper-division physics course, where students were "struggling already . . . it's like learning a completely new language." While other faculty suggested ways to integrate writing into her course without sacrificing content, Keya expressed reservations:

> The problem is it takes a lot of time and energy to actually write something well. I'm just saying . . . when I write a paper, we edit over and over and over again. . . . I guess we can expect- request- require certain things from the lab report. But I'm wondering if we should require a lot.

Keya raised concerns about "dilution," questioning whether "heap[ing] too much onto a course" would devalue both existing course content and writing instruction. For Keya, vertical integration reflected a "piecemeal" approach, and she doubted whether those pieces would add up to a substantive understanding of writing in physics.

Keya's concerns influenced her response to the Learning Goals: "So I (.) don't (.) see the value of this [short laugh] . . . whole thing. The way it's written right now. Because I feel like it's too general and too specific at the same time." Keya's concerns were closely tied to her own writing-instruction experience. She remarked that she was a "horrible" writer as an undergraduate student, and she grappled with the question, "What would have helped me?" Recognizing that she never had the importance of writing stressed for her as an undergraduate (she did not receive writing feedback until graduate school), Keya was still thinking through ways to address this gap as the focus group drew to a close. The diverse personal writing and teaching histories of focus-group participants shaped how they envisioned curricular goals, even as participants largely agreed that vertical integration was both challenging and necessary.

Altogether, the responses to the Learning Goals suggest that the focus groups did not provide sufficient time or space to build explicit awareness of tacit disciplinary conventions and differences. Faculty articulated very few discipline-specific changes to adapt the Learning Goals to their departments. While the CEE curriculum committee requested that WAES share the Learning Goals, and faculty members have drawn on them in individual, WAES-impacted course redesigns (Renna et al., 2022), vertical integration into curricula remains elusive. The focus groups provided a space for faculty to reflect on writing and writing pedagogy, but they expressed confusion and uncertainty about how the Learning Goals might inform coordinated curricular change.

Discussion

The focus groups provided us with important information about barriers and entry points to curricular change. With regard to the former, they illustrated the complex entanglement of classroom histories, tacit knowledge about writing, and institutional constraints affecting writing instruction. Faculty across focus groups expressed the belief that writing is a universal skill, rather than a set of practices that require understanding of different disciplinary values and expectations. Although faculty provided rich responses to student writing during the descriptive review, surfacing the tacit knowledge underlying those responses and engaging with the more abstract Learning Goals proved more challenging. Furthermore, a focus on current instructional demands foreclosed other ways of imagining writing instruction. For instance, Keya's constraints in teaching a challenging course with many content demands made it difficult to envision incorporating writing instruction in the physics curriculum as a whole without resorting to an ineffective, "piecemeal" approach. We find these barriers indicative of the discursive turbulence (Ware & Zilles, 2024) that emerges from pedagogical change. The framework of discursive turbulence reminds us to attend closely to the contradictions in faculty assessments of student writing; it also encourages us to see the disconnect between the two parts of the focus group as indicative of the long-term, turbulent nature of WAC work.

Entry points to building disciplinary goals and investment in vertical integration were also identified through the focus groups. While the responses to student writing were largely evaluative, the variety of rationales expressed by faculty helped to illustrate how values, histories of writing instruction, and beliefs surrounding scientific writing informed faculty evaluations. Following a WEC approach (Flash, 2016; Hughes, 2020), we name the conceptions of writing that emerged—such as the belief in writing as a universal skill and issues of passive voice and clarity—in order to better account for them in ongoing conversations with disciplinary faculty. The persistence of hedging also invites opportunities to make space for multiple flexible disciplinary writing goals and to build faculty confidence around giving writing feedback. Another entry point is how the descriptive-review method disrupted product-centered views and prompted faculty to co-construct process narratives. When asked to imagine what each sentence communicated about the author, faculty envisioned possible hurdles in the writing process and articulated shared experiences about working with student writers. These points of resonance could be stepping stones to collaborative initiation of pedagogical and curricular change. By imagining students' writing processes and leveraging moments of disagreement and hedging, WAC stakeholders can help faculty build more complex, concrete, and explicit disciplinary expectations, which can then be communicated more transparently to students via course instruction and curricular goals.

Although the focus groups provided important information, progress towards our initial aims was limited. While the descriptive-review process helped us begin to surface tacit faculty assumptions and expectations around writing, the single, fifty-to-eighty-minute sessions were too short to progress from tacit, individual faculty observations to explicit, shared disciplinary knowledge. This limitation is consistent with research demonstrating the long and turbulent process of conceptual change (Ware & Zilles, 2024). More importantly for our purposes, the bridge we envisioned connecting the descriptive review and the discussion of the Learning Goals was not realized. Perhaps another strategy for transitioning between the two parts of the focus group would have been more effective, or perhaps the disconnect reflects an inevitable difficulty in moving from something so concrete and familiar to something more abstract and unfamiliar. In all three focus groups, there was confusion around the purpose of the Learning Goals, along with questions and comments about their implementation, which limited the feedback on the goals themselves. Our third objective of working towards vertical (curricular) integration is a long-term one, not directly addressed in our plan (Appendix 1), but there was considerable conversation in the physics group around the purpose and feasibility of vertical integration. This conversation may have emerged in part because of generative tensions between WAES team members, faculty who had been involved in previous WAES interventions, and faculty unfamiliar with WAES. To our knowledge, all three of the departments involved in the focus groups continue to have faculty interested in vertical integration, but to date changes have largely been limited to individual courses.

One general limitation of our approach is that the group structure of the focus groups, combined with the high impact of curricular change on faculty labor, may lead members to focus on agreement rather than express divergent viewpoints. As Sim (1998) observes, this is a limitation of focus groups in general, and it can therefore be inaccurate to use focus groups as a measure of consensus. Furthermore, the focus groups represented only a portion of departmental faculty, of whom tenured faculty were an overrepresented population.

Future Work and Implications

To continue working toward the objectives we articulated in this paper, particularly those of surfacing tacit knowledge about writing pedagogy and fostering conversations about vertically integrating writing across engineering curricula, we are currently experimenting with more targeted conversations with faculty and with using the Learning Goals as a curricular assessment tool. One example of a more targeted conversation occurred at a recent crop sciences faculty meeting. We asked faculty to reflect on and discuss whether each value might be relevant to writing in crop sciences and whether it was (or was not) reflected in their courses. By involving a wider segment of departmental faculty, this strategy provided greater context about where writing values are showing up in crop sciences curricula, thereby helping us identify possible course connections and interventions. On the curricular assessment side, we have used the Learning Goals as a coding framework, assessing course materials to ascertain the placement of writing concepts and instruction across a single curriculum (Carzon et al., 2024). Our intent is to use these data about which elements of the Learning Goals are addressed by, or absent from, a curriculum as a basis for a more specific conversation with faculty. We hope to learn how the current state of the curriculum does and does not reflect their disciplinary values, using any disconnects between the two as a starting point for faculty to envision future changes. Following WEC approaches (e.g., Anson & Dannels, 2009), we aim to build awareness of existing writing instruction practices that could be made more explicit while providing a more concrete assessment of gaps in vertical integration.

For WAC/WEC stakeholders as a whole, our close analysis contributes to a better understanding of the powerful systems of disciplinary expectations among faculty, offering a starting point for pushing faculty to articulate tacit knowledge (Sheriff, 2021). Noting Jamila Kareem's (2020) call to center student goals, but also being sensitive to the ways in which the purposes and constraints of writing in the sciences and engineering influence faculty in these disciplines, we highlight two complementary needs: delving more into students' goals and diverse literacies, and better understanding the writing practices and values of STEM workplaces through studies such as Susan Conrad's (2017) linguistic analysis of civil engineering documents and Marie Paretti and Julie Ford's (2022) analysis of engineering workplace genres.

The focus groups demonstrated the difficulty of surfacing and articulating discipline-specific writing expectations and of translating those expectations into concrete pedagogical changes. The challenges we identified in the focus groups, along with their resonances in WAC/WEC literature, point to a need for an expanded tool kit of strategies—beyond the workshop and the writing-intensive course—that can be adapted to local contexts in order to surface disciplinary faculty's tacit writing knowledge and to collaboratively construct and implement disciplinary learning goals. While we do not know exactly what strategies are most likely to succeed in other institutional contexts, the focus groups, along with our work as a whole, emphasize the importance of long-term transdisciplinary relationships. Based on our experience, other key measures may include the assessment of student writing and departmental curricula (as is central in the WEC approach; e.g., Anson & Dannels, 2009; Flash, 2016), integrated, iterative research and intervention (such as a transdisciplinary action research model; see Stokols, 2006), and action-oriented approaches that give disciplinary faculty a clear entry point.

Despite—and in some ways because of—their limitations, the focus groups helped us recognize barriers to building longer-term investment in pedagogical and curricular change. Our findings illustrate how these changes lead to discursive turbulence, or the iterative and nonlinear adoption of writing conceptions and pedagogies (Ware & Zilles, 2024). The focus groups, along with our WAES FLCs and mentoring partnerships, have made it clear to us that STEM faculty recognize the importance of writing, but many lack the time, space, and tools to implement explicit writing pedagogies.

Acknowledgements

We thank the civil and environmental engineering, crop sciences, and physics faculty who participated in this research, and all the members of the WAES team for their contributions to the generative conversations about this research. We would particularly like to thank John Gallagher for providing feedback that improved this manuscript. This material draws upon work supported by the National Science Foundation under Improving Undergraduate STEM Education (IUSE) grant number 2013443. Additional support was provided by the Grainger College of Engineering's Strategic Instructional Innovations Program, the Center for Writing Studies, and the Departments of Civil and Environmental Engineering, Crop Sciences, and Physics at the University of Illinois at Urbana-Champaign.

References

Accreditation Board for Engineering and Technology. (2023). *Criteria for accrediting engineering programs, 2022–2023*. https://www.abet.org/accreditation/accreditation-criteria/criteria-for-accrediting-engineering-programs-2022-2023/

Anson, C. M., & Dannels, D. (2009). Profiling programs: Formative uses of departmental consultations in the assessment of communication across the curriculum. *Across the Disciplines, 6*(special issue), 1–15. https://doi.org/10.37514/ATD-J.2009.6.1.05

Anson, C. M., & Flash, P. (Eds.). (2021). *Writing-enriched curricula: Models of faculty-driven and departmental transformation*. The WAC Clearinghouse; University Press of Colorado. https://doi.org/10.37514/PER-B.2021.1299

Bartholomae, D. (1986). Inventing the university. *Journal of Basic Writing, 5*(1), 4–23.

Bohr, D. J., & Rhoades, G. (2014). The WAC glossary project: Facilitating conversations between composition and WID faculty in a unified writing curriculum. *Across the Disciplines, 11*(1), 1–10. https://doi.org/10.37514/ATD-J.2014.11.1.02

Bourdieu, P. (1977). *Outline of a theory of practice*. Cambridge University Press.

Carini, P. F. (2001). *Starting strong: A different look at children, school, and standards*. Teachers College Press.

Carzon, P., Mericle, M., Raley, J., & Zilles, J. L. (2024). Mapping writing concepts across an undergraduate physics curriculum. In *Engineering physics and physics division* [Paper presentation] ASEE Annual Conference and Exposition, Portland, Oregon, United States. https://strategy.asee.org/47761

Conrad, S. (2017). A comparison of practitioner and student writing in civil engineering. *Journal of Engineering Education, 106*(2), 191–217. https://doi.org/10.1002/jee.20161

Conrad, S. (2018). The use of passives and impersonal style in civil engineering writing. *Journal of Business and Technical Communication, 32*(1), 38–76. https://doi.org/10.1177/1050651917729864

Cox, M., Galin, J., & Melzer, D. (2018). Building sustainable WAC programs: A whole systems approach. *The WAC Journal, 29*(1), 64–87. https://doi.org/10.37514/WAC-J.2018.29.1.03

Crowley, S. (1998). The emergence of process pedagogy. In *Composition in the university: Historical and polemical essays* (pp. 187–214). University of Pittsburgh Press.

Flash, P. (2016). From apprised to revised: Faculty in the disciplines change what they never knew they knew. In K. B. Yancey (Ed.), *A Rhetoric of reflection* (pp. 227–249). University Press of Colorado.

Ford, J. D. (2012). Integrating communication into engineering curricula: An interdisciplinary approach to facilitating transfer at New Mexico Institute of Mining and Technology. *Composition Forum, 26*. http://compositionforum.com/issue/26/

Gallagher, J. R., Turnipseed, N., Yoritomo, J., Elliott, C., Cooper, L. S., Popovics, J. S., Prior, P., & Zilles, J. L. (2020). A collaborative longitudinal design for supporting writing pedagogies of STEM faculty. *Technical Communication Quarterly, 29*(4), 411–426. https://doi.org/10.1080/10572252.2020.1713405

Geisler, C., & Swarts, J. (2019). *Coding streams of language: Techniques for the systematic coding of text, talk, and other verbal data*. The WAC Clearinghouse; University Press of Colorado. https://doi.org/10.37514/PRA-B.2019.0230

Goffman, E. (1956). *The presentation of self in everyday life* (reprint). Doubleday Anchor.

Halasz, J., & Brincker, M. (2006). Making it your own: Writing fellows re-evaluate faculty "resistance." *Across the Disciplines, 3*(1), 1–13. https://doi.org/10.37514/atd-j.2006.3.1.03

Harichandran, R. S., Nocito-Gobel, J., Brisart, E., Erdil, N. O., Collura, M. A., Daniels, S. B., Harding, W. D., & Adams, D. J. (2014). A comprehensive engineering college-wide program for developing technical communication skills in students. *2014 IEEE Frontiers in Education Conference (FIE) Proceedings*, 1–8. https://doi.org/10.1109/FIE.2014.7044018

Hendricks, R. W., & Pappas, E. C. (1996). Advanced engineering communication: An integrated writing and communication program for materials engineers. *Journal of Engineering Education, 85*(4), 343–352. https://doi.org/10.1002/j.2168-9830.1996.tb00255.x

Hughes, B. (2020). Galvanizing goals: What early-career disciplinary faculty want to learn about WAC pedagogy. *The WAC Journal, 31*(1), 23–65. https://doi.org/10.37514/WAC-J.2020.31.1.02

Hyland, K. (1998). *Hedging in scientific research articles*. John Benjamins.

Jamieson, S. (2009). The vertical writing curriculum: The necessary core of liberal arts education. In J. C. Post & J. A. Inman (Eds.), *Composition(s) in the new liberal arts* (pp. 159–184). Hampton Press.

Kareem, J. M. (2020). Sustained communities for sustained learning: Connecting culturally sustaining pedagogy to WAC learning outcomes. In L. E. Bartlett, S. L. Tarabochia, A. R. Olinger, & M. J. Marshall (Eds.), *Diverse approaches to teaching, learning, and writing across the curriculum: IWAC at 25* (pp. 293–308). The WAC Clearinghouse; University Press of Colorado. https://doi.org/10.37514/PER-B.2020.0360.2.16

Kerri, M. (2017). Full-time faculty, threshold concepts, and the vertical curriculum. *Peer Review, 19*(1), 1–6.

Kovanen, B., Turnipseed, N., Mericle, M., & Roozen, K. (2022). Tracing literate activity across physics and chemistry: Toward embodied histories of disciplinary knowing, writing, and becoming. *Across the Disciplines, 19*(1–2), 62–77. https://doi.org/10.37514/ATD-J.2022.19.1-2.05

Kovanen, B., Ware, R., Mericle, M., Turnipseed, N., Coleman, J. P., Elliott, C., Popovics, J. S., Cooper, L., Gallagher, J. R., Prior, P., & Zilles, J. L. (2020). Implementing writing-as-process in engineering education. In *Promoting communication skills* [Paper presentation] ASEE Annual Conference and Exposition. https://peer.asee.org/34786

Mathison, M. A. (Ed.). (2019). *Sojourning in disciplinary cultures: A case study of teaching writing in engineering*. Utah State University Press.

Melzer, D. (2014). The connected curriculum: Designing a vertical transfer writing curriculum. *The WAC Journal, 25*(1), 78–91. https://doi.org/10.37514/WAC-J.2014.25.1.04

Paretti, M. C., & Ford, J. D. (2022). Written communication in engineering work. In R. Horowitz (Ed.), *The Routledge international handbook of research on writing* (2nd ed., pp. 460–474). Routledge. https://doi.org/10.4324/9780429437991-38

Patton, M. D. (2008). Beyond WI: Building an integrated communication curriculum in one department of civil engineering. *IEEE Transactions on Professional Communication*, *51*(3), 313–327. https://doi.org/10.1109/TPC.2008.2001250

Peters, R. A. (2009). Using focus groups and stakeholder surveys to revise the MPA curriculum. *Journal of Public Affairs Education*, *15*(1), 1–16. https://doi.org/10.1080/15236803.2009.12001539

Prior, P. (1998). *Writing/disciplinarity*. Lawrence Erlbaum Associates.

Renna, M. L., Avgoustopolos, R., Ware, R., Sooryanarayana, K. P., Popovics, J. S., & Zilles, J. L. (2022). Redesigning writing instruction within a lab-based civil engineering course: Reporting on the evolution across several semesters. In *Civil engineering division—Huh? What did you say? What does that mean?* [Paper presentation] ASEE Annual Conference and Exposition, Minneapolis, MN, United States. https://peer.asee.org/41443

Rhoades, G., & Carroll, B. (2012). Supporting a vertical writing model: Faculty conversations across the curriculum. *Currents in Teaching and Learning*, *4*(2), 42–50.

Sheriff, S. (2021). Beyond "I know it when I see it": WEC and the process of unearthing faculty expertise. In C. M. Anson & P. Flash (Eds.), *Writing-Enriched curricula: Models of faculty-driven and departmental transformation* (pp. 145–165). The WAC Clearinghouse; University Press of Colorado. https://doi.org/10.37514/PER-B.2021.1299.2.06

Sim, J. (1998). Collecting and analysing qualitative data: Issues raised by the focus group. *Journal of Advanced Nursing*, *28*(2), 345-352. https://doi.org/10.1046/j.1365-2648.1998.00692.x

Simon, R. (2013). "Starting with what is": Exploring response and responsibility to student writing through collaborative inquiry. *English Education*, *45*(2), 115–146. https://doi.org/10.58680/ee201322151

Stokols, D. (2006). Toward a science of transdisciplinary action research. *American Journal of Community Psychology*, *38*(1–2), 63–77. https://doi.org/10.1007/s10464-006-9060-5

Strauss, A., & Corbin, J. (1994). Grounded theory methodology: An overview. In N. K. Denzin & Y. S. Lincoln (Eds.), *Handbook of qualitative research* (pp. 273-285). SAGE Publications.

Vaughan, E. (2007). "I think we should just accept . . . our horrible lowly status": Analysing teacher-teacher talk within the context of community of practice. *Language Awareness*, *16*(3), 173–189. https://doi.org/10.2167/la456.0

Ware, R., Mericle, M., Prior, P., Gallagher, J. R., Elliot, C. M., Popovics, J. S., Cooper, L., & Zilles, J. L. (2022). Promoting pedagogical change around writing: Observations of discursive turbulence. In *NSF Grantees Poster Session* [Paper presentation] ASEE Annual Conference and Exposition, Minneapolis, MN, United States. https://peer.asee.org/42053

Ware, R., Turnipseed, N., Gallagher, J. R., Elliott, C. M., Popovics, J. S., Prior, P., & Zilles, J. L. (2019). Writing across engineering: A collaborative approach to support STEM faculty's integration of writing instruction in their classes. In *Liberal Education Division Technical Session 10* [Paper presentation] ASEE Annual Conference and Exposition, Tampa, FL, United States. https://peer.asee.org/33671

Ware, R. M., & Zilles, J. L. (2024). Tracing discursive turbulence as intra-active pedagogical change and becoming. *Written Communication*, *41*(1), 138–166. https://doi.org/10.1177/07410883231207105

Yoritomo, J. Y., Turnipseed, N., Cooper, S. L., Elliott, C. M., Gallagher, J. R., Popovics, J. S., Prior, P., & Zilles, J. L. (2018). Examining engineering writing instruction at a large research university through the lens of writing studies. In *Design, assessment, and redesign of writing instruction for engineers* [Paper presentation] ASEE Annual Conference and Exposition, Salt Lake City, UT, United States. https://peer.asee.org/30467

Yoritomo, J. Y., Turnipseed, N., Villotti, M. J., Tate, A., Searsmith, K., Perdekamp, M. G., Prior, P., & Zilles, J. L. (2019). A tale of two rubrics: Realigning genre instruction through improved response rubrics in a writing-intensive physics course. In *Engineering physics and physics division technical session 3* [Paper presentation] ASEE Annual Conference and Exposition, Tampa, FL, United States. https://peer.asee.org/32012

Appendix 1: Departmental Focus-Group Handouts with Student Samples

The following handout was given to department faculty at the beginning of each focus group.

The process of slow reading student work was developed by Patricia Carini in the K-12 educational setting, but it has since been used by researchers at the university level for faculty development and instructor training. We will use this method to spark conversations about ways to take into account what students know and what they need to know when setting objectives for writing across the curriculum.

The goal is primarily to take the opportunity to approach student writing at a slower pace (as we are often pressed by deadlines and busy schedules) and attend to what we value about student texts. It is a process of noticing and observing. According to Simon (2013), who carried out slow group reading in his work with student teachers, "the goal of the process [is] to remain descriptive rather than evaluative: situating our readings in 'what is' rather than focusing attention on what isn't working" (p. 124).

Slow Group Reading Process

1. Each sentence will be read three times by three different people. After you read the sentence, if you could, offer a brief observation about what you notice. Keep the following questions in mind to guide your observations:
    i   What is this sentence doing for the text?
    ii. What does this sentence communicate about the author?
    iii. What do you notice about the tone or style of the sentence?
    iv. What features (word choice, punctuation, syntax, etc.) in this sentence stand out to you?

Physics Samples

Sample 1 (excerpted conclusion from a first-year physics lab report):
The study conducted measured the speed of sound using an IOLab light and microphone sensors. In the experiment, a beam of light shined onto the IOLab was subsequently interrupted when a block of falling wood obstructed the light intensity and produced a soundwave registered to the IOLab. Using the equation: $V = D/\Delta t$, the distance between the block and the IOLab over the time difference between the interrupted light intensity and generation of a sound wave was used to calculate the speed of sound. . . . Over the course of the experiment, in order to minimize uncertainty, several measures were taken during the collection of the data. First, during the experimental setup, a flashlight was used instead of a laser pointer because the beam of light

needed to hit the light sensor of the IOLab consistently. The flashlight was also taped down onto a desk to insure that the distance between it and the IOLab did not vary. Moreover, the distance between the IOLab and the flashlight was taken using two meter sticks. Noticing that the two meter sticks may have shifted, we decided that the uncertainty for the measurement should be approximately +/- 0.02 m.

Sample 2 (full abstract from an upper-division physics lab report):

In this lab we measured the response of ferromagnetic materials to external magnetic fields. We were particularly interested in the mechanics of the phase transition between paramagnetic and ferromagnetic states. We used this data to produce B-H curves for toroidal materials within an inductor, from which we were able to observe the nature of the phase transition in terms of microscopic magnetic domains within each material. We then investigated how temperature affects this phase transition by comparing B-H curves taken at various temperatures, as well as measuring the magnetic susceptibility in response to a wide range of temperatures. We found that there is a critical temperature at which the dependence of magnetic susceptibility on temperature is nearly linear and decreases at a much quicker pace than below this critical temperature.

Civil and Environmental Engineering Samples

Sample 1 (abstract from an upper-division CEE lab report):

Bending tests were performed on notched specimens of 1045 hot rolled steel, 6061 aluminium, and PMMA. The notch types included sharp notch, also known as sharp cracks for all three materials, and rounded notches for just the metals. Bending test were performed using an Instron Model 4400 load frame. Photoelasticity tests were performed on PSM-1. Their visual stress distribution was discussed to learn the importance of photoelastic materials and tests. The metal specimens were both strengthened by the inclusion of a notch, the round notch being better for strengthening. The brittle PMMA specimen was weakened by the inclusion of a notch. A notch on the surface of tension will be weaker than a notch on the surface for compression. Finally, photoelastic properties are useful for the planning and design of elastic materials.

Sample 2 (conclusion from an upper-division CEE lab report):

The photoelasticity is useful for comparing stress concentrations between a specimen with a notch and a specimen without a notch. The photoelastic images can clearly show the differences between these two specimens. However, the photoelasticity cannot show the specific bending stress directly, which means it is not able to quantitatively compare the bending stress that specimens are subjected to. The results are only applicable to elastic materials rather than elastic-plastic materials. It is because elastic-plastic materials will yield in bending, which will change the stress concentration and the stress distribution at the notch.

Crop Sciences Samples

Sample 1 (hypothesis response assignment from a first-year crop sciences course):

Situation: You are house-sitting and realize that all of the indoor plants are wilting and fading in color.

Hypothesis: The plants in the house are wilting and fading in color because their pots don't have enough water.

Experiment: To test my hypothesis, I would separate the plants into two groups. I would leave one group without water (sorry homeowners) and water the other plants until their soil was damp every week. I would be sure to include plants from all sides of the house in each group to keep the confounding variable of sunlight at a minimum. Every day I would make observations on the two groups of plants; I would record their color as well as how wilted their leaves are. At the end of the experiment, I would compare the data collected from the two groups and decide if the water reduced the plants' wilting and fading in color. If this was the case, I would support my hypothesis.

Sample 2 (excerpt from a graduate student's fellowship proposal):

Motivation: While nitrogen-rich fertilizers have helped sustain the increasing human population, they are also damaging the environment[1]. Managing the nitrogen cycle is one of the 14 grand challenges for engineering today[2]. Seventy-five percent of the reactive nitrogen that is produced by humans is applied to crops, making this one of the greatest anthropogenic impacts on the nitrogen cycle[1]. Much of the nitrogen applied to crops is leached to water, lost to the atmosphere, or lost as food and human waste, leading to numerous negative environmental impacts including global warming, smog, acid rain, eutrophication, loss of biodiversity, and soil acidification[1,3]. Thus, it is imperative that we help manage the loss of nitrogen from these systems so that we can sustain the benefits of fertilizer use while reducing the negative consequences. The proposed research will investigate the differences in gaseous nitrogen emissions to the atmosphere from different farm management practices and study the influence of such practices in the dynamics of soil microbial populations. My ultimate goal is to use this information as input to coupled biogeochemical-farmer agent models to provide policy makers and farmers with information about realistic, affordable nutrient management strategies that will allow them to maintain current crop yields and reduce negative environmental impacts.

References: [1] Galloway et al. 2003. *Bioscience, 53*(4) [2] NAE. 2015. Grand Challenges for Engineering [3] Galloway et al. 2008. *Science*, 320

Group Discussion

2. After we've read two student examples this way, we'll open up to a conversation about patterns in observations that the group noticed.
    i. What kinds of features did you and your colleagues tend to notice?
    ii. What resonances or disconnects did you observe between the observations, particularly as each stood on its own without contestation or development from others?
    iii. Based on these examples, what would you say that you value about student writing, and what would you say that students struggle with when writing in your field?

Response to Learning Goals and Shared Values

3. To end today, we'll take a look at our current objective framework. Potential applications for this framework on a curricular level include using it to see what writing goals courses are already addressing, and where there might be gaps. On the level of faculty mentoring and course design, it can be used as a springboard to articulate what instructors want their students to work toward in specific courses.
    i. What overlaps do you see between the goals articulated in our conversation today and the objectives outlined here?
    ii. What potential disconnects or contradictions do you observe between our conversation and this objective framework?
    iii. *For physics:* Based on the way that you filled in this framework and your background in writing in physics, what would you say is consistent, and what needs to be changed? What points don't apply altogether that you would recommend cutting?
    iv. *For CEE and crop sciences:* When adapting these objectives to fit writing in [CEE/crop sciences], what would you say is consistent, and what needs to be changed? What points don't apply altogether that you would recommend cutting?

Appendix 2: Conventions for Transcription

We use the following symbols in the focus-group transcriptions:

[sigh]	brackets contain explanatory text or contextual additions
-	hyphens indicate an abrupt self-interruption
(.)	periods within parentheses indicate a pause
(..)	double periods within parentheses indicate a longer pause
...	ellipses indicate material removed from the transcript for concision
"Yes"	text within quotation marks indicates constructed dialogue
Italics	indicates emphasis placed on a word or phrase
!	exclamation marks are used to indicate rising intonation/excitement

We use conventional punctuation marks at the ends of sentences as well as periods to indicate slight pauses between phrases. We include repetitions of words but eliminate fillers such as "uh-huh," "mhm," and "uh."

Grammatical errors have not been corrected, and we have avoided the use of [*sic*] to avoid privileging some standardization/linguistic expectations over others.

Cross-Disciplinary Solidarity Through Labor-Oriented Research in WAC

LACEY WOOTTON

This article calls for increased attention to labor in WAC research and faculty development. In increasingly neoliberal and corporatized academic contexts, longstanding assumptions of divides among disciplines need to be replaced with solidarity. I argue that one step in achieving solidarity can be labor-oriented WAC research and labor-conscious faculty development. I draw on a study of emotional labor in writing-intensive disciplinary courses to demonstrate the potential for research revealing commonalities such as shared values and experiences of management. I close with calls for areas of inquiry in research and attention in faculty development.

In a recent article in the *Labor Studies Journal*, Seth Kahn and Amy Lynch-Biniek (2022) argue for a shift in emphasis from "activism" to "organizing." Discussing this shift in the context of ongoing needs for equity and inclusion in higher education, and noting that the burdens of activism can fall more heavily on traditionally marginalized groups, Kahn and Lynch-Biniek note that "organizing" foregrounds collaboration and group involvement, not the actions of individuals (pp. 324-325). Their proposed "rhetorical and structural shift" could, they argue, "build solidarity in the face of increasing precarity" (p. 321).

Shifts that support solidarity across disparate groups that might be invested in apparently differing or even competing interests remain as necessary as ever, if not more so, in the face of higher-education labor landscapes that continue their path toward neoliberal values, corporatization, and an academic gig economy. The Covid pandemic did not create these conditions, although it made them more visible for many faculty as institutions reduced budgets, enrollments fell, and faculty lost their jobs. But the ongoing crisis of academic labor has existed for decades.

Writing studies scholars and activists, such as Kahn and Amy Pason, have long called for attention to issues such as precarity and the rise of neoliberal and corporate values in academic institutions. Such attention requires an understanding of institutional contexts, in both local institutions and larger higher-education trends and forces. One important element of these contexts is managerialism—the institutional management of faculty labor, which faculty themselves often participate in. For example, Marc Bousquet (2003) critiques growing managerialism (and its accompanying divisions and discontents), urging rhetoric and composition scholars and managers to look away from managerial discourse and division in order to increase solidarity and resist forces that undermine the idea and power of faculty (p. 235). This urging is echoed in the call within the Indianapolis Resolution, the 2014 statement on labor conditions written by members of the Conference on College Composition and Communication Labor Caucus, to resist the managerialism that can accompany professionalism and to join professionalism with activism (Cox et al., 2016). Donna Strickland (2011) traces the history of managerialism in composition and argues that critiquing managerial power and relations is essential to improving material conditions for faculty. All of these critiques and calls highlight the importance of institutional structures, people, expectations, and values in shaping not only material conditions but also academic freedom.

Attending to these calls becomes even more crucial in the context of a higher-education landscape characterized by fears of declining student enrollments and shrinking budgets—fears that occur in institutions that are also embracing corporate and neoliberal values and practices. Under these conditions, austerity measures, values that are more corporate than academic, and precarity are potential conditions for all faculty. For example, in the introduction to their collection of essays on austerity and composition, Tony Scott and Nancy Welch (2016) describe some of the dangers of an austerity culture, including a reductive emphasis on metrics and a turn to a "corporate audit culture" (p. 12); and noted that these conditions are now affecting all disciplines (p. 5). Scott (2016) cautions that a turn toward entrepreneurialism (encouraged in the cash-strapped neoliberal university) could undermine higher education's service of the public good; although he focuses on its effects in the field of composition, entrepreneurialism can be found in departments across most universities.

Not only do precarity and contingency affect those in the contingent positions, but widespread contingency has broader negative effects on academia: it undermines faculty governance (Cross and Goldenberg, 2009), academic freedom and faculty power (Ginsberg, 2011), and the ongoing stability of higher education itself (Bousquet, 2008). Austerity, accountability, and audit regimes can also affect faculty well-being, whether through tenure reviews (Sheffield and Muhlhauser, 2021), the scope and quantity of everyday employment expectations (Lackritz, 2004), or work-life balance (Jacobs and Winslow, 2004). As Anicca Cox et al. (2016) argue, the spread of neoliberalism in higher education can lead to feelings of "inevitability, enormity, and isolation"—and then despair (p. 41). These effects can be felt by all faculty, no matter their discipline or rank.

This sampling of warnings and critiques indicates problems with institutional structures and conditions across the curriculum and thus the need to address them in solidarity, across all disciplines and ranks. The cross-disciplinary connections of writing across the curriculum (WAC) programs could well be a fruitful source of such solidarity wherever possible—including in the faculty development connections between writing studies faculty and administrators and disciplinary faculty teaching writing. Finding the possibilities for those avenues and then forging the connections will require new research in WAC, with a focus on disciplinary writing instruction as labor, particularly in local political-economic institutional contexts, and with attention to both the commonalities among faculty and the managerial structures and conditions that affect their labor.

Since "labor" has been extensively theorized and variously defined, I want to offer a brief explanation of how I understand "labor" and "management." I am using here Kahn and Pason's (2021) concept of labor, which insists that labor comprises both the tasks involved and the worker's relations with management. As Kahn and Pason explain, "[I]f we're not talking about how work is managed, we're not talking about labor issues" (p. 114). This concept of labor has the benefit of aligning with calls in WAC faculty development for attention to local institutional contexts and managerial structures (e.g., Condon et al., 2016, p. 31). Furthermore, this emphasis on managerial structures aligns with institutional ethnography's emphasis on the coordination of people's activities as an object of study (as I will discuss later) and with concerns in academia about the effects of administrative values and choices on faculty and their labor. "Management" is a crucial component of academic labor: institutional policies, practices, and procedures influence what faculty do, how they are held accountable, how (and whether) they are compensated and rewarded, and whether the material support for their labor is sufficient. At the same time, as I will discuss, the nature and degrees of management have fostered division among faculty instead of prompting solidarity. Using these concepts, I am calling on WAC researchers and faculty developers to normalize the consideration of labor issues in research and faculty development, and I offer an example of what such research might look like.

In 2015, Michelle LaFrance made a similar call: "It is time to make labor concerns a central component of forthcoming statements in WAC/WID [writing in the disciplines] programmatic work and a more central component of research in this subfield of writing studies" (p. A15). LaFrance focused mainly on the labor conditions of contingency and emphasized the importance of labor-oriented research for the sustainability of WAC programs, a focus and emphasis more specific than the broader solidarity issues that I am considering. It is notable that though she pointed to these gaps and limitations in WAC research in 2015, little has been done to address them since then.

While WAC research has not examined the labor of disciplinary writing instruction directly, some scholarship has at least implicitly acknowledged labor and management issues such as rewards and workloads. For example, in the conclusion of their study of faculty development, William Condon et al. (2016) note that universities must materially value and reward teaching and faculty development in order to support an institutional culture that values teaching (p. 123). Faculty development and changes to teaching methods that require additional labor should be institutionally recognized and compensated. For example, Jody Swilky (1992) describes a faculty member who, after participating in faculty development, wanted to revise his course to incorporate more writing instruction, but he did not do so because of the increased labor that it would require. A further structural constraint on faculty development appears in Condon et al.'s (2016) finding that nontenure-track faculty were reluctant to significantly innovate because of fears of the effects on their student evaluations (pp. 64–65). Pamela Flash (2016) touches upon the institutional context of labor in the conclusion of her discussion of reflection and faculty development, questioning whether economic forces could undermine the sustainability of faculty-development efforts (p. 248). Studies such as these fleetingly acknowledge the realities of academic labor, the political economy and managerial choices that might constrain faculty in their desire to support student writing and learning.

In this article, I call for more research to explore the political economy of academic labor, as well as the ways faculty experience that labor in disciplinary writing instruction. I argue that in doing so, we can add new dimensions to our understanding of disciplinary writing instruction, building additional bridges to faculty development and labor solidarity. In particular, I am arguing that with more research into faculty's experiences of the management of their writing-instruction labor, writing studies faculty can find common ground and cause with their colleagues across the university. As faculty better understand the institutional structures that shape both material conditions and academic culture, they can thus perhaps better navigate and influence those structures. I will first describe signs of separation between writing studies faculty and faculty in other disciplines. I will then present insights into disciplinary faculty's values and methods in teaching writing and into the institutional structures that affect that labor. I draw from a study of emotional labor in writing instruction in the disciplines that used institutional ethnography, a methodology well-suited for an exploration of structures and management. I will close with some suggestions and questions for labor-conscious faculty researchers and developers to consider.

Signs of Separation: Disciplinary Siloing across the University

While writing studies faculty and disciplinary faculty do collaborate within WAC initiatives, potential commonalities and connections—bridges to understanding and solidarity—are sometimes overlooked, and even undermined, in WAC literature, perhaps in part due to a history of disciplinary faculty questioning the disciplinarity of writing studies or criticizing the "products" of first-year writing classes. For example, in his plenary talk at the 2021 International Writing Across the Curriculum Conference, Chris Thaiss listed addressing the complaining questions of colleagues in other disciplines ("Why doesn't the English department / writing program do its job?") as part of the "fearlessness" required in WAC labor (p. 9). These types of questions suggest that such interactions with colleagues are something that we might fear.

Even when conversations with colleagues in other disciplines do not involve the potential for critique, defensiveness, fear, or courage, they sometimes occur across pedagogical and dispositional gaps. Thaiss, for example, highlighted the "complacent walls of disciplinary jargon," "awkward conversations," and "our own ignorance of others' expertise" (pp. 8–9). While he urged WAC faculty to listen, "and keep listening to, and learning from people across an institution whose views on students and the goals of education differ from our own" (p. 9)—a laudable call to bridge differences—the emphasis on separation, on difference, remains. There are efforts to achieve common ground, but within an assumed context of a lack of it.

Faculty developers, too, have sometimes operated from a position of separation and difference. Joan A. Mullin (2008), for example, highlights the frequency of this position even as she seeks to bridge it. She criticizes "a traditional, missionary form of knowledge transmission," in which a more knowledgeable WAC faculty developer engages with a disciplinary faculty member who needs to be "converted" (pp. 498–499). Instead, she argues for a more collaborative relationship grounded in rhetorical listening. While in this case the writing studies expert is not in a position of "fear" or defensiveness, the assumption of difference and separation remains.

Such assumptions potentially undermine the kinds of connections and collaboration that support understanding and solidarity. Moreover, they can exacerbate the tendency among writing studies faculty to identify as victims—the "wound attachment" and "rhetoric of subjection" that Laura Micciche (2007) describes (p. 36). When we believe that we require fearlessness to engage with our colleagues in other disciplines, or that we must overcome resistance or convert them, we inadvertently solidify a long-standing set of perceived power relations in which composition sits near the bottom. Moreover, as Micciche argues, when we maintain an attachment to the subjected identity, "[c]omposition's emotional and institutional subordination then functions as an identity marker rather than a source of critique and change" (p. 40). It is difficult to effect change, whether in disciplinary writing instruction or labor conditions, when one is in a defensive crouch.

This is not to say, of course, that there are no differences between writing faculty and faculty teaching writing in other disciplines, nor that institutional systems and individual faculty do not devalue composition. There are, and they sometimes do. In fact, there is a body of literature devoted to exploring the sources, history, and meaning of that divide, particularly, but not exclusively, as it appears within English departments. Feminist scholars often point to the historically gendered demographics and perceptions of composition: a predominantly female faculty, engaged in what was perceived as "care" (Schell, 1998, ch. 4) or hygiene (Strickland, 2011, p. 40) work on a contingent basis. These characteristics contributed to composition's lower status, especially in comparison to disciplines engaged in the supposed "real" work of the university, not the "clean-up" of callow first-year students. Also emphasizing the role of gender and feminization in composition's separation and low status, Susan Miller (1991) explores these dynamics in detail in her history and analysis of the relationship between composition and literary studies, pointing to the broader political and hegemonic systems that both determined the fate of composition and were sustained by it.

As Miller describes, institutional values, systems, and practices contributed to the separation of composition from literature and other disciplines; in other words, these separations occur within institutional structures and managerial and cultural practices in which all faculty are enmeshed. For example, Kahn (2020) argues that while institutions might claim to "value" teaching, they often do not, and this devaluing is signaled through lower pay, contingency, larger class sizes, and implicit characterizations of teaching as punishment—conditions that affect faculty in all disciplines. Courses and faculty most associated with teaching (general education courses, first-year writing, contingent faculty) feel the negative material effects of this devaluing the most, along with marginalization in relation to other courses and faculty.

When these structural and managerial forces are more overt, as in first-year writing (Strickland, 2011), this association with managerialism can contribute to the separation between writing studies and other disciplines instead of fostering solidarity born out of commonalities. Scott (2009) and Bruce Horner (2016) both argue that the perceived association among bureaucracy, management, and composition can lead to separation between writing studies and other disciplines. Scott distinguishes between "professionals" and "bureaucrats": professionals (scholars and faculty in more managerial roles) have more autonomy, expertise, and prestige, while bureaucrats (among whom are composition faculty) "are more highly managed" and lack prestige (pp. 43–44). Horner, too, argues that composition's "low academic status" is not due to any actual lack of disciplinarity but to other disciplines' discomfort with the ways that the material labor conditions of composition reveal structures and relationships that other disciplines would like to pretend do not exist (p. 167). In other words, composition confronts faculty in other disciplines with the labor realities of academia, including the reality that academic labor is in fact managed—realities to which they are subject, too, as I have described above.[1] Thus, one of the foundations of separation between writing studies and other disciplines is actually grounded in our common condition of laboring within institutional structures that affect our teaching labor.

The particularities of separation between writing studies and other disciplines, despite shared challenges, occur within academic cultures prone to widespread division and silos. In arguing for greater coordination among different employee cohorts in universities, Daniel Scott and Adrianna J. Kezar (2019) claim, "For too long in higher education, different worker groups have conceived of themselves as separated by distinct, even competing interests and priorities" (p. 101). These self-conceptions, according to Scott and Kezar, undermine efforts to engage in the activism and solidarity that Kahn and Lynch-Biniek call for: "The isolation of different types of higher education workers reduces communication, fosters unawareness of common interests, and hinders the ability to effectively collaborate in solidarity. . . ." (p. 101). In times of austerity and calls for individual entrepreneurship, these silos may well extend beyond departments and cohorts to include faculty who feel compelled to look out for themselves. Efforts to bridge the separations between writing studies and other disciplines must thus also attempt to account for the myriad other separations that undermine solidarity and faculty activism—separations that may benefit institutional structures and individuals who want to heighten forms of management that work against faculty power.

Because WAC is inherently collaborative and involves bridge-building across disciplines, especially in faculty development, it is an important site for exploring the spread of detrimental labor conditions and the possibility of solidarity and activism. But by focusing on differences, separations, and dismissals, and by assuming that broad gaps and strong resistance exist, writing studies scholars and faculty developers might be coming to these relationships with their guard up—and their minds made up—already casting themselves as different, separate, and even lesser before their colleagues have the chance to do so. I believe that further exploration of disciplinary writing instruction as labor, in its local institutional context and within larger institutional structures, can mitigate such tendencies because (as I discuss in the next section) it can reveal commonalities and insights that can serve as the foundation to labor solidarity and action.

---

1. In fact, WAC courses serve as especially fruitful sites of research into curricular and pedagogical management in other disciplines because they often require courses to include certain pedagogical elements and practices, and they might also insist that WAC faculty participate in faculty development.

What Labor Research Can Reveal: Insights from an Institutional Ethnography of Disciplinary Writing Instruction

In order to overcome perceived differences in values and status and lay the groundwork for navigating and changing managerial practices that negatively affect faculty, WAC administrators and faculty can find sources of commonality and solidarity by researching the labor of disciplinary writing instruction. The latter involves exploring the practices and experiences of faculty whose teaching tasks are managed, not only because of the requirements of a WAC program but also because they are employees subject to the policies, requirements, and expectations of an academic institution. I undertook such a study in the fall of 2020, conducting an institutional ethnography of the emotional labor of faculty teaching "W2" courses (writing-intensive courses that fulfilled a second-level university writing requirement) at a mid-sized, R1 private university. In this section, I will present two areas of insight—the values and the experiences of institutional structures and management—that demonstrate some of the potential of labor research in general and institutional ethnography in particular.

Institutional ethnography (IE) is a fruitful methodology for research into WAC labor, in part because IE is intended to examine workplace activities as they are managed (or coordinated, in IE terms) and experienced. As Michelle LaFrance (2019) says in her book on IE and writing studies research, "IE enables us to systematically study the hierarchical systems of labor, professional systems of value, and notions of expertise and prestige that structure the realm of higher education, the field itself, and our local actualities as these are manifest in, around, and through writing" (p. 12). Developed by sociologist Dorothy Smith (2005), IE provides an epistemological framework and research methods that surface the often-overlooked relationships among employees, their activities, management structures, and the norms and values of the institution. It directs attention to particularities and calls on the researcher to resist broader generalizations or prior theorization; it also relies on the researcher's rigorous, iterative, impressionistic interpretation (instead of relying only on the coding) of the various connections, coordinations, and disjunctures (Campbell and Gregor, 2004, pp. 84–85). Smith (2005) argues that institutions coordinate employees' activities, usually via institutional texts, and that this coordination reveals the "ruling relations" (the norms and values) of the institution (p. 227). Crucially, IE insists that individuals participate in their coordination; coordination is not control. However, IE also highlights the institutional accountability structures that track, evaluate, and reward or criticize individuals. Moreover, an important component of IE research that pertains to my study is the recognition that there might be gaps, resistances, and disjunctures in institutional coordination.[2] IE can therefore reveal the complexities

---

2. LaFrance (2019) provides multiple examples of IE's power to illuminate labor conditions in writing studies. IE has been used elsewhere to study academic labor, although not WAC labor or teaching labor; see, for example, McCoy (2014) and Wright (2014).

of managerial functions in an institution, as well as the values and norms embedded in those functions and the ways that faculty experience them.

The study that I undertook involved eighteen participants from a variety of faculty cohorts (adjunct, term, tenure-track) and disciplines (arts, sciences, humanities, and social sciences; professional schools of public affairs, international service, and business), and a mix of age ranges, teaching experience, and genders. Three participants were faculty of color, roughly reflecting the broader demographics of faculty teaching W2 courses. I conducted focus groups with fifteen of the participants; with the other three, I met for three individual interviews throughout one semester. In keeping with the principles of IE, I drew on participants' experiences as a source of knowledge and expertise. Also in accordance with IE, I collected documents that were disciplinary (e.g., accreditation standards), institutional (e.g., personnel policies, W2 requirements, department-level learning outcomes), and course-specific (e.g., syllabi, feedback on student writing). I used these documents to trace the institutional management of participants' activities and compared that tracing to participants' descriptions of their experiences.

These faculty had taken advantage of various forms of support for teaching W2 courses. The proposal form for creating a new W2 course, or converting an existing course to a W2, required faculty to understand elements of writing pedagogy such as high- and low-stakes assignments, writing-to-learn activities, interactive feedback, and information literacy; the general education program and the faculty committee overseeing the W2 courses offered workshops to help faculty learn these concepts and prepare their proposals. Six participants had been members of faculty-learning communities for faculty teaching W2 courses. All three interview participants indicated involvement in some form of professional development related to writing instruction, whether it was a university-sponsored workshop, a disciplinary conference session, or social media or blogs by colleagues knowledgeable in pedagogy. Nonetheless, most participants expressed at least some feeling that they did not know enough about teaching writing.

In the discussion that follows, I will focus on participants' experiences and their feelings about those experiences. I will highlight two areas of insight drawn from this study: participants' values regarding writing instruction and their experiences of institutional management. I believe that these areas serve as examples of the rich material that can be garnered from labor research—material that can provide a foundation for better understanding managerial structures and experiences and thus for labor solidarity and action.

Participants' Values for Writing Instruction

As we explored their emotional labor, study participants described values concerning teaching and learning, including a deep sense of obligation to student learning and satisfaction in their identities as teachers, that will appear familiar to faculty in writing studies. They clearly gave a great deal of their intellectual attention to pedagogy, including ways to support student writing development. All of these professed values indicate shared ground with writing faculty, a foundation of care and commitment that could ground common cause in labor solidarity, an understanding of shared structures, and even labor-oriented faculty development.

In their study of WAC faculty development, Condon et al. (2016) found that contrary to conventional wisdom that disciplinary faculty only care about research, "teachers care deeply about their teaching" (p. 62). The participants in this study, too, consistently expressed that they cared about their teaching and about student learning, including student writing development. Sam,[3] a government professor in one of the focus groups, put it simply: "But I'm also a teacher, because I'm interested in doing a good job for my students and with my students." Sam not only embraced the identity of "teacher" but also equated that identity with supporting his students.

Participants also revealed that they recognized their own responsibility for student writing development, although they often worried that they lacked the means to fulfill that responsibility. Eight of the focus-group participants and all of the interview participants indicated a lack of confidence in their ability to teach writing. For example, Karen, a psychology professor, voiced both her feelings of inadequacy in her writing-pedagogy knowledge and her obligation to still support students' writing development: "So I definitely have an incredible respect for the people who do this, and this is their job, to teach undergraduates how to write, and I, I don't even know that I would know the first place to start to do it according to maybe general practices and principles, but I do my best." Similarly, Miriam, who teaches art history, expressed both anxiety and obligation: "I do feel like a little bit panicked, actually, when I, when a student like replies, and it's like, Oh, I need even more specific advice, and I think, oh, you know, I hope I'll be able to do this." These faculty understood what their jobs required of them in the W2 classes, but they worried that they might not be able to fulfill those requirements.

Despite such concerns, ten of the focus-group participants and all of the interview participants expressed a belief in the requirements, demonstrating that they shared the values expressed in the W2 course-development materials. An international studies professor, Joseph, explained that he had already been supporting student writing, but the W2 framework helped him to do so: "Because it had always been a writing-intensive course, but [the W2] gave us a frame to actually, you know, really emphasize that part of it." The W2 label and structure facilitated Joseph's efforts to teach students to write in his discipline. Others who had not already been emphasizing writing expressed some initial resistance but subsequently experienced a shift

---

3. All names mentioned in this study are pseudonyms.

in their views. Miriam described the process in this way: "I was reading [student papers], thinking, that one was pretty good, actually. And I read another one. And then it came to me, hey, this might be the W2 actually working. I couldn't believe it! I didn't think it would actually work. And it's like, they're quite well written." What is notable here is that not only did Miriam realize the effectiveness of a writing-in-the-disciplines approach but also, even before that realization, she was able to implement the W2 approach. She sufficiently valued the importance of student writing development, and the role of disciplinary writing in that development, to go along with the W2 requirements, do her best to implement them, and help students improve their writing.

All the study participants held strong feelings of obligation and accountability for student learning. This accountability was not codified in university policies (nor did the student evaluations of teaching capture it); instead, participants constructed accountability for themselves—what, based on my research, I am calling "deep accountability," a multifaceted feeling of obligation constructed from professional identity and values, institutional and cultural influences, and a humane sense of care for students. Participants' desire to do what the W2 framework required of them was rooted in deep accountability: they believed that the W2 requirements would benefit students' writing development, and so they tried to follow them and deployed emotional labor to support their students in achieving the W2 learning outcomes.

These faculty often expressed their feelings of deep accountability quite directly. For example, Carl, who teaches chemistry, described a lofty disciplinary purpose for his writing instruction: "But in, in the sciences now, being able to finesse and, and be a good communicator and understanding how to communicate your research topic or just your scientific results in general is just critical, both to the success of your profession, but also this, you know, global enterprise that we're all in right now." But Carl also recognized the more specific obligations to students who would have jobs in laboratories: "So you know, if a student goes out and is working at a testing facility, they need to be able to write their, their technical reports in a very specific way, and, and so our students are comfortable doing that on, at graduation, they're going to be better off when they go to their job. So we all see it as part of our responsibility that this kind of training is important in general." In both of these cases, Carl constructed a connection between writing instruction and his students' future writing endeavors. There was no institutional accountability for this preparation, but Carl still believed in it and in the role of his labor in creating successful outcomes for his students.

As I have noted, however, participants also believed that they lacked sufficient knowledge of writing instruction to fully support students. To satisfy their sense of accountability, they supplemented what knowledge they did have with knowledge they felt confident in: their understanding of students as people and their ability to engage in relational and emotional labor.[4]

Emotional labor involves emotional self-management, and all study participants described experiences of managing or repressing their own feelings so that students could maintain a positive disposition and motivation. Joseph articulated this tension between the frustration or irritation that a teacher might feel and the desire to maintain students' investment and motivation: "I want to write something really, really direct, almost brusque, right now. And I guess to convey the feedback, I need to frame it in something that's a bit more, hopefully, you know, thought-provoking for the student, but also doesn't just instantly frustrate them with me saying, no, you're wrong." Although Joseph had not been trained in providing constructive feedback, he believed in his knowledge of student motivation, based on his years of teaching experience, and used that knowledge to guide his feedback approach. That approach was a form of emotional labor, requiring him to manage the expression of his emotional response—irritation—in order to prompt the desired response in the student writers—motivation to continue to try to improve. Such deployments of emotional and relational labor will likely seem familiar to writing studies faculty—as will the experiences of exceeding what an institution explicitly requires of its faculty.

Indeed, it is important to emphasize that in fulfilling their perceived obligations through time- and energy-consuming emotional labor, participants were not fulfilling explicit institutional requirements, nor would they be held directly accountable for them. Their own sense of professional accountability and their values drove them to exceed what institutional policies explicitly required for writing instruction in their discipline. In other words, they followed the actual W2 requirements and then exceeded those requirements and others related to teaching—demonstrating a commitment to student writing development that surely will seem familiar to writing studies faculty. Yet these insights also indicate complexities and nuances in institutional requirements, structures, and management that might not be immediately visible to faculty, beyond the sense that their labor is not accounted for, recognized, or rewarded.

Institutional Context for the Labor of Writing Instruction

These experiences of the labor of disciplinary writing instruction demonstrate that the study participants believed in the importance of their labor and strived to engage

---

4. I am relying on Arlie Russell Hochschild's (2012) definition of emotional labor, which involves, in the course of one's job, managing one's own emotions in order to create the desired emotional outcomes in others. Emotional labor has been extensively discussed in writing studies (e.g., Jacobs and Micciche, 2003; Lamos, 2016; Micciche, 2007; Sicari, 2020; Wooten et al., 2020) but not as it pertains to disciplinary writing instruction.

in the labor in ways that would benefit student learning. The experiences occurred within institutional structures, policies, and management that coordinated their labor, but only partially, as these faculty exceeded what was explicitly required in that coordination. Other insights from this study underscore the importance of the context in which labor occurs, the institutional supports and constraints. Participants described complicated relationships with their institution. As I explained above, they believed that the W2 structure aligned with their values of supporting student learning; even those who initially questioned its merit and felt some resistance agreed with it once they saw the positive effects on student writing. Although, as I have noted, some writing studies scholars have argued that the management and bureaucracy associated with composition contribute to composition's low status in institutional hierarchies (e.g., Scott, 2009; Horner, 2016), the participants in this study did not object to the management of their labor when they saw it as benefiting their teaching and their students, and they even described positive changes to their teaching practices resulting from the W2 requirements.

But when these faculty believed that the institution was not acting in the best interests of teaching and learning, they were more critical—and yet they continued to engage in the labor they believed would satisfy the deep accountability they had constructed. These complex relationships of labor and institution provide potentially valuable insights for labor advocates and those who would engage in labor-conscious faculty development, who might build on the shared values and impulses described above to better understand and act in response to labor management.

One such area of insight was the awareness of insufficient institutional material support for disciplinary writing instruction, as ten focus-group participants attested. An area of concern was institutional choices related to class size, which influenced their ability to support student writing development. For example, Steven, a marketing instructor and interview participant, had seventy-five students in three sections of his W2 course. He described his thought process when reading a set of papers in this way: "I mean, right now I'm—you know, 75 papers. I started out really strong and I'm putting in a lot of effort. But then as I look at, okay, well, that just took me 30 minutes, I've got seven—you know, like, it's, okay, I've got to try to shorten this down. And so I want to treat each paper fairly and give them the proper attention and feedback. But you know, there's only so many hours in the day, and you've got to kind of prioritize." Steven felt obligated to give each paper more attention, but he also recognized the material reality of the number of papers that needed attention and the unrealistic labor burden that it entailed.

Similarly, Karen, the psychology professor, responded to my question about institutional expectations for her writing instruction by pointing to class size: "The expectations for me come from the class size. So if you're going to make a W2 class

30 people, and I'm the only instructor, and it's three credits, one semester. . . . Then there's only so much I can do. So you're, you're setting the expectations of how much time I can spend working with students as writers. If there were *ten*, then they'll get better writing instruction. If there's 30, then they're going to get, you know, less—less writing instruction." Like Steven, Karen could see how material conditions directly affected teaching: there was less time for written feedback and for engagement—emotional and pedagogical—with students.

It is notable that although these faculty were aware that the institution did not create the most positive conditions for their writing-instruction labor, they continued to feel accountable to students. Their desire to support students' writing development and their sense of deep professional accountability compelled them to find ways to do the best they could within those constrained conditions.[5]

Moreover, they did so with the awareness that the institution often did not value or reward this labor. All three interview participants felt that the institution did not sufficiently value teaching in personnel evaluations, including those for term and adjunct faculty, whose primary duty is teaching. Carl said, "I think a lot of the things that we do in, in instruction, it's hard to see where doing well and, and actually having students be proficient and, and good at what we're training them for, I don't think that's really reflected in, in my tenure or advancement progression, or in our term faculty lines progression, either." (Carl, a tenured professor, serves on committees that review term faculty.) Others expressed uncertainty about how "good teaching" might even be institutionally defined. Miriam was not certain that such a definition existed in her department's guidelines for term reappointment and promotion: "I can't, I can't bring to mind any kind of definition of satisfactory teaching in there, but I know one, one aspect of, for example, the additional things you can submit for your reappointment. One of them is a syllabus, and in there it says specifically, like, that the sources you have in your syllabus are like really up to date."

Without clear expectations and rewards for teaching, these faculty developed their own sense of deep accountability to student learning, often exceeding the labor explicitly required of them. These dynamics indicate a complicated and often fraught relationship between faculty and the institutional structures and policies that coordinate/manage their labor. Participants pointed to alignments between their professional values for student writing and institutional policies for the W2 classes, but they also highlighted a lack of institutional support and acknowledgement of their labor, including the emotional labor that exceeded explicit requirements. Uncovering these

---

5. As a result, unfortunately, these faculty sometimes seemed to participate in their own exploitation. In other words, instead of resisting or trying to change potentially exploitative conditions, they tried to make the best of those conditions.

complex relationships through research can open the door to the types of understanding that benefit labor solidarity and action.

Conclusion: Inquiry and Action

Revealing alignments and divergences between those who labor and institutional structures is a hallmark of institutional ethnography (IE). IE allows researchers to examine the particularities of labor experiences and structures and then "look up" to comprehend the broader institutional structures, values, and norms that influence those particularities. As LaFrance (2019) concludes, "As we continue conversations about how IE may enable us to tell stories differently, to uncover what can only be seen when we 'look up,' 'study up,' or 'stand under,' we are also discussing how it is that our research prepares us *to act* alongside others" (p. 136). That is, comprehension leads to action in solidarity with others.

In this IE study of emotional labor in disciplinary writing instruction, participants expressed feelings of obligation, accountability, and care for students and their writing development, as well as a lack of institutional support and recognition—all of which will likely sound familiar to writing studies faculty. Labor conditions often assumed to be the unfortunate lot of composition faculty have now spread across disciplines and faculty ranks: "Today, workers across different groups in higher education face more similar conditions than in past times. Most workers at non-executive levels face job insecurity, shrinking wages, a lack of benefits, de-skilling and de-professionalization, as well as mounting accountability pressures" (Scott and Kezar, 2019, p. 102). This labor study reveals values and experiences that could serve as the foundation to stronger commonalities and solidarity among faculty from different disciplines: deep accountability to student writing development, labor exceeding (often unclear) local institutional expectations, and often inadequate material support and rewards. Moreover, this study reveals successes and insufficiencies in management, both support for improved teaching of writing and policies that do not reward, or even undermine, that teaching.

It is difficult to imagine a path to labor action that does not involve understanding the institutional context in which that labor happens, especially the complexities of the management of that labor. In the case of my study, helping disciplinary faculty to "look up" and recognize their own sense of accountability and obligation, the labor they perform in response to that sense, and the insufficiency of official personnel procedures and policies to reward that labor creates possibilities for change, including action to improve personnel mechanisms. In addition, demonstrating to writing studies colleagues that faculty in other disciplines share not only our values but also our experiences of institutional management creates a foundation to overcoming long-standing separations, leading to solidarity and shared action. Moreover, these study findings could be useful to faculty developers interested in accounting for labor conditions. For example, WAC faculty development might help faculty reflect on their sense of accountability and obligation to create more effective ways to meet those obligations, or faculty might consider how to deploy emotional labor as efficiently and effectively as possible. Or, perhaps, WAC faculty developers could incorporate analyses of labor conditions and possibilities for solidarity and action into their definition of "faculty development"; for example, in the case of this study, they could consider how to communicate instructors' labor in personnel files or even strategize to improve personnel policies so that they reward the labor of teaching writing.

More broadly, IE and other forms of research into the labor of disciplinary writing instruction could take a variety of paths that would create a better understanding of writing instruction in the disciplines, WAC academic labor and management, and WAC faculty development—as well as paths to labor solidarity and action. What follows are some suggestions for future paths.

Areas of Inquiry for Labor-Oriented WAC Research

WAC research that brings labor into the picture, either as important context or as the topic of research, can generate new lines of inquiry that provide a fuller picture of disciplinary writing instruction. Researchers might ask questions such as the following:

- How do institutional policies for WAC and for personnel processes associated with teaching occlude power relationships that might exploit or marginalize the labor of women and BIPOC faculty?
- What affordances do disciplinary faculty draw on to help them in the labor of disciplinary writing instruction, especially in the absence of institutional support?
- How do institutional accountability measures for the labor of teaching (such as student evaluations) align with or diverge from faculty's own sense of accountability to student writing development?

In asking questions such as these, WAC researchers will not only reveal insights that support faculty development and improve instruction: they will also start to forge paths to solidarity by surfacing commonalities among disciplines and premising their research on the idea that labor matters.

Areas of Consideration for Labor-Conscious Faculty Development

WAC faculty development has always been a site of bridge-building across disciplines, and faculty development arising out of labor-oriented research can further support solidarity by continuing with the premise that labor matters—and that this labor, of disciplinary writing instruction accomplished by committed, caring individuals, should be valued. Labor-conscious faculty developers might consider the following:

- If faculty feel undervalued and unsupported, how can WAC faculty development value and support them? How can faculty development be crafted so as not to perpetuate exploitation via additional burdens and expectations beyond what is explicitly required by personnel policies?
- What unacknowledged resources do disciplinary faculty bring to writing instruction? How can emotional labor, for example, become less of a burden and more of a powerful affordance in conjunction with fuller knowledge of writing pedagogy?
- What role does labor advocacy play in faculty development? Should solidarity and self-advocacy fall under the umbrella of faculty development?

WAC faculty developers already have a great deal on their plates, of course, and so attention to the resources and exploitation of disciplinary faculty must be reflected in attention to the burdens that faculty developers bear. But recognition of the role of labor in disciplinary writing instruction and WAC faculty development might also lead to faculty development that is not only more ethical but also more efficient.

Exigence for Action: We Need to Act Together

WAC initiatives and faculty development have always fostered connections across disciplines, thereby resisting academic siloing. A political economy of increasing precarity and corporatization, though, calls for greater attention to ways of forging connection and solidarity. As Scott and Kezar (2019) argue,

> Without collaborating in solidarity across different worker and other constituent groups, members of the higher education community may not be able to resist the harmful trends that have been transforming the sector over the previous decades. Neo-liberal trends like shifting towards increasingly exploitative employment and labor management practices, eroding worker involvement in governance, and lowering the quality of working conditions have been undermining the ability of higher education to serve its students, perform community service, and achieve its research missions. (pp. 101–102)

WAC research, instruction, and development have the potential to be important sites of collaboration in solidarity and of resistance to one of the dangers of neoliberalism:

"Neoliberalism has thus replaced an emphasis on collectivism and the public good with an emphasis on individual competition and entrepreneurialism, converting higher education workers from people with shared interests to a motley collection of individuals who compete with one another for scarce resources" (Scott and Kezar, 2019, p. 110). Scrambling for resources, with an "every-person-for-themselves" attitude, can place faculty into positions of complicity with an exploitative system.

Labor-oriented research and faculty development in WAC are not a panacea, of course, and will not suddenly eliminate corporatization and neoliberal impulses. Solidarity is difficult to achieve, and creating a healthier, more humane political economy in academia is even more difficult. But gaining deeper insights into the labor of disciplinary writing instruction, and then using those insights to support faculty and forge connections with them, can at least be a site of resistance and create important steps toward cultural and institutional change.

References

Bousquet, M. (2002). Tenured bosses and disposable teachers. *Minnesota Review*, 58, 231–239.

Bousquet, M. (2008). *How the university works: Higher education and the low-wage nation*. NYU Press.

Campbell, M., & Gregor, F. (2004). *Mapping social relations: A primer in doing institutional ethnography*. AltaMira Press.

Condon, W., Iverson, E. R., Manduca, C. A., Rutz, C., & Willett, G. (2016). *Faculty development and student learning: Assessing the connections*. Indiana University Press.

Cox, A., Dougherty, T., Kahn, S., LaFrance, M., & Lynch-Biniek, A. (2016). The Indianapolis Resolution: Responding to twenty-first-century exigencies/political economies of composition labor. *College Composition and Communication, 68*(1), 38–67. https://secure.ncte.org/library/NCTEFiles/Resources/Journals/CCC/0681-sep2016/CCC0681Indianapolis.pdf.

Cross, J. G., & Goldenberg, E. N. (2009). *Off-Track profs: Nontenured teachers in higher education*. The MIT Press.

Enos, T. (1996). *Gender roles and faculty lives in rhetoric and composition*. Southern Illinois University Press.

Flash, P. (2016). From apprised to revised: Faculty in the disciplines change what they never knew they knew. In K. B. Yancey (Ed.), *A rhetoric of reflection* (pp. 226–249). University Press of Colorado.

Ginsberg, B. (2011). *The fall of the faculty: The rise of the all-administrative university and why it matters*. Oxford University Press.

Hochschild, A. R. (2012). *The managed heart: Commercialization of human feeling*. University of California Press.

Horner, B. (2016). *Rewriting composition: Terms of exchange*. Southern Illinois University Press.

Jacobs, D., & Micciche, L. R. (Eds.). (2003). *A way to move: Rhetorics of emotion and composition*. Boynton/Cook.

Jacobs, J. A., & Winslow, S. E. (2004). Overworked faculty: Job stresses and family demands. *The Annals of the American Academy of Political and Social Science*, *596*, 104–129. http://www.jstor.org/stable/4127652

Kahn, S. (2020). We value teaching too much to keep devaluing it. *College English*, *82*(6), 591–611. https://library.ncte.org/journals/ce/issues/v82-6/30805

Kahn, S., & Lynch-Biniek, A. (2022). From activism to organizing, from caring to care work. *Labor Studies Journal, 47*(3), 320–344. https://doi.org/10.1177/0160449X221112060

Kahn, S., & Pason, A. (2021). What do we mean by academic labor (in rhetorical studies)? *Rhetoric and Public Affairs*, *24*(1–2), 109–128. https://doi.org/10.14321/rhetpublaffa.24.1-2.0109

Lackritz, J. R. (2004). Exploring burnout among university faculty: Incidence, performance, and demographic issues. *Teaching and Teacher Education*, *20*(7), 713–729. https://doi.org/10.1016/j.tate.2004.07.002

LaFrance, M. (2015). Making visible labor issues in writing across the curriculum: A call to research. *Forum: Issues about Part-Time and Contingent Faculty*, in *College Composition and Communication 67*(1), A13–A16. https://library.ncte.org/journals/CCC/issues/v67-1/27445

LaFrance, M. (2019). *Institutional ethnography: A theory of practice for writing studies researchers*. Utah State University Press.

Lamos, S. (2016). Toward job security for teaching-track composition faculty: Recognizing and rewarding affective-labor-in-space. *College English*, *78*(4), 362–386. http://www.ncte.org/journals/ce

McCoy, L. (2014). Producing "what the deans know": Cost accounting and the restructuring of post-secondary education. In D. E. Smith & S. M. Turner (Eds.), *Incorporating texts into institutional ethnographies* (pp. 93–119). University of Toronto Press.

Micciche, L. (2007). *Doing emotion: Rhetoric, writing, teaching*. Boynton/Cook.

Miller, S. (1991). *Textual carnivals: The politics of composition*. Southern Illinois University Press.

Mullin, J. A. (2008). Interdisciplinary work as professional development: Changing the culture of teaching. *Pedagogy*, *8*(3), 495–508. https://doi.org/10.1215/15314200-2008-008

Schell, E. (1992). The feminization of composition: Questioning the metaphors that bind women teachers. *Composition Studies*, *20*(1), 55–61. https://www.uc.edu/journals/composition-studies.html

Schell, E. (1998). *Gypsy academics and mother-teachers: Gender, contingent labor, and writing instruction.* Boynton/Cook.

Scott, T. (2009). *Dangerous writing: Understanding the political economy of composition.* Utah State University Press.

Scott, T. (2016). Animated by the entrepreneurial spirit: Austerity, dispossession, and composition's last living act. In N. Welch & T. Scott (Eds.), *Composition in the age of austerity* (pp. 205–219). Utah State University Press.

Scott, D., & Kezar, A. J. (2019). Intergroup solidarity and collaboration in higher education organizing and bargaining in the United States. *Academic Labor: Research and Artistry, 3*(10), 100–125. http://digitalcommons.humboldt.edu/alra/vol3/iss1/10

Scott, T., & Welch, N. (2016). Introduction: Composition in the age of austerity. In N. Welch & T. Scott (Eds.), *Composition in the age of austerity* (pp. 3–17). Utah State University Press.

Sheffield, J. P., & Muhlhauser, P. (2021). When enough *isn't* enough: Rhetoric and composition tenure-track scholars' perceptions and feelings toward tenure processes. *College English, 83*(3), 200–234.

Sicari, A. (2020). Complaint as "sticky data" for the woman WPA: The intellectual work of a WPA's emotional and embodied labor. *The Journal of the Assembly for Expanded Perspectives on Learning, 25,* 99–117. https://doi.org/10.7290/jaepl2599gi

Smith, D. (2005). *Institutional ethnography: A sociology for people.* AltaMira Press.

Strickland, D. (2011). *The managerial unconscious in the history of composition studies.* Southern Illinois University Press.

Swilky, J. (1992). Reconsidering faculty resistance to writing reform. *Writing Program Administration, 16*(1–2), 50–61. http://wpacouncil.org/journal/index.html

Thaiss, C. (2021). WAC fearlessness, sustainability, and adaptability: Part one. *The WAC Journal, 32,* 8–15. https://doi.org/10.37514/WAC-J.2022.32.1.02

Wooten, C. A., Babb, J., Costello, K. M., & Navickas, K. (Eds.). (2020). *The things we carry: Strategies for recognizing and negotiating emotional labor in writing program administration.* Utah State University Press.

Wright, S. (2014). Knowledge that counts: Points systems and the governance of Danish universities. In A. I. Griffith & D. E. Smith (Eds.), *Under new public management: Institutional ethnographies of changing front-line work* (pp. 294–337). University of Toronto Press.

Special Forum: Adulting with WAC

Introduction: Adult Learners in the Composition Classroom

MACY DUNKLIN

My college experience was not traditional. My fellow high-school graduates dove headfirst into their collegiate experience, but I left after one semester and got a real job, as they say, to avoid accruing college debt. After being a terrible student in high school, I was not expecting to go further than an associate's degree after a couple night classes at the local community college. Most of us taking night classes at Central Piedmont Community College were there for reasons other than academic interest. Some may have been delayed for the same reasons as me—financial need or lack of interest—but all of us had practical motivations for returning to school. My status as a recent high-school graduate was an unexpected addition to the classroom rather than the norm. At my community college, at 6:00 p.m. on a Tuesday in a town with a handful of four-year institutions, the typical student was an adult learner returning to remedial courses after taking extended time off from their educational journey.

Thanks to my time with my older classmates, however, I learned to interrogate my desire for an education and appreciate its value. When I complained about yet another essay, my classmates relayed a variety of experiences, such as getting a middle-school son involved in the essay as a moment to teach the importance of education and writing. Indirectly, they showed me the value I could bring to my assignments by connecting them to my values, which led to my first understanding of transfer. When group projects came around (with a professor who thankfully had us work on our projects in class), I was amazed to find group work functional. My classmates collaborated more like an on-site team at work than students begrudgingly meeting deadlines. They openly shared their other priorities and negotiated workloads and meetings, which taught me how to professionally advocate for myself in and out of the classroom. Moreover, they demonstrated how there is more to learn from a writing assignment than simply writing: experiences off the paper informour ability to address multiple audiences in ink.

Nevertheless, these classes were not an oasis for returning students. A technician had to drop because she was moved to the night shift. Even if we could normally attend class, student absence policies generally do not include stipulations for sick children or being late due to a boss holding you for a meeting at work. In addition to these struggles, we regularly faced the challenge of going to work, attending classes, *and* completing assignments in the same day. Despite my age, I shared some of my older classmates' struggles as a fellow working student. The education system felt set up for college first, work second.

My time with older students shaped and strengthened my mental capacities to even handle a postsecondary education, and the advocacy they did on their own behalf revealed to me the inflexibility and ableism of most university policies. I had my fair share of troubles as a part-time student living in a different town, but the coursework had been prepared for people like me—the recent high-school graduate. The curriculum did not include space for revisiting core skills learned in junior- and senior-level English classes, nor did it provide additional courses to help students "catch up." If anything, the opposite was true. Early college programs were on the rise and younger students were showing up in classrooms, making it more difficult for older students to adapt.

As I started teaching amid these shifts, I wondered, how am I supposed to teach all these people, arriving in the classroom at diverse stages in their education, how to write? I searched existing writing studies literature and found few answers. Instead, I saw that age was not part of the classroom diversity discussion. Where was the conversation happening, and what were people learning?

As I returned to this question in the middle of my doctoral journey, I received the chance to be a guest editor of *The WAC Journal*. This special forum on adult learners was made possible by the Will Hochman New Scholar Fellowship offered by the WAC Clearinghouse. My experience as the first Will Hochman scholar has been empowering, enlightening, and rigorous. Over the course of the last year, I have worked closely with the Pearce Center for Professional Communication at Clemson University and members of the WAC Clearinghouse to complete two interrelated tasks: (1) to create a special forum around a topic of importance to myself and the WAC community, and (2) to direct the first journal-based mini conference as an extension of this special forum. For the first rendition of the fellowship, I chose the journal's topic to be adult learners, expanding the discussion for the conference to include age and the WAC/WID classroom.

Under the guidance of the editor of *The WAC Journal*, Allison Daniel, and the director of the Pearce Center, Dr. Cameron Bushnell, I developed the administrative and professional skills required to accomplish these goals while also being given the space to generate my own ideas and design for the special forum and accompanying conference. As a Will Hochman fellow, I had the opportunity to spotlight an area of WAC/WID pedagogy that warranted more (and ongoing) discussion as well as to bring together those who are already passionately working towards the same goals as me.

The purpose of a mini conference based on a journal special issue is to invite scholars into a curated space to discuss key issues in the field. I believe that at our inaugural conference in May of this year, we achieved that goal. The publication of this special forum, which includes voices from the conference, continues the discussions we had and prompts others to join the conversation by responding to, applying, and citing the work presented here. I would like to draw the reader's attention to how the articles I briefly introduce next all include the voices of adult learners. Rather than talking about them at a distance or viewing them, in an objectifying manner, as a study sample, the manuscripts presented in this special forum are an expression of the passion and power of these students and their collaborators in writing education.

Jamie Hudson interrogates how innovative writing practices may create new and nuanced barriers despite the intent for new practices to be progressive and inclusive. Through reflections on participating in experiential education projects as an adult learner, Jamie provides critical feedback on how to not only include adult learners but also integrate experiential learning at work or through career opportunities. In a similar manner, **Kendon Kurzer, Natasha J. Lee, Amy Macias-Stowe, Mary Her, and Nieva Manalo** reflect on how recent programs at their university better serve learners of different experiences and education levels. By discussing their own experiences as students and teachers in a preparatory writing course, they elaborate on what elements of a writing classroom are most beneficial to resumers, a term coined to describe students resuming their education. Similarly, **Collie Fulford, Yaseen Abdul-Malik, Stefanie Frigo, Thomas Kelly, Adrienne Long, and Stuart Parrish** describe their round-table discussion groups to show how adult learners in the classroom can be beneficial to students who feel behind their peers. Lastly, **Gabrielle Kelney** presents insights from a program focused on continuing educational opportunities for adult learners. She details how her institution started a writing support group for adult learner alumni, who continue to grow their skills in a shared environment with scholars who recently resumed their academic careers.

Each of the voices in this collection targets a different area of concern for adult learners—applying new skills in their immediate environments, navigating how current curricula may or may not meet the needs of resumers, being seen as collaborators, and accessing or developing educational resources tailored to their needs. It is my hope that the stories presented here will inspire more and ongoing conversations about how we can recognize, accommodate, and empower learners of all ages in our WAC/WID classrooms.

The Adult Learner in the Writing Classroom: Creating Value through Experiential Education

JAMIE HUDSON

Introduction

During my college experience as an adult learner, it was through my internship, undergraduate research experience, and in-class chances to work with clients that I gained the confidence to seek out the job I wanted and the necessary expertise to succeed in the writing and editing field. It was these experiential education opportunities that helped me receive the education I came back to get. Without these experiences, my portfolio would have been dismal, consisting only of college essays and a certificate in technical communication with little proof that I could competently write and edit in various genres. While my experience returning to college helped me build durable skills, the opportunities I enjoyed may be inaccessible to many adult learners. Also called nontraditional students, adult learners are typically over the age of twenty-five and possess characteristics that separate them from the traditional learner population (Chen, 2017; Choy, 2002; Lodewyck, 2021).

One challenge faced by adult learners in higher education is the transition from workplace writing to academic writing because it can be difficult for them to leverage their valuable work/life experiences in the classroom (Johnson, 2017). Thus, an emerging academic identity may be in tension or competition with other senses of self or identities, such as professional or personal identities. These identities affect the writing these nontraditional students do. For these learners, the establishment of an academic identity is made challenging by the different discourses and different linguistic features that may be alien to the work-based learner (Mason and Atkin, 2021). As Sacha Mason and Chris Atkin state, the "discoursal self is represented by the work-based learner as an interconnection between the academic and the professional. It is within academic writing that these emerge and interact with each other in a dynamic, and often challenging way" (p. 23). These interactions make it critical to consider how adult learners need particular support in the classroom to integrate their identities and have their unique needs met.

While all students need to develop strong writing and communication skills to prepare them for success in the workplace, this need is particularly acute for the adult learner. Adults may return to college for many reasons, but a main factor is financial considerations: many adult learners realize that higher education can provide both economic and career opportunities (Bellare et al., 2023; Bowers and Bergman, 2016; Choy, 2002; Klein-Collins, 2011). Whether adults communicate professionally or are full-time professional communicators, advanced skills in writing, speaking, and visual design are often crucial to career success and advancement. Despite this need, many academic programs include minimal, if any, education in professional communication skills (Shriver, 2012). While some faculty do incorporate relevant assessments into writing-intensive courses across the curriculum, too often faculty fail to design writing activities that tap into the valuable workplace writing experiences that their nontraditional students bring to the classroom (Cleary, 2011; Marinara, 1997). Experiential education offers one approach to bridge this gap. Experiential education is one of the best methods to help adult learners connect their professional and academic experiences and develop skills through activities like collaborative research, writing with faculty mentors, workplace internships, and service learning (McKenzie, 2013).

The Association for Experiential Education (2024) defines experiential education as "a teaching philosophy that informs many methodologies in which educators purposefully engage with learners in direct experience and focused reflection in order to increase knowledge, develop skills, clarify values, and develop people's capacity to contribute to their communities" (para. 1). Both this association and Jay Roberts (2015) distinguish experiential "education" from experiential "learning." Roberts argues that experiential learning is informal, while experiential education includes a broader pedagogical process (p. 24). He believes that experiential education is not simply how we learn experientially but, instead, how moments are created through the systematic process of experiential education. Research supports the effectiveness of more experiential learning approaches in teaching and learning (Roberts, 2015).

There were additional valuable experiential education opportunities I received as a result of faculty investing in me personally. The capstone professor for my associate degree referred me to a local magazine to write articles as a freelancer. My persuasive writing professor recommended me for two Presidential Writing Awards, something I knew nothing about prior to my conversation with her. In addition, my technical editing professor also referred me for multiple freelance editing jobs. All of the skills I learned through each experiential education opportunity were immediately transferable to my workplace and gave me confidence to volunteer for workgroups and writing assignments for which I previously would not have had the expertise. Immediately after graduation, I was awarded additional hours at work, where I could apply my newly acquired knowledge and experience in numerous different areas.

However, finding and taking part in experiential education opportunities can be difficult for nontraditional students, who may be full-time working professionals, caregivers for children or other family members, disabled, or neurodivergent (Klein-Collins, 2011; Remenick, 2019; (Woldeab et al., 2023). Unfortunately, faculty and university program structures may fail to create equitable opportunities in which adult learners can fully participate, or faculty may fail in their communication by not inviting adult learners to writing activities. Experiential educational opportunities should support the success of adult learners in the classroom and allow them to gain desirable writing skills and expertise that are transferable to their career paths (Woldeab et al., 2023). In addition, universities need to utilize creative new ideas to ensure these opportunities are made available to traditional and nontraditional students alike and to increase retention rates (Cleary, 2011). Due to various barriers encountered by both students and faculty, adult learners often miss out on valuable chances for experiential education. To address this issue, writing-across-the-curriculum (WAC) faculty can aim to create more equitable access to these learning opportunities. This article will review the typical adult learner experience with writing in higher education; explore student, faculty, and university barriers to incorporating writing in experiential education opportunities; and provide recommendations for improving access to these opportunities for this student population.

What Writing-Focused Experiential Education Can Provide for Adult Learners

While all students need opportunities to connect writing in the classroom with what they would do as professionals, adult learners in particular want to know that their courses will lead to improvement in their income and career prospects (Leggins, 2021). Nontraditional students are more likely to value experiential education opportunities that include writing and communication assignments that teach valuable skills transferable to the workplace. Karen Shriver (2012) explains that while there are parallels between communication in classroom and workplace settings, three requisites of professional communication make it unlike most classroom experiences:

1. The need to orchestrate writing knowledge and strategy with visual design knowledge and strategy
2. The need to engage multiple stakeholders with a given body of content
3. The need to negotiate the social, political, and cultural landscapes of the workplace (p. 281)

Writing is a necessary form of communication that is vital to any profession. Having excellent writing skills can make an employee indispensable to their team or company. These writing skills are also one of the best ways to remain consistently employable, be more attractive to prospective employers, and advance in existing careers, regardless of the profession. Technical knowledge about workplace writing conventions, company-specific style guides, and formatting for different rhetorical situations is valuable to employers (Solomon, 2021). Neil Urquhart (2022), a veteran communications trainer, coach, and facilitator, says that "knowing how to write well and with impact is an essential skill to flourish in the professional world" (para. 1). But these writing skills, which support business and professional goals, take time and experience to master (Solomon, 2021). However, once learned, these skills can fast-track career success (Oliveri et al., 2021). Although there is widespread agreement that advanced skills in writing, speaking, and visual design are crucial for career advancement, do current pedagogical approaches meet the communication and writing needs of adult learners? Why would adult learners particularly benefit from experiential education?

Returning to the university with eighty previous credits as a working mom in my thirties, I chose to enroll in the Interdisciplinary Professional Studies (IPS) program at Boise State University that is designed for adult learners. Because this program accepted my previous credits and allowed me to tailor my degree to earn specific certificates in chosen areas, it was the best value for my money. This program targets adult students and allows them, depending on their degree emphasis and elective choices, to complete their degree completely online (Boise State University, 2024). My desired emphasis (technical communication), however, was outside of the online options offered by the program. The disconnect between the required courses and skills learned in my certificate program versus the overall degree program meant that I was on my own for researching any experiential education opportunities in the field of technical writing and communication. I didn't even know what kinds of opportunities were possible until my technical editing professor, Heather Smith (pseudonym), offered to complete an independent study with me. This idea had never been shared with me by advisors as an option within my degree plan.

This experiential education opportunity afforded me an enormous amount of valuable writing experience, taught me best practices for research methods, and provided multiple chances to publish my research. In addition, my faculty mentor told me about a paid research opportunity (which I was awarded) and helped me apply and be accepted to share my research during the undergraduate poster presentations at two conferences (one at my university and one in another state). These presentations taught me how to design an effective research poster and describe my research and gave me ample practice at public speaking. Additionally, my employer now wants me to show my poster, along with other research done for the organization for which I work, during a presentation at a department-wide meeting. I was also fortunate to complete an internship with the company where I work by making connections within the department and, prior to applying for the internship, scheduling a meeting with the director to ensure compatibility. The director was willing to have me intern in his department, and he completed all the necessary paperwork and assisted me with the application process. This internship was instrumental in helping me improve my writing and editing skills in multiple genres. It also provided me with a portfolio of over forty published articles in both internal and external company communications, and gave me an amazing network of professionals with whom to stay in contact, all while earning college credit.

As demonstrated by my experiences, adult learners benefit from the personalization of learning and an emphasis on practical utility (Chen, 2017). Unfortunately, many traditional methods used for classroom writing assignments are overly prescriptive and don't draw on skills that students can transfer to the workplace (Hendrickson and Garcia de Mueller, 2016). Adult learners desire meaningful coursework that develops usable professional skills (Woldeab et al., 2023). Reflections are one way for students to draw valuable connections between coursework and career. However, writing assignments that ask students to reflect on an experience, merely to encourage writing in the course, create busywork rather than a beneficial assessment that can provide skills for advancement in the workplace. Michael J. Michaud (2013) argues that "[a]s students, [adult learners] would be well-served by literacy instruction that takes as its starting point not those things teachers and institutions perceive such students to be lacking but, instead, the complex and evolving role that literacy already plays in such students' lives" (p. 91). In other words, adult learners may be more motivated to learn when the knowledge they receive directly relates to their needs (Bowers and Bergman, 2016; Woldeab et al., 2023). Ashley J. Holmes et al. (2022) describe how WAC programs could benefit from using an approach called Lifewide Writing Across the Curriculum, which helps WAC programs and administrators better understand the diverse roles in students' multiple spheres of writing. An understanding of the diversity and complexity of students' lives outside the classroom should inform the approach of writing-based initiatives across the curriculum. This lifewide approach validates students' writing experience and their experiences in the various spheres they inhabit, such as professional and internship spheres, and uses this knowledge to inform writing-intensive pedagogies (p. 53). Reflections are one assignment often used in writing instruction to help students become more knowledgeable and better equipped for future writing tasks, leading to increased college success (Taczak and Robertson, 2017).

For example, I experienced great variations in the value of writing assignments in courses that sought to include reflective learning for their adult students. In a course on emotional intelligence, students were assigned to write reflections regarding how the week's content could be applied to their personal and professional lives, which was a positive experience. Writing about considering others, putting yourself in their shoes, and thinking about why someone may react in a certain way are valuable practices that have immediate relevance to the workplace. Kara Taczak and Liane Robertson (2017) note, "As reflective writing practitioners, students learn to develop the repertoire of integrated knowledge useful for future writing situations (whether that situation is for another college course, everyday writing practices, or a current or future job)" (p. 214). Additionally, reflective assignments are valuable if they "allow learners to bring in all parts of self: motivations, emotions, goals, previous knowledge and experiences, and world views, to integrate them, creating a space where they can communicate their growing competence" (Galeucia et al., 2023, p. 7). However, in some required classes for my online program, I was assigned such overly prescriptive writing assignments that I sometimes failed to understand what was expected of me. In these cases, I frequently found myself frustrated with "writing just to write" rather than having authentic assignments that clearly outlined their purpose and benefit. Thus, for the adult learner, authentic writing assignments and assessments are crucial to learning because these assignments allow students to reflect on and replicate writing styles that occur outside of the academic context (Wargo, 2020). This kind of writing is more likely to occur within experiential education opportunities, such as internships where students can be asked to write critically about their own performance and ways to improve.

Student Barriers to Accessing Writing-Based Experiential Education Opportunities

While we see that adult learners can particularly benefit from opportunities to develop writing skills through experiential education, they face barriers to getting those opportunities. In an email interview, an adult learner who completed an internship through her degree program at my university said that because students invest so much money and time pursuing a specific career path, they would greatly benefit from learning essential skills directly in that industry via internships. She argues that students who are equipped with such skills will be more successful, especially when transitioning out of college (personal communication, October 31, 2023). The National Association of Colleges and Employers (2023) describes internships as

> a form of experiential learning that integrates knowledge and theory learned in the classroom with practical application and skills development in a

professional workplace setting (across in-person, remote, or hybrid modalities). Internships provide students [with] the opportunity to gain valuable applied experience, develop social capital, explore career fields, and make connections in professional fields. In addition, internships serve as a significant recruiting mechanism for employers, providing them with the opportunity to guide and evaluate potential candidates. (para. 1)

Thus, internships help students get experience that supports their future success. However, students in my online program had to find their own internship opportunities and then figure out how to incorporate them into their degree plan.

This lack of guidance can be particularly burdensome to adult learners because their time is limited and strained due to numerous obligations outside of the classroom, including working and caring for dependents, sometimes as a single parent (Choy, 2002; Woldeab et al., 2023). The process of searching and applying for internship opportunities may be prohibitive for some adult learners due to these other responsibilities and demands, such as working long hours and then transitioning directly to caring for children. In addition, students may receive little to no guidance on where to look for specific kinds of internships but are nonetheless expected to inquire at companies where they would like to be considered for acceptance. Despite the clear benefits of such experiences for students, employers are sometimes reluctant to extend internship opportunities, which creates another barrier for many applicants. When I spoke with the director of the program for which I was interning, he confided that he would like to have more interns but was skeptical of opening that door to the university since he had heard many horror stories about terrible interns (D. Mediate, personal communication, September 18, 2023). I was selected for my internship due to my previous interactions with the director, but students shouldn't have to rely solely on existing connections to gain access to these kinds of opportunities.

In addition to structural factors that create barriers, individuals may have misunderstandings about what opportunities are available to them. Many adult learners are unable to take part in experiential education opportunities that would benefit them because they didn't know they could ask—they believed that these opportunities were not for them since traditional students tend to receive the majority of resources from colleges and universities (Chen, 2017). In an interview for an IRB-approved study of adult learner experiences with experiential learning, a nontraditional student said that he always thought internships and experiential education opportunities were meant for traditional students, not adult learners: "We were not thought of as the core audience for the current opportunities and the times they are available. If I saw I was considered in the creation of those opportunities I would feel like I could consider taking it on" (personal communication, March 12, 2024).

While students need to accept responsibility for steering the direction of their own education, they also need to be made aware of what is even possible. After all, how can one be self-motivated to take part in opportunities that one doesn't know exist? Another adult learner said that they tried to look up possible opportunities on the university's website, but you'd have to think of every possible way to search since the website organization is poor and makes it extremely hard to find things. The student also stated, "You're on your own, so much is word of mouth. They may not want to publish all opportunities if they're trying to be selective, but that creates further inequity" (personal communication, March 12, 2024). Adult learners in online courses are especially at a disadvantage when it comes to the communication and offering of these experiences: they often miss communications that are physically posted around campus, designed to catch the eye of students as they go from class to class (McDaniel, 2017). Clearly communicating the availability of experiential learning opportunities to all students from the start of their college education helps provide equitable access to these resources. Once students are made aware of what opportunities are available and who can pursue them, then they can take the initiative to determine how they might participate. Students should also be encouraged to speak to faculty to see if there are flexible options, since considerable responsibilities and obligations already sit on the shoulders of adult learners (Chen, 2017). Faculty can then ensure higher levels of participation from adult learners by taking the time and effort to work with these students to create flexibility (McDaniel, 2017; Remenick, 2019).

Another barrier to accessing experiential education opportunities that adult learners face is the difficulty of building relationships with faculty. Due to their unique circumstances, not all adult students have the opportunity to make these valuable connections. Because of the relationships I formed with multiple professors, they singled me out for experiential education opportunities. These professors believed that I excelled in writing and knew my background and work experience, so I received attention and opportunities specifically related to this expertise. These experiences were deeply impactful for me as a writer. However, handpicking students for these learning opportunities creates a clear inequity because these opportunities are only being offered to a select few who perform well because they are not struggling to balance commitments and/or have the time to build strong relationships with faculty. Some adult learners cannot allocate as much time to their studies due to extensive demands from their work and home life (Choy, 2002), which may negatively affect their classroom performance—they do not perform to their full potential because of competing demands on their time. These students are not less deserving of these learning opportunities but may appear less committed (Campbell, 2016), and thus they are less likely to be selected for internships or offered a chance to do an independent study. Adult learners would be greatly served by having experiential education opportunities that are designed to help them reach their goals, scheduled at times when they can participate, and clearly communicated so there is no confusion as to who can join.

Faculty Experience in Teaching WAC

If these writing skills are so vital to career advancement and success, then how can WAC faculty help adult learners find experiential education opportunities to gain these skills? If faculty take the time to develop experiential education activities and practices that reflect the diversity of students' experiences, then adult learners can relate their personal knowledge to the classroom (Remenick, 2019). For many adult learners, faculty play a key role in making college a deeper, more successful learning environment, as in my experience. Experiential education experiences are engaging and effective for adult students as they tend to be immersive, requiring students to have close interaction and collaboration with faculty (Roberts, 2015). It is at the intersection of these relationships with faculty and experiential education that adult learners derive a great deal of value from their education.

Developing special relationships with faculty often provides adult learners with additional support and can help them feel more successful. Adult learners who don't have the opportunity to build such relationships are often frustrated and may feel marginalized (Kasworm, 2010). Furthermore, adult students bring a wide range of literacy histories and workplace literacy practices with them when they return to higher education and pursue their degrees (Michaud, 2013), and faculty often miss the chance to tap into these valuable professional experiences. Michaud (2013) explains that "for those who work with adult students pursuing bachelor's degrees, it may be important to get a sense of the relative value and investment such students feel towards workplace literacy practices" (p. 91). Peter Felten and Leo M. Lambert (2020) explain how decades of higher-education research have found that "student-faculty relationships are a primary factor in learning, belonging, and persistence. . . . Faculty are central to relationship-rich education" (p. 2). Faculty are vital in helping students integrate classroom learning with their experiences outside of the classroom (p. 14).

If faculty take the time to get to know adult students and develop activities and practices that reflect students' diverse experiences and skills, then it can allow adult learners to relate their personal knowledge and experiences to the classroom (Remenick, 2019). High-impact practices, such as active learning and collaborative learning—both of which can take place in experiential education—are as important for adult learners as they are for traditional learners (McDaniel, 2017). Research has shown that when faculty help students practice and complete assignments as though they were in a professional role rather than only having writing assignments that are embedded in coursework, students more effectively develop valuable communication skills that are applicable to future careers (Paretti, 2008). These situated learning practices can be a form of experiential learning and can take place during internships, independent studies, research projects, and more.

Faculty cannot remove all situational barriers faced by adult learners, but they can assist in mitigating dispositional barriers (e.g., fear of failure, low self-efficacy, etc.) and provide learning opportunities that support the learning environment (Howell et al., 2023). Professors should understand the power their words and actions hold for their students, and they should endeavor to build their students' potential and provide opportunities for adult learners to gain necessary expertise in various aspects of writing and communication. As Mason and Atkin (2021) assert, "[e]motions surrounding writing affect academic identity and self-efficacy both positively and negatively[,] and these can be equally empowering or paralysing where 'fear and anxiety can cripple early writing endeavours'" (p. 17). One way to assuage these fears is through building faculty relationships during experiential education activities. Marie C. Paretti (2008) found that students made the greatest progress when engaged in meaningful participation and interaction in the desired areas of learning. A requirement for effective situated learning is that faculty create assignments that not only function as a vehicle for a grade but also encourage mediated social interaction and design creativity, leading to a deeper understanding of the work and how it translates to the real world.

However, constraints faced by faculty can limit student access to the types of relationships and educational opportunities that are most valuable. An associate professor in the department of writing studies at my university, Heather Smith, transparently shared how she sees structural inequities affecting even her ability to choose which students to involve in experiential learning opportunities, like an independent study. She explained, "Since I'm working under resource constraints, I try to approach who I work with cautiously. If a student has developed a relationship with me and I know they are able to work independently, I'm more inclined to grant a request for independent study" (personal communication, November 13, 2023). During the IRB-approved study previously mentioned, I was able to learn that Armand Gunderson (pseudonym), also a professor in the department of writing studies, likewise believes that experiential education opportunities are important and that when students can take part, they are so much better for it. Professor Armand explained that if he is looking to research a subject that a student is also interested in or working on, he will consider asking them to collaborate to publish work together. He says this kind of collaboration has been a positive experience for both him and the students involved, allowing the students to get some publications under their belt before they even graduate. Faculty like Heather and Armand are drawn to collaborating with student researchers, which means they look for opportunities to write and conduct research with a student that not only supports learning but also earns them another publication. Heather has already published two pieces with students and currently has one out for review that was collaboratively written with a team of students from a course she taught. "I am [all] for a mix of benefits to the students that they may not otherwise have available as well as benefits for my own work," she said. Faculty should consider how they may also benefit from writing collaborations and see if this gives them more chances or freedom to extend experiential education opportunities to more adult students.

Armand believes that courses in technical communication tend to attract adult students who may have already tried out an academic major or career change and are coming back to college after an extended break. Being aware of the strengths adult learners bring to the classroom primes Armand to build in opportunities for students to write in ways that build on their experiences outside the classroom. Additionally, he understands that traditional students probably don't have a wealth of work experience or life experience, so it is not always on their radar to pursue some sort of experiential education, like an internship, working closely with faculty, etc.; in contrast, some nontraditional students step back on campus already looking for such valuable opportunities. This approach to education leads the adult learner to think about how they can make a connection between what they're doing to make money and what they're studying in the classroom. In over thirty years of teaching adult learners in a college setting, Armand has observed the value of experiential education for this population, as well as barriers faced by faculty: "[E]ven though I may think, hey, this is a good idea, this is a good student to work with. The workload is crushing. There's no way I would say yes to experiential learning right now. I don't want to say yes to something and then the student disappears for a month at a time, and I'm just trying to finish this darn thing up and get it off the books. Now it's a hassle."

Structural university barriers are also an issue for many faculty like Armand. He explained that to become tenured and promoted to associate professor, faculty must produce a lot of scholarship and peer-reviewed work. Armand says that while the university does value these experiential education experiences, he does not see those values represented or rewarded in promotion or tenure meetings. No matter how many students he's worked with, what the university cares about is how many peer-reviewed publications he's produced or how much outside grant money he's brought in. If he is working with students and not producing scholarship, then it's going to affect his chances of promotion. As a university faculty member and administrator, Emily Henderson (pseudonym) agrees with Armand: "[W]hat we say we value and how we allocate our resources are not in alignment." Emily believes that the university needs to make a concerted effort to help faculty understand the current population of students and their needs. She says that having a clear understanding of who students are and what their needs are can help create an infrastructure with support built in, and faculty need acknowledgement by the university that experiential education is a rewardable way to exert energy. Additionally, she says there are important questions to ask: How do we reach these adult students who would specifically benefit from experiential education? Which departments are teaching writing that isn't programmatic? Where is writing taught, and where and how is it included in the curriculum? The university concentrates on traditional student experiences, but it needs to look at nontraditional students and design experiences for these students, too. University culture should value engagement with students over prestige (Felten and Lambert, 2020, p. 62). Faculty can only do so much, and the institution needs to build structures that support their efforts.

How WAC Programs Can Respond

Individual faculty can only do so much, but programs can tackle structural barriers through WAC approaches. A challenge shared by WAC faculty is addressing "the need to build a foundation upon which consultants and disciplinary faculty members can work together, honoring both their own and the other's disciplinary traditions." There is a universal need to build a way for WAC faculty and consultants to have their expertise valued and used by faculty across the curriculum (Vrchota, 2015). Furthermore, partnerships between campus programs are needed to create experiential education opportunities for adult students to gain expertise in writing and communication. These partnerships can provide writing support for faculty across campus, allowing them to share ideas and discuss what is and is not working in the classroom. Additionally, developing and offering credit-based career development courses/programs helps create more opportunities for adult learners to obtain the skills and expertise they need to achieve their career goals (Albertson et al., 2013).

Despite the barriers faced by faculty and administrators, there are numerous programs across the country that are successfully implementing experiential education and raising the retention rates of adult learners. University programs can enhance what they're already doing to incorporate writing in a valuable way for adult learners by learning from these examples. If the university retains more adult learners by ensuring that its offerings meet the needs of these students, then the institution earns more money. Programs must demonstrate to prospective adult learners that their time spent at college will result in better career opportunities, or there will continue to be those who dismiss college education as a waste of money (Albertson et al., 2013, p. 2).

For instance, Michelle Navarre Cleary (2011) describes how DePaul University's School for New Learning (SNL) has been saving the university money by working on perfecting their Writing Workshop, which serves students from across the curriculum:

> Students use these assessments to develop and implement a plan to build upon their strengths, address their most pressing challenges, and find resources for their ongoing writing development. As a result, rather than having set assignments, students work on writing tasks that are important to them. Thus, by encouraging students to write about what engages them and giving them the tools they need, Writing Workshop builds on the research of Carroll, Sternglass, Herrington and Curtis, and Beaufort and exemplifies SNL's commitment to personalized, lifelong learning. Because it is individualized and focused on developing writers rather than pieces of writing, Writing Workshop works for students with a broad range of learning styles, prior knowledge, goals, and needs. (p. 43–44)

Cleary explains that even though DePaul's Writing Workshop students tend to be weaker writers than those in a writing-intensive program, the retention rate for these students is higher than national averages. The Writing Workshop also found a unique way to balance its small class size, capped at ten students every quarter, with financial and teaching challenges. The group started by asking, "[H]ow can a tuition-dependent university afford to run classes with ten or fewer students and still pay instructors enough to make it worth their while to teach these classes?" (p. 46). The university saves money even running small classes when more students are successful, even if only one student is enrolled. How is this possible? The university found that if that one student dropped out in their first year, the university would lose an estimated three thousand dollars. In order to raise the retention rate of students and save money, the university offered the flexibility necessary to support the increasingly diverse population of students and worked to help them develop as writers. The Writing Workshop also provides a teacher's tool kit to new faculty, who are observed during their first quarter and provided with feedback and assistance. DePaul has found that the Writing Workshop improved support for struggling writers, who are now being retained at higher rates, and is also attracting other students from across the curriculum who seek assistance with improving their writing skills. "If universities wish to retain and graduate the growing majority of 'nontraditional' students, then we need more such experiments," Cleary concludes (p. 47).

Just as DePaul's Writing Workshop raised retention rates by implementing a program that helped struggling students improve their writing skills, Louisiana State University's holistic Communication across the Curriculum program created an initiative called the Distinguished Communicator (DC) Medal program to improve communication education through mentoring, in-depth coursework, and leadership training (Galeucia et al., 2023). This program helps students develop their ability to communicate who they are, what they are capable of, and how their classroom experiences are relevant to their career goals. Galeucia et al. explain that "the process DC candidates use to construct their ePortfolio is a student learning experience, to help students reflect, frame, and integrate their disciplinary learning with intention" (p. 5). The portfolio work also provides students with opportunities for learning valuable skills, such as metacognition and audience analysis, that are related to their goals. This program believes that the lessons and structures it has outlined "can help other institutions reflect on the role of a highly customized showcase or signature ePortfolio and correlated mentoring model amid concerns about institution-wide assessment versus programmatic assessment, the utility of developing rubrics that focus on higher order thinking and communication concerns, and faculty/staff bandwidth" (p. 5). The program's criteria allows each student to showcase their skills and knowledge by using multimodal forms of real-world communication (p. 6). "We've also worked to create greater transparency about the reasoning behind the prompts and guidelines, which gives us the opportunity to connect with students on a more effective level than simply providing hoops to jump through and the promise of a reward at the end," program leaders stated (p. 24). The adults in this program are finding value in this approach, whereby they develop communication skills to demonstrate their professional skill sets. The program's leaders hope to inspire other colleagues to be more comfortable using a process like this as a springboard to explore other concerns:

> For us, this reflective experience has cemented that much of what we did because we felt it streamlined work also led to streamlined, deep, and meaningful learning experiences for students that transcended a single project or degree. One might suggest, in fact, that by modeling backward design in portfolio development we were able to identify prompts and rubrics that nudged us closer to higher-order concerns for our students. (p. 25)

Programs designed specifically for adult learners are an excellent place to start when looking into what kinds of experiential education writing are successful in helping this population. For example, the Interdisciplinary Professional Studies (IPS) program at Boise State University was designed to help adult learners utilize the credits they've already earned from previous colleges (Boise State University, 2024). The IPS program recognized the need for more experiential education opportunities for its adult learners. To address this issue, the program is implementing a new course in the fall of 2024 called Work Integrated Learning. This course is designed to connect students' professional experiences with classroom readings and assignments on workplace topics in order to promote writing transfer (Felten and Lambert, 2020, p. 90). This experience allows nontraditional, working students to turn their workplace into a laboratory of experimentation and observation, and it empowers students to apply theory to the workplace situations that they encounter each day. By writing reflections about how they might implement the things they learn each week, students are encouraged to grow their career through active experimentation. This model asks participants meaningful questions to help them make immediate connections between classroom learning and the workplace.

A great example of a writing-specific course that incorporates experiential learning is Consulting with Writers, a three-credit course at Boise State University. Students in this course engage with evidence-based instructional practices, including, but not limited to, the following:

- Writing Center pedagogy and tutoring theory
- Language acquisition theory
- Foundational rhetorical theory
- Genre theory and writing in the disciplines
- Cognitive learning theories
- Inclusivity and diversity studies
- Rhetorical grammar

Students also complete professional development workshops throughout the year, giving them opportunities to participate in experiential education. Some students in the course are also chosen as writing consultants for Boise State's Writing Center. This one-credit internship takes students' learning to the next level, helping them make immediate connections between classroom learning and the workplace. Writing consultants are chosen from all majors across campus, allowing for a variety of educational backgrounds and identities and for breadth of knowledge. The peer-to-peer consultations not only help the writers seeking feedback but also allow the consultants to practice with fellow students the strategies they learned in the classroom. Research shows that this kind of one-on-one interaction with peers and faculty positively influences the level of student learning, retention and graduation rates, and students' development of critical thinking and communication skills (Felten and Lambert, 2020, p. 5).

The above examples show how change can take place at a departmental level. For example, if a large number of adult students are enrolled in a program, then faculty in that department should collaborate on curricula, being intentional in thinking deeply about the needs and strengths that returning adult students have. Faculty across the curriculum should be encouraged to "purposefully creat[e] opportunities for eliciting students' lifewide writing knowledge and experiences" (Holmes et al.,

2022). Drawing on lifewide writing knowledge, faculty are encouraged to assign meaningful writing assignments related to a diverse range of genres, purposes, and audiences; this way, students have the opportunity to compose academic writing as rhetorically complex as the forms of communication in their other spheres of experience. Holmes et al. believe that being transparent about writing complexities and challenges helps students understand how they learn and can reduce systemic inequities (p. 55). Other efforts, though smaller, can have a significant impact; for example, McDaniel (2017) suggests that faculty hold office hours outside of the typical nine-to-five schedule in order to make time for adult learners outside of the classroom. Evening office hours, including virtual options, can help adult learners connect with faculty since they are often working or picking up children from school during typical office hours.

By breaking down the barriers to experiential education opportunities for the adult learner population, WAC programs can retain more learners and raise graduation rates. Administrators and faculty can target issues of communication, accessibility, and unproductive assignments to meet the needs of nontraditional students and provide them with an education that prepares them for career advancement. The university must support and reward faculty and value student experience over prestige.

Conclusion

To make WAC more equitable, WAC directors and faculty should think critically about their practices and respond to the needs of nontraditional students. To alleviate the financial constraints of universities and the workloads of faculty members, creative "experiments" and open, ongoing discussions should take place that focus on relevant topics and the current needs of the growing adult learner population. Adult learners need to be informed of the opportunities that are open to them and, considering their work and family obligations, whether there is flexibility that makes these experiential education opportunities possible. This communication helps encourage adult learners to take responsibility for their education and enables them to find appropriate experiential education opportunities that best align with their personal and professional goals. Faculty cannot be held responsible for resolving each situational barrier that adult learners face, but they should understand the role they can play in mitigating dispositional barriers and creating writing assignments that help learners make connections between classroom learning and the workplace. There are numerous examples of successful experiential education programs at universities across the country, and administrators can support faculty by encouraging and supporting the implementation of such programs and practices. If adult learners are shown how experiential education opportunities during their college education can lead to better economic outcomes, then they are more likely to remain in school and prevent the university from losing money. These better retention rates help alleviate costs related to improving access to these opportunities for nontraditional students, creating a better situation for all involved. While I would have probably remained a student and graduated due to my own motivation and to meet my family's needs, I was far more motivated to continue my studies and to do my best work because experiential education opportunities bridged the gap between classroom learning and gaining workplace skills. I saw the value of my education and its direct connection to what I wanted to do after graduation, and my education is now more powerful because it has prepared me for the work I want to do.

References

Albertson, R., Austin, D., Bishop, K., Brinkley, T., Buchanan, C., Collins, J., Curran, S., Daw, M., DuPont, J., Foskett, M., Howard, C., Keiser, P., Leadem, S., Leavitt, N., Lambert, L., O'Connell, M., Powers, P., Presnell, M., & Selverian, M. (2013, May). *A Roadmap for transforming the college-to-career experience: A crowdsourced paper* [Paper presentation]. Rethinking Success, Winston-Salem, NC, United States.

Association for Experiential Education. (2024). *What is experiential education?* https://www.aee.org/what-is-experiential-education

Bellare, Y., Smith, A. R., Cochran, K., & Garcia-Lopez, S. (2023). Motivations and barriers for adult learner achievement: Recommendations for institutions of higher education. *Adult Learning, 34*(1), 30–39. https://doi.org/10.1177/10451595211059574

Boise State University. (2024, April 11). *Interdisciplinary professional studies.* https://www.boisestate.edu/online/interdisciplinary-professional-studies/

Bowers, A., & Bergman, M. (2016). Affordability and the return on investment of college completion: Unique challenges and opportunities for adult learners. *The Journal of Continuing Higher Education, 64*(3), 144–151. https://doi.org/10.1080/07377363.2016.1229102

Campbell, S. (2016, February 9). *Differences in adult learning and motivation.* Council for Adult and Experiential Learning. https://www.cael.org/resouces/pathways-blog/differences-in-adult-learning-and-motivation

Chen, J. C. (2017). Nontraditional adult learners: The Neglected diversity in postsecondary education. *SAGE Open, 7*(1). https://doi.org/10.1177/2158244017697161

Choy, S. (2002, August). *Nontraditional undergraduates.* National Center for Education Statistics. https://nces.ed.gov/pubs/web/97578e.asp

Cleary, M. N. (2011). How Antonio graduated on out of here: Improving the success of adult students with an individualized writing course. *The Journal of Basic Writing, 30*(1), 34–63. https://doi.org/10.37514/jbw-j.2011.30.1.03

Felten, P., & Lambert, L. M. (2020). *Relationship-rich education: How human connections drive success in college.* Johns Hopkins University Press.

Galeucia, A., Bowles, B., Baumgartner, J., & Burdette, R. (2023). Using ePortfolios to help students reframe, reflect, and integrate their learning. *Across the Disciplines, 20*(3–4), 5–30. https://doi.org/10.37514/atd-j.2023.20.3-4.02

Hendrickson, B., & Garcia de Mueller, G. (2016). Inviting students to determine for themselves what it means to write across the disciplines. *The WAC Journal, 27*, 74–93. https://doi.org/10.37514/WAC-J.2016.27.1.05

Holmes, A. J., Yancey, K. B., O'Sullivan, I., Hart, D. A., & Sinha, Y. (2022). Lifewide writing across the curriculum: Valuing students' multiple writing lives beyond the university. *The WAC Journal, 33*, 32–61. https://doi.org/10.37514/WAC-J.2022.33.1.02

Howell, S. L., Johnson, M. C., & Hansen, J. C. (2023). The innovative use of technological tools (the ABCs and Ps) to help adult learners decrease transactional distance and increase learning presence. *Adult Learning, 34*(3), 181–187. https://doi.org/10.1177/10451595221149768

Johnson, S. M. (2017). *Teaching adult undergraduate students.* Vanderbilt University. https://cft.vanderbilt.edu/guides-sub-pages/teaching-adult-undergraduate-students/

Kankiewicz, K. (2018). *Using service-learning in writing courses.* The WAC Clearinghouse. https://wac.colostate.edu/repository/teaching/guides/sl/

Kasworm, C. E. (2010). Adult learners in a research university: Negotiating undergraduate student identity. *Adult Education Quarterly, 60*(2), 143-160. https://doi.org/10.1177/0741713609336110

Klein-Collins, R. (2011). Strategies for becoming adult-learning focused institutions. *Peer Review, 13*(1), 4–7. libproxy.boisestate.edu/login?url=https://search.ebscohost.com/login.aspx?direct=true&db=aph&AN=60071930&site=ehost-live

Leggins, S. (2021). The "new" nontraditional students: A look at today's adult learners and what colleges can do to meet their unique needs. *Journal of College Admission,* (251), 34–39. libproxy.boisestate.edu/login?url=https://search.ebscohost.com/login.aspx?direct=true&db=aph&AN=152118025&site=ehost-live

Lodewyck, R. F. (2021). *What is adult learner.* IGI Global. https://www.igi-global.com/dictionary/postsecondary-program-design-for-adult-learners/711

Marinara, M. (1997). When working class students "do" the academy: How we negotiate with alternative literacies. *Journal of Basic Writing, 16*(2), 3–16. https://doi.org/10.37514/jbw-j.1997.16.2.02

Mason, S., & Atkin, C. (2021). Capturing the struggle: Adult learners and academic writing. *Journal of Further and Higher Education, 45*(8), 1048–1060. https://doi.org/10.1080/0309877X.2020.1851663

Mcdaniel, R. (2017). *Teaching adult undergraduate students.* Vanderbilt University. https://cft.vanderbilt.edu/guides-sub-pages/teaching-adult-undergraduate-students/

McKenzie, M. (2013). Rescuing education: The rise of experiential learning. *Independent School, 72*(3), 24–28. libproxy.boisestate.edu/login?url=https://search.ebscohost.com/login.aspx?direct=true&db=aph&AN=85748138&site=ehost-live

Michaud, M. J. (2013). Literacy in the lives of adult students pursuing bachelor's degrees. *Open Words: Access and English Studies, 7*(1), 72–95. https://doi.org/10.37514/opw-j.2013.7.1.06

National Association of Colleges and Employers. (2023, June). *Internship meaning and definition: A NACE guide.* https://www.naceweb.org/internships

Oliveri, M. E., Slomp, D. H., Elliot, N., Rupp, A. A., Mislevy, R. J., Vezzu, M., Tackitt, A., Nastal, J., Phelps, J., & Osborn, M. (2021). Introduction: Meeting the challenges of workplace English communication in the 21st century. *The Journal of Writing Analytics, 5*(1), 1–33. https://doi.org/10.37514/jwa-j.2021.5.1.01

Paretti, M. C. (2008). Teaching communication in capstone design: The role of the instructor in situated learning. *Journal of Engineering Education, 97*(4), 491–503. https://doi.org/10.1002/j.2168-9830.2008.tb00995.x

Remenick, L. (2019). Services and support for nontraditional students in higher education: A historical literature review. *Journal of Adult and Continuing Education, 25*(1), 113–130. https://doi.org/10.1177/1477971419842880

Roberts, J. W. (2015). *Experiential education in the college context: What it is, how it works, and why it matters.* Routledge. https://doi.org/10.4324/9781315774992

Schriver, K. (2012). What we know about expertise in professional communication. In V. W. Berninger (Ed.), *Past, present, and future contributions of cognitive writing research to cognitive psychology* (pp. 275–312). Psychology Press.

Solomon, G. (2021, December 10). *Why mastering writing skills can help future-proof your career.* Forbes. https://www.forbes.com/sites/gretasolomon/2018/08/09/why-mastering-writing-skills-can-help-future-proof-your-career/?sh=f8ba03d58317

Taczak, K., & Robertson, L. (2017). Metacognition and the reflective writing practitioner: An integrated knowledge approach. In P. Portanova, J. M. Rifenburg, & D. Roen (Eds.), *Contemporary perspectives on cognition and writing* (pp. 211–229). The WAC Clearinghouse. https://doi.org/10.37514/PER-B.2017.0032.2.11

Urquhart, N. (2022, January 6). *What are the foundation stones of good writing?* AIM & Associés. https://aim-associes.com/learning/what-are-the-foundation-stones-of-good-writing-neil/

Vrchota, D. A. (2015). Cross-Curricular consulting: How WAC experts can practice adult learning theory to build relationships with disciplinary faculty. *The WAC Journal, 26*, 56–75. https://doi.org/10.37514/wac-j.2015.26.1.04

Wargo, K. (2020). A conceptual framework for authentic writing assignments: Academic and everyday meet. *Journal of Adolescent & Adult Literacy, 63*(5), 539–547. https://doi-org.libproxy.boisestate.edu/10.1002/jaal.1022

Woldeab, D., Punti, G., & Bohannon, R. (2023). The lived experiences of adult learners in an individualized program: Empowerment, responsibility, tensions, and anxiety. *Journal of Adult and Continuing Education, 29*(2), 524–543. https://doi.org/10.1177/14779714221149601

Resumers in and beyond a Writing-Intensive Preparatory Course: Challenges, Assets, and Opportunities

KENDON KURZER, NATASHA J. LEE, AMY MACIAS-STOWE, MARY HER, AND NIEVA MANALO

This paper features the experiences of three resuming students in and beyond a writing-intensive (WI) preparatory course at a large public university. The resumers (who are paper coauthors to elevate the voices of resuming students) identified key course themes as being particularly valuable as they transition into higher education after extended time away and prepare for their required WI courses: discipline-specific genre conventions, source integration and citation norms, audience awareness, collaboration via course discussions and group projects, and reviews of general academic composition conventions. Key areas that could strengthen the course for future resumers and highlight their role as classroom assets include emphasizing the value of their lived experiences in course discussions and formal assignments, regularly soliciting information about students' anxiety levels to provide increased support, and better tailoring content to student needs (such as linguistic features).

Introduction

In college writing classes, returning/resuming/adult students (various terms have been used; we use the term *resumers* since several authors of this paper self-identify with that label) often stand out among traditionally aged students. This distinction may be felt most acutely by the resumers themselves (Colvin, 2013), but their classmates and instructors contribute by projecting reductive stereotypes onto them. This demographic of resuming students actually encompasses great diversity in age, family status, motivation for continuing school, occupation, prior academic experience, and more (Grabowski et al., 2016; Lin, 2016). Every resumer has personal challenges and goals, but each may encounter a common barrier in the writing classroom: the transition (back) to academic writing (Frankenfield, 2018; Gillam, 1991; Peters et al., 2017). Resuming students may be separated from prior classroom writing by years spent writing in specific professional contexts, writing for personal means, or barely writing at all (Cleary, 2012; Gillam, 1991; Peters et al., 2017). An instructor and curriculum should acknowledge and account for this distance, especially in introductory writing classes, or students may lose confidence in their writing abilities, which can snowball into insecurity over their place in the university (Gillespie, 2001; McLeod, 1995; Warren, 1992).

Transitioning to Academic Writing through Resumers' Personal Experience

A well-established strategy to reintroduce students to academic writing is incorporating their personal experiences into assignments. Common models include low-stakes journaling, free-writing exercises, or discussion posts (Bardine, 1995; Khoo & Kang, 2022; Thompson, 2011; Warren, 1992), but student experiences can also be integrated into more formal—while still flexible—writing assignments. This flexibility includes affording students agency in choosing their own writing prompts and topics, whether personal or disciplinary (Cleary, 2012). Resuming students likely have more varied experiences than traditionally aged students, and these events are central to their more developed core identities (Gillam, 1991). The fact that students find writing assignments with which they have a personal connection more engaging (Eodice et al., 2017) is especially pertinent for resuming students who are particularly mindful of their commitment to classes because of their sacrifices made when returning to school (Colvin, 2013; Ruecker, 2021). This mindfulness can lead to an appreciation of, pride in, and ownership of writing as a directly applicable skill for resumers (Gillespie, 2001; Warren, 1992).

In more general writing courses, asking students to explore their own academic subject is also an opportunity to introduce WID values. Stressing WID themes highlights how the specialized knowledge that resuming students have can be purposefully used in academic writing. Students returning to academia from the workplace may have recent writing experience, but they may be aware that they are dealing with different expectations and methods now. While their prior skills can be applicable to academic writing, the transition "requires rhetorical consciousness on the part of the writer," even "the most competent writers" (Peters et al., 2017, p. 4). Of major concern are the specific academic conventions for target audience, tone, and purpose (Gillam, 1991; Gillespie, 2001; Peters et al., 2017). Implementing these conventions as expected in a particular discipline can be irritating and confusing for resumers, especially if they have a defeatist approach toward their own ability (McLeod, 1995; Warren, 1992). Effective strategies to help resumers practice these conventions include frequent low-stakes assignments, explicit definitions of terms, scaffolding major assignments, and models of effective writing (Cleary, 2012).

Anxiety as a Barrier to Successful Academic Transitions

Giving students control over their writing process is important for resuming students with nontraditional academic backgrounds although asking students to blend their life experiences with academic writing expectations can induce anxiety. Michelle Navarre Cleary (2012) shares how a resuming student struggled to write a research essay about ballet, a subject she had extensive experience with, because of her insecurity with school and miscommunication with her instructor. The student had never considered ballet in an academic sense before, and the perceived uncrossable distinction prevented her from realizing that the purpose of this assignment was to introduce her to academic research through a familiar domain. Without structured support, resuming students may find tackling both the unfamiliar nuances of academic writing and personal anxiety difficult. This example also demonstrates the importance of understanding the root cause of writing anxiety, which is crucial to combating it.

While instructors may be aware of resuming students' anxiety about writing, they cannot understand how to address this anxiety without coming to know the student individually. Resumers likely have many sources of writing anxiety, including generalized anxiety and insecurity over being a nontraditional student (Colvin, 2013). Gender-related anxiety plays a role, with female resumers often feeling more insecure and anxious than male counterparts (Lin, 2016; Thompson, 1981). Instructors can evaluate students' anxiety levels directly through surveys or individual conferences (McLeod, 1995; Warren, 1992) and then follow up with personalized feedback. Resuming students may prefer constructive criticism and distrust praise, which they might interpret as patronizing and unhelpful (Hattie & Timperley, 2007). Other studies report that resuming students appreciate encouraging, positive feedback, especially when such feedback is empathetic to their position in the classroom and affirms their progress (Cleary, 2012; McLeod, 1995).

Finding the right balance and strategy for each student is difficult, but it is a key part of student empowerment and improvement. Alice M. Gillam (1991) recommends that at the beginning of the course, students produce "an experience portfolio including a prose vitae describing significant life experiences, a writing history and writer's profile, and writing samples" (p. 12). Such an assignment compels students to reflect on their experience with writing in different domains and provides them with instructor feedback; it also opens discussions about acknowledging different forms of writing, student attitudes, and self-perception of ability, which can reassure resumers that they are not alone in their experience or anxiety. These discussions can also be held via informal digital class forums to help resumers form supportive communities within the classroom (Khoo & Kang, 2022; Ruecker, 2021). Both the resuming student and instructor benefit from acknowledging and addressing anxiety in the classroom instead of letting it prevent constructive feedback and genuine writing improvement.

Instructors' Role in Resumers' Success

Instructors may assume that they are prepared to teach resuming students, but this expectation may be unfounded. Many introductory writing classes are taught by teaching assistants who may be inexperienced writing teachers (Winzenried, 2016) or untrained to work with nontraditional students (McLeod, 1995). Although graduate students are increasingly resuming students themselves and thus may foster empathetic connections with undergraduate resumers (National Center for Education Statistics, 2023), they still benefit from resources such as professional development workshops. Writing across the curriculum (WAC) workshops can be especially useful as they spark conversations between instructors about pedagogical approaches or student trends that administrators may miss (McLeod, 1995).

Instructors have the potential to significantly impact students' success. Many resuming students cite disagreements or perceived disrespect from their instructor as a major detriment to their academic performance, especially in already anxiety-inducing writing classes (Cleary, 2012; Fairchild, 1999). Common issues include strict policies around attendance or late work, which can unfairly exclude resuming students who have more responsibilities outside of school (Ruecker, 2021). While instructor-student interactions primarily occur through academic avenues such as feedback on assignments or lectures, more personal connections frequently form within the classroom. Susan H. McLeod (1995) shares how a spontaneous talk between a resumer and their writing instructor concerning the student's anxiety about standing out led to the instructor sharing her own experience as a resuming student. The instructor continued to give encouraging feedback throughout the course, which ultimately led to the student wanting to take more writing courses. These empathetic moments create valuable spaces for the resumer to feel acknowledged and empowered in college. To better create these spaces, writing program administrators can foster connections between instructors who are themselves resumers by highlighting,—with instructor permission–that fact on instructor profile websites and in advertisement materials.

Resumers' Access to Resources outside the Composition Classroom

While resumers can conceivably access resources outside the composition classroom, these resources may not always be readily available given resumers' extracurricular constraints. For example, writing centers can provide personalized feedback from tutors and introduce WAC values (Salem, 2014; Soven, 2011), but resuming students may be unable to access writing center support as many campus systems are not designed for students with business-hour commitments, like jobs or family responsibilities, or those unfamiliar with navigating campus infrastructures (Colvin, 2013). Resources and communities that accommodate resuming adult students' needs are important, but targeted support systems are still needed at many institutions (Bay, 1999; Ruecker, 2021).

A few scholars have explored resumers' experience in WAC/WID writing classes, such as Diane S. Thompson (2011), who shows how experience with discipline-specific writing instruction can increase confidence, and Kathleen J. Cassity (2005), who discusses how nontraditional students should draw upon their personal experiences in WAC contexts. Similarly, Margaret Jeanine Rauch (2020) calls for proactive instructional approaches that address both discipline-specific techniques and student anxiety. However, the field still experiences a dearth of relevant research; moreover, much of the existent research either does not distinguish resuming students from the even broader category of nontraditional students or centers models of first-time or graduate students (Bardine, 1995; Gillespie, 2001; Peters et al., 2017). While these studies begin to frame critical facets of learning for resumers, we risk strengthening the barriers against resuming undergraduate students by largely ignoring their unique experiences. Using a WAC/WID model, instructors and program administrators can effectively address the needs of resuming students by explicitly acknowledging their transition back to academic writing, their individual life experiences, and the barriers they face.

This project contributes to the literature on resumers in WAC contexts by centering the voices of three resumers as coauthors of this paper: Amy Macias-Stowe, Nieva Manalo, and Mary Her, all of whom took a WAC course taught by Kendon Kurzer designed to prepare them for their junior-level writing-intensive (WI) requirement. While Kurzer has guided the framing of this project, each of the three resumers bring their own voices and perspectives.

Our Context

At California State University, Sacramento (CSUS), students are required to fulfill writing requirements at various stages of their undergraduate experiences: first-year composition, second-year composition, and the Graduation Writing Assessment Requirement (GWAR), which is a California State University system-wide requirement. At CSUS, the GWAR includes a placement score and a writing-intensive (WI) course that is typically taught by a faculty member in a student's major department. (Most majors require that their students take certain WI courses, while some do not require specific courses; students in these majors may take any WI course available to them.)

Prior to enrolling in their WI course, students obtain a GWAR placement score either via a portfolio submitted early in their junior year or a WI preparatory class.

The class, titled "English 109W: Preparing to Write in the Disciplines," is a three-unit course designed to prepare students to succeed in their WI courses. As much of the work associated with WAC and student support occurs in the context of writing centers (Salem, 2014) or graduate programs (Soven, 2011), our course is somewhat unique: it is a formal, credit-bearing undergraduate course positioned to support students, like the resumers noted in this project, who come from a wide range of backgrounds.

Our Resumers

When teaching this course during the fall of 2023, Kurzer was happy to discover that the course featured several resumers, three of whom expressed a willingness to participate in this project documenting their experiences with the WI preparatory class and into the first part of their WI course. This section introduces the resumers who contributed to this project. As their backgrounds are essential to informing their experiences, quite a few details are provided.

Amy Macias-Stowe is a fifty-two-year-old Mexican American new grandmother who grew up in a bilingual household and who routinely code-switches between English and Spanish. Spanish continues to be a central part of her life today although Macias-Stowe considers English to be her primary language. Macias-Stowe retired from the beauty industry after twenty-five years as a licensed cosmetologist and now works for the university as a service coordinator.

A communications major/Spanish minor, Macias-Stowe enrolled in junior college out of high school and dropped out after two years to enroll in cosmetology school. Macias-Stowe then returned to junior college in 2008, taking one or two classes per semester toward her associate's transfer degree due to family and work demands. After changing her major three times, she finished her degree and then took a five-year break before enrolling in a four-year university. Prior to our class together, Macias-Stowe had been at CSUS for four semesters on a part-time basis, taking a few required general education courses and many communications classes. Macias-Stowe questioned whether she should enroll in the WI preparatory courses or attempt for a passing portfolio. Ultimately, she decided to take the course because she had not written extensively in roughly six years and lacked confidence in her writing ability.

Nieva Manalo is a forty-one-year-old Filipina mother who currently works as a full-time nurse while pursuing her bachelor's degree in nursing. She speaks Tagalog and Visayan, another Filipino language. Manalo returned to school the semester she took the WI preparatory course (along with two other core nursing classes) after a 17-year break after finishing her associate's degree in nursing.

Because she had last written an essay seventeen years ago, Manalo opted to take the WI preparatory course. She did not feel confident submitting a written portfolio and wanted to be prepared for her WI course the following semester. She initially felt intimidated and nervous about the WI preparatory course but knew it was "a necessary evil" to prepare her for her future writing demands.

Mary Her is a sociology major in her senior year and an administrative assistant at a private therapy clinic. Like Manalo, Her took the WI preparatory course (in addition to a few core sociology courses) during her first semester back in school after a ten-year hiatus. While the other resumers had associate's degrees from community colleges, Her's previous higher education experience was also at CSUS. Because of this previous experience, and unlike the other students, Her was required to enroll in the WI preparatory class. While she could have challenged this requirement, she decided to simply take the class.

Her felt stressed and worried on the first day of class after seeing how many writing projects Kurzer had scheduled. She knew that she would have to spend more time on this class because writing is "one of [her] weakest subjects." Unfortunately, due to changes in her work schedule, Her ended up needing to drop her WI course at the time of writing this paper; she plans on taking it a subsequent semester.

Our Writing-Intensive Preparatory Class

Using a WAC framework, Kurzer's WI preparatory course primarily featured assignments that required students to identify which WI course they were expected to take—along with the specific writing assignments required in that course—and research discipline- and career-specific genres and writing expectations they likely would encounter in their upper-division major classes and beyond (similar to Winzenried, 2016). The first assignment was a combination of a literary reflection and an analysis of artifacts (syllabi and assignments, if available) of the WI course students would take. In this assignment, Kurzer hoped his students would reflect on their reading and writing journey within the context of upcoming WI expectations as a way to connect their past learning with their future disciplinary literacy development (as discussed in Gillespie, 2001). The second assignment was a genre analysis that required students to find several samples from different genres about a related topic and analyze certain features (audience, purpose, rhetorical tools, support, structure, language, etc.). Students had the option of writing this assignment in partnerships or small groups based on shared disciplines. The collaborative third assignment was a writing guide in which students shared their research on disciplinary conventions and expectations, including a discussion of some common genres. This group project also included a presentation.

When Kurzer started the class (which he taught for the first time the semester of this study despite teaching similar classes at other institutions, and he has extensive experience teaching WAC/WID classes), he anticipated that the students would typically have progressed through the first- and second-year writing requirements and thus would be prepared to dive into disciplinary discourse expectations quickly. However, that proved not to be the case, as many students expressed the desire to discuss basic academic writing expectations first. Accordingly, classroom discussions early in the term featured introductions to some foundational topics like organization, idea development, and source use, prior to getting into content like discipline-specific norms and genre awareness.

Resumers' Positive Experiences in the WI Preparatory Course

All three resumers named in this paper identified various features of the WI preparatory course that they appreciated as they embarked again on their higher education journey. First, the resumers valued the emphasis on discipline-specific genre conventions in course discussions, which explicitly featured discipline-specific audience needs and expectations. As a result, Macias-Stowe felt more prepared to produce writing in communications contexts, and Manalo was better able to understand which forms and genres of writing are likely to be emphasized in and beyond her nursing classes. Class discussions and course assignments gave students space to explore these academic and professional expectations in an authentic manner. The three resumers, who had career experiences to draw on, especially saw the benefit in breaking down the types of writing they would be expected to produce.

Macias-Stowe and Her both appreciated the salient focus on audience awareness within particular disciplines. Her noted that she wanted to ensure that she was adhering to academic norms for discipline-specific audiences, which is a prevalent concern for resumers (Peters et al., 2017). The course also covered style and citation conventions (APA in the case of the three resumers, though MLA and Chicago were also discussed) as well as source integration techniques (for instance, Kurzer emphasized the importance of relying on paraphrases over extensive direct quotes to ease reader comprehension).

Manalo noted that she valued the critical thinking and analysis skills emphasized and presented in the class, while Macias-Stowe appreciated the first assignment (the literacy reflection/WI course introduction assignment) as a refresher in academic writing and found that she had retained more knowledge on the fundamentals of writing than she previously thought and thus felt more confident in her abilities. Manalo similarly felt better prepared for her WI course because of the guidance afforded by that assignment. These sentiments are echoed by other resumers, who often report gaining confidence in their academic abilities after taking writing classes that feature clear, comprehensive instructions and frequent writing practice (Cleary, 2012; Warren, 1992).

Similarly, the resumers all noted and appreciated the collaborative writing afforded by the class (especially as students could write several assignments with partners or in small groups). Macias-Stowe mentioned that collaborating with others allowed her to share some of her knowledge and understanding of academic writing. Her recognized her role in fostering a collaborative atmosphere and accordingly felt that she was an asset in enhancing the students' overall learning experience. These experiences align with the recommendations of Mary K. Morrison (1994), who promoted collaboration as (1) a way to assimilate older students into the classroom community, which is typically dominated by younger students, as an opportunity for them to share their unique personal expertise; (2) a reassurance that other students are not perfect writers either; and (3) a more engaging and valuable approach for adults than traditional lecturing.

The resumers also reported that they felt like they were explicitly treated as assets in this WI preparatory course, a value strongly valued by Morrison (1994). For example, Her noted that she actively participated in course discussions by sharing her lived experiences beyond higher education. Manalo similarly commented that because she possessed a mindset that, in her own words, was "more mature and purposeful" (common characteristics of resumers mentioned in Bay, 1999), she was more open-minded than some of her younger peers in class and could serve as a mentor to help guide them, especially regarding what might be impactful in terms of content and expressing thoughts in writing. These and similar dialogues can help resumers reconcile their coexisting identities of being experienced working adults and inexperienced students, resulting in positive self-reflection and academic production (Gillespie, 2001).

Beyond the class, Macias-Stowe is invested in the project represented by this article as she hopes that it will assist other students in understanding the challenges that come with returning to writing in academia at a "later age" (her words). She hopes to reflect the idea that if she can be a successful academic writer "at her age," then anyone can. This goal is shared by many older female resumers who experience structural challenges and a subsequent determination to succeed upon returning to the university (Fairchild, 2019). Kurzer would like to note that Macias-Stowe has always been quite invested and self-motivated in her learning and thus should recognize her own role in contributing to her success.

Resumers' Experiences in Their Writing-Intensive Courses

While Her needed to withdraw from her WI course due to her work schedule shifting last minute—highlighting a common issue for resuming students (Colvin,

2013; Grabowski et al., 2016)—Macias-Stowe and Manalo both enrolled in a WI-requirement-fulfilling course the semester after taking our preparatory course; at the time of writing this paper, they had been enrolled in the class for roughly four weeks, although the first week was impacted by a faculty strike. Both Macias-Stowe and Manalo shared that they felt much more prepared to succeed in their WI course because of their efforts and instruction in our preparatory course.

Partway through the semester of her WI course, Manalo reported that she felt more confident in her ability to break down the prompts of the WI course and organize her responses. She feels increasingly intentional and reflective about her approach to writing, and thus she is now a strategic writer who plans meaningfully as she writes. Manalo commented specifically on her confidence regarding her preparation for writing her first essay for her nursing WI because of what she learned from our preparatory course, stating that it "helped [her] immensely." Macias-Stowe also feels more confident and noted in particular that she has "reached another level of academic learning" and feels prepared to succeed. In particular, she feels that the preparatory course helped her better analyze meaningfully and develop appropriate content, rather than being distracted by other concerns like formatting or organizing the paper as she appreciated the review of the fundamentals of academic organization expectations we covered.

Macias-Stowe also commented that the preparatory course "perfectly covered the fundamentals of academic writing" as it stressed skills that are essential in her WI course, like synthesizing materials and producing papers supported by course readings. Macias-Stowe noted that her WI course builds on the foundations laid by the preparatory course by challenging students to analyze course readings in a more nuanced, complete manner. She was grateful for the practice afforded by assignments like the genre research project from our course that required analysis. Such practice can be very effective when explicitly linked to discipline-specific analysis, which includes both reading and writing in a certain style (Winzenried, 2016).

In hindsight, Manalo appreciated the preparatory course's focus on audience awareness that has enabled her to think critically about who would be reading her work and why (echoed in Schneider, 1988). She now tailors her content and approach to be more effective in her WI course. Macias-Stowe similarly appreciated the explicit guidance on APA formatting and identifying wordiness markers, like excessive passive voice, which she identified as one of her continuing biggest challenges in crafting tight, effective prose in her academic papers.

Collectively, Macias-Stowe and Manalo's initial experiences indicate that the WI preparatory course adequately prepares resuming students to succeed in their WI course, which is taught in their home departments by disciplinary faculty who are not explicitly trained to teach writing. While many students test out of the WI preparatory course by submitting a passing portfolio, and though (as Macias-Stowe noted) taking an extra course may feel unnecessary, moving forward with confidence into the challenge of upper-division writing may be worth the effort and time required to take an additional class, especially for resumers (Rauch, 2020).

Suggestions for Strengthening the WI Preparatory Course, Specifically for Resumers

The three resumers identified the WI preparatory course as an environment that, while conducive to their learning and enabling them to succeed in their WI courses, still did not fully embrace their roles as returning students. Although Kurzer's class included multiple low-stakes assignments and scaffolded major projects—an approach that has been shown to effectively support resuming students (Cleary, 2012)—more targeted support for these particular students' needs would have been welcome. One suggestion is to take more time at the beginning of a term to solicit thoughts from students regarding what they hope to learn from the class; while Kurzer uses a general survey to ask students about their perceptions of their mastery of academic reading and writing, a more effective survey could get into specifics—such as organization, source use, idea development, and language support—and then the instructor and students could craft the schedule of topics to be covered in the class together (similar to a suggestion from Cleary [2012], who asked students to describe their prior learning experience and their traits as a writer.) Giving students opportunities to frame the course and its focus would be one way of better ensuring that resumers' more diverse needs are adequately addressed.

While the resumers felt like they were assets to the environment of the WI preparatory course, Kurzer in hindsight noted that several of the assignments could be more deliberately leveraged to highlight the contributions of the real-world experiences of the resumers. For example, the first assignment, a literacy narrative that asks students to reflect on their previous writing experiences and then connect to their future writing expectations for their specific WI course, could be reframed to include writing on the job (as highlighted in Gillam, 1991, and Peters et al., 2017) rather than assuming that students have just written for academic purposes prior to taking our class. That inclusion would emphasize and validate the experiences of our resumers. Similarly, in later assignments in which students research writing expectations in their target careers, Kurzer could again emphasize that some students can speak authentically to those expectations of writing in various careers. Manalo, for example, as a practicing nurse, could share her experiences (beyond the spur-of-the-moment in-class discussions in which she brought up those experiences).

Additionally, while the resumers recognized the value of collaboration in writing via peer reviews and the extra support afforded by writing papers with a partner, they noted that they occasionally felt that they shouldered more than their fair share of the work. They also recognized that such collaboration resulted in challenges regarding aligning schedules and deciding who would cover which topics. Some resumers may be uninterested in working with younger classmates, which can lead to further social isolation and age-related insecurity (Ruecker, 2021). Still, research indicates that collaborative activities can be valuable, especially for female resumers, who may be more comfortable with the supportive, reciprocal dynamics of peer-review work, while also familiarizing students with audience awareness (Schneider, 1988).

The resumers also shared that they experienced the anxiety that research shows is particularly common to returning female students (Colvin, 2013; Fairchild, 2019). Macias-Stowe felt anxious when presenting her research findings on writing expectations in communications contexts. Manalo felt overwhelmed and intimidated by all the prompts and topics covered in the preparatory course, especially as she was also juggling a full-time job and family responsibilities (a common stressor for resuming students, as seen in Bay, 1999). She was sometimes unsure of how to formulate ideas and responses. Accordingly, Kurzer plans to be more deliberate about soliciting information on students' anxiety levels and to pay particular attention to resuming students. While he frequently holds individual student conferences (per McLeod, 1995), more routine surveys (Warren, 1992) could be used to track anxiety levels and help him better refine his teaching to be more supportive.

Furthermore, the resumers felt that they would have benefited from more support with regard to language and grammar. Her explicitly advocated for more explicit discussion of linguistic and sentence-level features. While the preparatory course covered punctuation and briefly discussed key grammatical themes like sentence structure and concision—which Macias-Stowe mentioned that she appreciated—Her felt that she struggled to apply these concepts in her writing. More grammatical lessons and exercises, especially regarding how to apply these concepts in students' own writing, would have helped. One possibility, at least for WI preparatory classes that are sheltered for multilingual students (which this course was not, although sheltered courses are offered at this institutions), would be to include some activities using Dynamic Written Corrective Feedback (DWCF). This is a particular method of coding linguistic errors in short pieces of student work, which are then edited and recoded with accompanying reflective components (see Evans et al., 2010, and Kurzer, 2023, for more information).

Conclusion

Overall, the structure at CSUS of providing a WI preparatory course that satisfies the Graduation Writing Assessment Requirement (GWAR) in addition to a portfolio option works well for many students, especially resumers who benefit from the additional support. The assignments of the course—which included reflection pieces, literacy experiences, and several genre analyses—align well with the needs of resumers as they work toward succeeding in their WI courses.

The elements of the WI preparatory course that Macias-Stowe, Manalo, and Her found most valuable include the following:

- Explicit instruction on, and practice researching and presenting, discipline-specific genre conventions
- Instruction on discipline-specific source integration norms and citation styles
- Instruction on audience awareness in discipline-specific contexts and how audience determines disciplinary norms for communication (also found in Gillam, 1991, and Peters et al., 2013)
- Collaboration via course discussions, peer review, and partner/group-produced papers and presentations (although collaboration could place undue responsibility on resumers to carry their peers at the same time) (Morrison, 1994)
- The opportunity to review and refine understanding of general academic composition conventions like organization, idea development, and clear and concise writing

These themes most prepared the resumers for their specific WI courses and thus should continue to be included and emphasized in preparatory courses like this one, even if many of the students do not need as much explicit review (as may be the case if they have proceeded through composition instruction on campus as typically expected).

On the other hand, some possible avenues for strengthening the WI preparatory course, especially for resumers, include the following:

- More explicit emphasis on the values resumers' experiences bring to the classroom in course discussions and on major assignment prompts (Cassity, 2005; Colvin, 2013; Morrison, 199)
- More systematic and/or regular solicitation of information about students' anxiety levels to better gauge and react to issues in a timely manner (McLeod, 1995; Warren, 1992)
- Better tailoring of course content to student needs (e.g., increased time spent reviewing academic composition norms, increased attention to linguistic forms, etc.) (Cleary, 2012; Gillam, 1991)

- More explicit guidance on group/peer expectations regarding collaborative assignments to ensure that resumers are not being asked inadvertently to perform the bulk of the work (Schneider, 1988)

Naturally, these are only a few possibilities for creating a classroom environment that better supports resumers in a WI preparatory course like that investigated here. But these possibilities should be explored to better ensure student success.

A course design that recognizes the unique challenges resumers face and assets they bring to our classroom would create increased opportunities for all students—and teachers—to learn from each other. By emphasizing resumers' voices and experiences in and beyond our classrooms—as attempted in this article—our writing programs can become more inclusive and supportive for all students, especially those facing the challenges of returning to university learning.

References

Bardine, B. A. (1995). Using writing journals in the adult literacy classroom: Teacher to teacher. Ohio Literacy Resource Center, Kent State University.

Bay, L. (1999). Twists, turns, and returns: Returning adult students. *Teaching English in the Two-Year College, 26*(3), 305.

Cassity, K. J. (2005). *Bringing lived cultures and experience to the WAC classroom: A qualitative study of selected nontraditional community college students writing across the curriculum* (Publication No. 3171037) [Doctoral dissertation, University of Hawai'i]. ProQuest Dissertations Publishing.

Cleary, M. N. (2012). Anxiety and the newly returned adult student. *Teaching English in the Two-Year College, 39*(4), 364–376.

Colvin, B. B. (2013). Where is Merlin when I need him? The barriers to higher education are still in place: Recent re-entry experience. *New Horizons in Adult Education and Human Resource Development, 25*(2), 19–32. https://doi.org/10.1002/nha.20014

Eodice, M., Geller, A. E., & Lerner, N. (2017). What meaningful writing means for students. *The Peer Review, 19*(1), 21–29.

Evans, N. W., Hartshorn, K. J., McCollum, R., & Wolfersberger, M. (2010). Contextualizing corrective feedback in L2 writing pedagogy. *Language Teaching Research, 14*(4), 445–463. https://doi.org/10.1177/1362168810375367

Fairchild, S. D. (2019). Breaking the silence, reimagining justice: Voices of returning women students in community college. *Feminist Teacher, 28*(1), 1–16. https://www.jstor.org/stable/10.5406/femteacher.28.1.0001

Frankenfield, J. (2018). *Treating the writing trauma: Managing anxiety and promoting transfer among adult learners with workplace writing pedagogies* (Publication No. 13422277) [Master's thesis, State University of New York]. ProQuest Dissertations Publishing.

Gillam, A. M. (1991). Returning students' ways of writing: Implications for first-year college composition. *Journal of Teaching Writing, 10*(1), 1–20.

Gillespie, M. (2001). Research in writing: Implications for adult literacy education. In J. Comings, B. Garner, & C. Smith (Eds.), *The annual review of adult learning and literacy: Volume 2* (pp. 63–110). Jossey-Bass.

Grabowski, C., Rush, M., Ragen, K., Fayard, V., & Watkins-Lewis, K. (2016). Today's non-traditional student: Challenges to academic success and degree completion. *Inquiries Journal/Student Pulse, 8*(3), 1–2. http://www.inquiriesjournal.com/a?id=1377

Hattie, J., & Timperley, H. (2007). The power of feedback. *Review of Educational Research, 77*(1), 81–112. https://journals.sagepub.com/doi/10.3102/003465430298487

Khoo, E., & Kang, S. (2022). Proactive learner empowerment: Towards a transformative academic integrity approach for English language learners. *International Journal for Educational Integrity, 18*(1), 1–24. https://doi.org/10.1007/s40979-022-00111-2

Kurzer, K. (2023). Dynamic written corrective feedback: A scoping review. *Feedback: Research in Second Language, 1*, 93–108. https://doi.org/10.32038/frsl.2023.01.06

Lin, X. (2016). Barriers and challenges of female adult students enrolled in higher education: A literature review. *Higher Education Studies, 6*(2), 119–126. http://dx.doi.org/10.5539/hes.v6n2p119

McLeod, S. H. (1995). Pygmalion or golem? Teacher affect and efficacy. *College Composition and Communication, 46*(3), 369–386. https://www.jstor.org/stable/358711

Morrison, M. K. (1994). "The old lady in the student lounge": Integrating the adult female student into the college classroom. In M. Reynolds (Ed.), *Two-Year college English: Essays for a new century* (pp. 26–37). The National Council of Teachers of English.

National Center for Education Statistics. (2023). *Characteristics of postsecondary students*. https://nces.ed.gov/programs/coe/indicator/csb/postsecondary-students

Peters, D. L., Goldstein, M. H., & Lax, J. (2017, June). *From industry to graduate school: How returners (re)learn how to write* [Paper presentation]. 2017 American Society for Engineering Education (ASEE) Annual Conference & Exposition, Columbus, OH, United States.

Rauch, M. J. (2020). *Perceptions of academic writing from first generation non-traditional students* (Publication No. 1850) [Doctoral dissertation, University of Mississippi]. Electronic Theses and Dissertations.

Ruecker, T. (2021). Retention and persistence in writing programs: A survey of students repeating first-year writing. *Composition Forum, 46*.

Salem, L. (2014). Opportunity and transformation: How writing centers are positioned in the political landscape of higher education in the United States. *The Writing Center Journal, 34*(1), 15–43. https://www.jstor.org/stable/43444146

Schneider, H. M. (1988). The peer approach to adult learning. *Equity & Excellence in Education, 24*(3), 63–66. https://doi.org/10.1080/1066568880240318

Soven, M. (2011). Curriculum-Based peer tutors and WAC. In S. H. McLeod, E. Miraglia, M. Soven, & C. Thaiss (Eds.), *WAC for the new millennium: Strategies for continuing writing-across-the-curriculum programs* (pp. 200–232). The WAC Clearinghouse.

Thompson, D. S. (2011). *No more a stranger: The development of academic literacy in adult English language learners in community college* (Publication No. 12066) [Doctoral dissertation, Pennsylvania State University]. Electronic Theses and Dissertations for Graduate School.

Thompson, M. O. (1981, October). *The returning student: Writing anxiety and general anxiety* [Paper presentation]. Northeast Regional Conference on English in the Two-Year College 1981, Baltimore, MD, United States.

Warren, S. (1992, March). *Grandmothers in the classroom: How college English teachers can help those non-traditional students* [Paper presentation]. Annual Meeting of the College English Association 1992, Pittsburgh, PA, United States.

Winzenried, M. A. (2016). Brokering disciplinary writing: TAs and the teaching of writing across the disciplines. *Across the Disciplines, 13*(3). https://doi.org/10.37514/ATD-J.2016.13.3.11

In Our Own Words: Adult Learners on Writing in College

COLLIE FULFORD, STEFANIE FRIGO, YASEEN ABDUL-MALIK, THOMAS KELLY, ADRIENNE LONG, AND STUART PARRISH

In this article, we—two faculty and four alumni—reflect on the writing and learning experiences of adult undergraduates at North Carolina Central University (NCCU, or "Central"), a historically Black public university where 18 percent of students are over the age of twenty-four (National Center for Educational Statistics, 2021a). That age marker for adulthood is somewhat arbitrary, as many NCCU students under the age of twenty-five have significant adult responsibilities, such as parenting and/or being financially self-supporting. These responsibilities are among the broader criteria that qualify students as independent, irrespective of age, per the Free Application for Federal Aid (Cruse et al., 2018). Nonnegotiable commitments to work and family can set independent students apart from their classmates because of limitations on the time available for writing, research, and other academic and social activity (Wladis et al., 2022). However, as the alumni authors of this article disclose, more than just time constraints can separate this group from their peers. Each adult learner brings a unique constellation of experiential assets and perspectives to their studies. The heterogeneity of the adult undergraduate population at NCCU makes generalizing about these students' intersecting identities, educational histories, and experiences with writing a tall order. Nevertheless, their differences provide standpoints from which it is possible to rethink higher education—including the teaching and learning of writing across the curriculum.

When Collie, one of the faculty authors of this article, saw the call for this special section of *The WAC Journal*, she was already immersed in research about the writing lives of adult students. Her review of literature in writing studies had revealed a paucity of work representing this population of writers, despite their strength in numbers. Students over the age of twenty-four account for about a quarter of US undergraduates (National Center for Educational Statistics, 2021b). Yet aside from research about veteran students and writing

(Blaauw-Hara, 2021; Doe & Langstraat, 2014; Hart and Thompson, 2020) and scholarship about community college writers that mentions adult students (see Hassel & Phillips, 2022; Sullivan, 2020; Tinberg and Nadeau, 2010), scholarship about postsecondary writers rarely includes adult students and even more rarely centers this marginalized population. As Michael J. Michaud (2013) pointed out more than a decade ago, this absence is especially pronounced in writing research about students seeking bachelor's degrees. Collie was therefore glad that *The WAC Journal*'s call for articles invited scholars to focus on this population: it offered a critical opportunity to foreground adult students' vantage points on writing across the curriculum. Her frequent research collaborator, Stefanie Frigo, and four NCCU alumni with whom Steff and Collie have worked extensively as research partners all expressed interest in coauthoring for this issue.

The four authors who write the student perspectives in this article are Adrienne Long, Thomas Kelly, Yaseen Abdul-Malik, and Stuart Parrish. Here they represent their own distinctive standpoints that have been shaped by complex matrices of identity and experience. Their ages at the time of graduation span from late twenties to early sixties. Although two decades apart in age, Adrienne and Yaseen both prioritized degree completion when they returned to college: both attended continuously, full-time, while also working and parenting. They needed to realize the economic benefits of their degrees as soon as possible. In contrast, Stuart and Thomas integrated college into their lives intermittently across multiple decades; each adopted the practice of "dipping in and out" (Barton, 2009, p. 55) that is characteristic of a subset of adult learners who do so to accommodate shifting life priorities and changes to the conditions that make study possible. These four have completed bachelor's degrees in history (Yaseen '19), psychology (Adrienne '21), and interdisciplinary studies (Stuart '21 and Thomas '24). They have written for classes and extracurriculars, for their jobs, for their families, and for themselves. Remarkably, they all took up collegiate activities beyond coursework despite the extent of their other responsibilities. For instance, in recognition of the need for belonging and advocacy, the three oldest alumni authors of this article served as officers of NCCU's Adult Learners Student Organization; Adrienne was its founder and first president. Since advocacy and equitable representation of adult learners are also important in scholarship, the six of us (in different configurations) have conducted participatory research about the adult learner population at NCCU across multiple collaborative projects—including a study of adult students' writing lives—which we describe elsewhere (Frigo & Fulford, 2025; Fulford, 2022; Rosenberg et al., 2024). Because of their involvement in this research, Adrienne, Thomas, Yaseen, and Stuart are well positioned to provide insights about writing across the curriculum from adult learners' perspectives.

We structure this article as a roundtable to suggest a teaching approach that can work equally well in groups of adult learners and in age-integrated spaces. Roundtables, focus groups, and small-group work all prioritize the contributions of the discussants. Small-group discussion and project-based collaborative learning are established teaching approaches that honor the social nature of learning and knowledge production. These methods are familiar to democratically oriented faculty who decenter themselves in favor of what can emerge from and among students. These practices shift the locus of authority from the teacher to the students, thereby flattening classroom hierarchies. We argue that it is important to intentionally employ these kinds of collaborative approaches in age-integrated learning settings to achieve two benefits—one for adult learners, and the other for the overall community of learners. First, decentralized strategies demonstrate to adult learners that faculty respect their existing social, rhetorical, and process knowledge. By using these approaches, we show that we trust them to contribute experiential wisdom. Second, many adult learners are accustomed to taking the lead in collective decision-making about significant matters in their jobs and family lives; thus, in mixed-age groups, they can model efficient problem-solving and generous ways of interacting.

We coauthors know each other well through our work on multiple joint projects. Our roundtable approach used to be a deliberate, constructed practice, but at this point we fall into it without consciously thinking about process. Working literally around Steff's kitchen table (and via many video meetings, emails, and texts), our group collaboratively reviewed the call for articles and decided how to write our response. In an iterative, digressive, messy, and enjoyably social process, we jointly developed a set of questions to try to unpack the experiences of adult undergraduate writers that would speak to *The WAC Journal* readership. Adrienne, Yaseen, Thomas, and Stuart then engaged with these co-constructed guiding questions:

1. What did you bring to academic writing as an adult learner?
2. What happened in your classes, in your interactions with other students and with professors?
3. What challenges and support have you experienced as an adult learner and writer?
4. What relationships do you perceive between your academic writing and where you are now?

Their forthright responses reveal what may not otherwise be evident to faculty who teach writing across the curriculum in mixed-age institutions.

Roundtable

Question 1: Who are you, and what did you bring to academic writing as an adult learner?

Yaseen Abdul-Malik

I'm a thirty-three-year-old, African American Muslim elementary school teacher who hated education for a long time. My family moved overseas in the early 2000s, and I was raised in a world where nationality, gender, and race governed what you could and could not do in the workplace. My ability to speak both English and Arabic pushed me into education to make ends meet. I received my teaching certification from Cambridge University and got my TESOL certification in Dubai and Abu Dhabi. With each new certification, I discovered the advantages of an education—and the systemic barriers that prevented others from having access to that education. Writing was how these systems of power identified and measured what I knew. I knew how to communicate through speech. I could illustrate my competencies in conversation, but these systems that gate-kept power, money, and freedom were built on narrow and rigid understandings. To fulfill my passion, I had to write my way out. Taking technical writing classes in college helped me create narratives of competency that transferred into the business sphere, making me marketable in new ways.

Thomas Kelly

I am a mid-fifties white man. I made several attempts at getting a college degree over the last three decades, but it wasn't until my early fifties that I finally accumulated the right credits to receive my AA degree at Durham Technical Community College and was able to attend North Carolina Central University as a junior and graduating senior. Over the last thirty years, I have made several runs and false starts at getting into a four-year college, and I had an impressive amount of unusable credit hours going into NCCU. Earning a living, having a life, and honestly, being a lazy man all kept me from committing to a four-year school. I was so impressed when I began to understand the lives that Yaseen and Adrienne led. They had far more adult responsibilities than I—a childless spinster—and they were going to school full-time as well! Once I started taking junior- and senior-level classes, I could only manage two courses a semester. I am a dilettante. And a hippy, so by my fifties I could make enough money part-time as a self-employed carpenter to afford college. I received my AA at the age of fifty-two from Durham Technical Community College, and now at fifty-six I am graduating from North Carolina Central University with a BA in Interdisciplinary Studies—the choose-your-own-adventure degree.

I used the opportunity to choose my classes to further my writing interests. I chose primarily psychology and writing courses, and my academic writing became a vehicle for my creative pursuits. Everything I wrote became an chance to shoehorn my personality into my writing, and the professors had to read it! Being read was the realization of a lifelong dream.

My experience at NCCU was profound. My age and experience added empathy and depth to my writing, and the professors teaching my junior and senior classes mentored me in the creation of a written voice that is unique to who I am after all these years. I did my best writing (so far) at NCCU.

Adrienne Long

I am a divorced, fifty-one-year-old African American female whose passion for advocating for adult learners developed while completing my bachelor's degree at NCCU in psychology. Much like Tom, I feel that age paired with empathetic depth as an adult learner afforded me the opportunity to infuse generational wisdom into my writing. A large portion of the writing I did as an undergraduate student had a mature tone and was informed by my "real-life" experiences. Having lived longer than most traditional students in my courses proved an advantage with regard to knowing and understanding the larger context of the subjects I wrote about. I grew to appreciate this about myself over time, and I was more grateful for the experience of being back in school overall despite the challenges. I was happy to be back in school, but jumping into new technology – like learning management systems and discussion boards – was the scariest part for me. I had to learn new tools just to submit a term paper. It was mostly assumed by professors that all the students in their class had recent exposure to something similar.

I quickly realized that if I really had the desire to complete school, now would be the time. Otherwise, I was prepared to quit. Every day that passed, I remember thinking to myself, "Why are you doing this?" Having started the Adult Learner Student Organization, I knew there were others like me that felt the same way. From there, I decided that I needed to do something while in school that could make "the difference" for someone else. I, too, wanted and needed the normalcy that I felt my younger counterparts were enjoying.

I remember meeting Tom Kelly for the first time at an interest reception for the Adult Learner Student Organization that I started at NCCU. Because of the conversation we were having on the challenges we shared as students, I realized that I really wanted to make a difference that would bring more visibility to the challenges and the emotional hurdles we face. The organization became a passion as I used writing as a way to give it a voice of its own. Yes, I was a student, but I was an adult first. Because of that, my writings displayed a serious and persuasive tone to get things established or considered for the students that were members.

Stuart Parrish

I'm a sixty-five-year-old white male, married. I took classes part-time at Duke, UNC, Louisburg, Wake Tech, and Durham Tech over many years. I had some professional certificates, but it wasn't until I took technical writing at NCCU that I really settled down with firm goals and commitment. Now I see myself as hopelessly creative, and maybe not too well suited for academics, but I definitely benefited from doing a lot of the hardest intellectual work of my life under tough circumstances— with an aging mother, selling the family home, and becoming the family's main support member for her. Naturally, younger students will have a different sense of voice and identity than I do. When I'm off base, I have muscle memory. I know to ask myself how to simplify what I'm trying to do into discrete steps or ask for help.

At NCCU, I really enjoyed learning where research and writing could lead me, like presenting at my first conference with Jamal Whitted and Collie.[1] Jamal told me about Steff's interdisciplinary studies intro class. Students write a portfolio for it, and he was so enthusiastic about how all the assignments blew his mind, expanding his self-awareness, making him really think through liminal areas of his plans and dreams. That writing really bore fruit for me, too, inspiring growth and clarity. That class was also where I met Tom, and it was a revelation for us to be two guys over (harumph) years of age in the same class, finding things in common. I think that was the first time that happened to me at NCCU. It was a very welcome initiation into what it could be, what I maybe hoped college would be.

Question 2: What happened in your classes between adult learners and more traditional learners? Between you and your professors? Between you and other adult learners? Why do these interactions matter?

Adrienne

Most prerequisite undergraduate classes have a large mixture of every kind of student. But by the time you reach classes in your major, the dynamic begins to shift. Adult students desiring to do well will oftentimes sit closer to the front of the class so they will not be distracted. Over time, everyone in the class with similar goals will gravitate to one another, commiserating over the coursework needing to be completed. A mutual bond eventually forms from common threads when, over time, everyone realizes they have the same goal—completion!

---

1. Stuart, Jamal, and Collie presented their research about adult students at a diversity, equity, and inclusion conference. As insider researchers, Jamal and Stuart framed the talk by discussing their own higher education histories as adults in relation to findings from surveys and interviews (see Parrish et al., 2019).

Providing input based on prior knowledge of subjects was often well received by my professors and at times heavily relied upon for deeper explanations of the subject matter. Too often, though, it felt like because I looked "old" enough, I was automatically considered a subject-matter expert. I once had a psychology professor ask me my opinion about a point in time that I am not old enough to have lived through. At that moment, I felt singled out from the rest of my classmates.

Adults can tend to feel less inferior as older students, and more assimilated into student life, when professors foster cross-generational learning relationships. Doing this helps students on both sides of the age spectrum share with their classmates their backgrounds, personal influences, ideologies, and opinions, which may not be shared when there is a lack of collaborative activities. In my general psychology course, the professor once hosted a panel to discuss gender roles and relationships with audience participation during a Q&A. It was well received because it allowed students to gain wisdom while providing real-world views that matter or relate to all ages.

Stu

I didn't play unofficial TA, but I tried in little ways to let classmates know when I could be helpful. Then I let them make the move if they wanted some assistance. I benefited from that, too. In service to others, I felt more included. I'm older, more mature. This self-awareness might make the teachers' jobs easier. Knowing more about myself, my limitations and strengths, as well as what I mention above—all of this comes with intrinsic motivation. I know learning is a never-ending process of refinement, so that understanding was built into my expectations; I could talk about that with my professors, and we could plan together how I could improve.

Peer review is great, too—exchanging papers, reading each other's work, and offering a critique. Also, working in groups outside of class, like video group assignments. The dynamic changes when we share a common goal and when we don't feel as graded or scrutinized. You can hear people's register or tone change when the prof leaves and they are speaking in a room (or Zoom) full of peers only. I noticed that when we abruptly transitioned to online classes due to COVID safety concerns. We were given group assignments and we had to meet up online, and this was an environment where the professor wouldn't be present. Traditional students expressed feeling homesick, lonely, and isolated. I don't know how, but it seems that allowing us to interact like that created a broader bandwidth of communication and connection.

Yaseen

There are two types of people who go to college: people who want to, and people who need to. I needed to go to college. I circumnavigated this truth for many years but eventually realized that to get to the next level, college was a necessity. Unlike traditional students, I did not go to college to find myself. I had neither the luxury nor the time to be undecided. I needed a stamp on a paper. I went in with no illusions. While sitting in dorm rooms and talking to my peers, though, something changed. I listened to traditional students talk in class about new discoveries. Some of them spoke with a romance that made me feel like there was more to this place than just grades. They talked of home as a faraway place, a place that they could retreat to, not a place that they were responsible for. I wanted what they had. I felt that without it, I wasn't getting what I was paying for.

To create the illusion that I was one of them, I took the bus to campus early in the morning. I texted a friend to let me into his dorm so I could walk with my friends to the café for breakfast. I would call out of work to go to kickbacks and parties. I didn't correct people who thought I was younger than I really was. There was a hope I had—I wanted to travel backwards. To no longer be the kind of person who needed to go to college, but to be a person who wanted to go. A person who had time to volunteer for free, who formed lasting relationships with roommates and line brothers. I had missed that, but maybe I could get it back.

I couldn't. A nontraditional student must balance the world outside campus with the world on campus. The more energy I put into the world on campus, the more the real world left me behind. Rent was due, electricity was due, my family needed me. Taking the bus home, I realized that college was an island, and I was not an islander. It was then that I realized that being a nontraditional student was not an academic designation. It was an illustration of a class system.

Thomas

Though I was in the class of students who wanted to be at Central, and I did not have the outside pressure of family and finances that both Yaseen and Adrienne had, my age felt isolating. Also, I was a white dude in a primarily nonwhite space. I was, however, prepared for that; it is the reason I chose Central. What I wasn't prepared for, however, was how much younger most of the students were at a four-year university than they had been in community college. It was lonely and strange. Being at Central, I deeply desired some human connection. Someone who could understand what I was going through. The professors presented an odd dilemma. The social construct of professor and student and the relative power dynamic was vexing. I am not sure what they felt, but I felt (and probably misread) that social structure strongly—perhaps a leftover from when I had been a young man in the harsher power dynamics of the 1980s. With my professors, I had this needy desire to have some social connection, adult to adult. But I was stymied by my reading of what was socially acceptable, given my perception of the power differential. It wasn't until I found Adrienne and her Adult Learners group (and, later, Stu—it was so nice to not be the only old guy in class) that I felt some of the collegiate solidarity and camaraderie that younger students seem to enjoy.

Question 3: What challenges and support have you experienced as an adult learner, especially regarding writing?

Yaseen

Can you write a paper if you have work in the morning? Can you write a paper if you have to get to a parent-teacher conference right after class? If your car breaks down and you have to take the bus to and from campus, can you write a paper then? Can you write a paper if you're taking care of your sick relative? What time will you make for research? What time do you have left for drafting? These are the questions that nontraditional writers in higher education deal with all the time. I went to college when I was twenty-two years old, and I brought my responsibilities with me. In my first year, my wife had our first son. With no money for sitters and no housing provided for us by the school, I had to work and keep my grades up. We brought our son to class. I wrote papers on the bus, during breaks, and in other classes. I did this because I understood what I was working towards and what a college education meant for me and my family. Even traditional students arrive at college in different circumstances, so the word *nontraditional* infers a normality that does not exist. I wonder what ideas I would have discovered if I had been in a system that was able to consider my outside life.

I did not take a writing class in high school. My high school was a collection of books I received once a month through an online program. MLA style was a foreign concept, and I had to reteach myself. Relearning these formats for writing in addition to the writing itself was difficult for me during my collegiate studies. The formulaic archetypes that college papers share create a foundation of uniformity, but this also has the unintentional effect of making part of the writing process tedious.

Stu

I really identify with the feelings and scenarios Yaseen describes because I had my share of similar experiences—but different. I have this self-knowledge, which was a big plus, but looking back, I also felt that I had to really lean in and trust and depend on all the help I could get. I tried to use office hours, Zoom, phone calls, email, anything I could because I felt strongly that I needed a lot of feedback to stay on track. Maybe Yaseen, Tom, and Adrienne had more self-assurance than I did . . . perhaps a more robust internal writing infrastructure? You can't paint all adult learners with the same brush. I needed structure and help with formatting and time management. I look back and feel like I was just beginning to make inroads towards good habits and writing practices. For instance, during my internship, a graduate-student mentor came up with a method that I still use today when I can. She used a big conference-room screen during our editing sessions. Getting the text off of laptops and onto a big scale somehow afforded me more distance from my own words and made editing feel more objective. As she effortlessly demonstrated how technology could help with a difficult task, I overcame my lack of confidence and adopted this new skill.

Adrienne

The challenges that I faced were related to the rules of writing versus me writing how I speak normally. I hadn't been in school for a long time, and my writing style had been shaped by what I knew from working in corporate and not having someone critique my writing. My class assignments were more structured and often had rules I had to follow.

It was during the summer between my junior and senior years that I wasn't sure if I would be able to graduate. I decided to write a letter to the chancellor of my school to advocate for myself, but also to advocate for the rights of all the other adult students in my position. I was eager to illustrate in my email the severe disappointment his pending decision would cause if he were to not let me continue school. This style of writing works well in corporate, but could I convey my thoughts and feelings effectively to persuade the chancellor? I wanted the email to express how I emotionally felt but also be inclusive of how my peers felt as well. I knew this was my one shot. The email was designed to capture his attention and to express the overall distress that I carried in my heart about students being mandated to come back to campus during the COVID-19 pandemic. I submitted the email to him at 10:59 p.m., sure that I was right in my position to ask for something more than the constant "no" that I'd been given up to this point. But I was told that I couldn't be a part of the distance learning program, that it was full! I only had five classes standing between me and graduation and moving on with the rest of my life. I sent a second email, sure that I would hear nothing back. But by 2:00 p.m. of the following day, I received a call from my school's student advocate informing me that I was registered for the next semester and would graduate. That email, along with my style of writing from an adult's perspective regarding the sacrifices I made and the challenges I faced to get to that point, is what I want to believe captured the heart of my reader and inspired him to make the one phone call that would change everything!

Thomas

While the classes and especially the newer technologies were challenging, I had expected the final two years of college at a real four-year university to be difficult. Other than my experience being a highly visible outlier in my classes, my time at Central was smooth, and the students and professors were lovely. I had great writing and English instructors throughout my early mishmash of college years, and I hope that community college gets the respect it deserves in academia. By the time I came to Central, I understood that I should seek out and destroy all passive sentences. Every writer needs to edit, edit, edit, then come back two weeks later and edit some more. What can be said in three sentences can also be said in two; slash every useless word without mercy. The professors at Central were enthusiastic because I was not just trying to meet the requirements of the assignment but was also working to write something someone might actually want to read.

Question 4: What relationships do you perceive between your academic writing experiences and where you are now?

Stu

I am working on local history and genealogy, music, songwriting, and integrating new technology into my music. Writing and editing has changed how I think about musical possibilities. I think of practice as research and experimentation, and that leads to composition, which I then collate, edit, and practice in new arrangements. I love the quote, "The map is not the territory it represents"; but if the map is correct, then the territory will have similar structures, and therein lies its usefulness. I am used to blurred boundaries, but I often get lost in thought or in the chaos of creation. The structures of writing practices, flipping a set of questions into an outline/rubric, asking myself holistically to dive deep and then surface, simplify, clarify—all of that is invaluable and transferrable to my music practice. By *practice* I mean time spent doing, being free to explore without self-editing, as well as the more crafty work. I learned from my undergraduate studies that there aren't any shortcuts, and even professors have to carve out time and make writing a priority because nothing writes itself. I met an editor of a journal recently and described where I was at, and he reminded me, "Write two hours every day, and that stuff will begin to sort itself out."

Adrienne

Before participating in research about adult student writers, I never thought much about my writing. I was right in the middle of completing my degree. When asked several questions during the research project about how I developed my writing style, I was forced to reflect on my experiences and growing up as a whole. This research experience then led me to an internship opportunity, which allowed me to explore how different words and styles of writing can bring to life other people's voices. I am more passionate than I was before simply because I know how to use the power of my experience to express what I wanna say.

Yaseen

Speaking is in the moment, writing is forever. It took years for me to understand this truth, and it is one of the things that make me such an avid reader and writer now. I have always had ideas; storytelling is my passion. But it wasn't until I took writing classes in college that I discovered that my voice could resonate through sound and space. It could be kept in a thing—a thing that could be discovered and rediscovered forever. That made learning how to write important. Through these classes, I learned that certain types of writing must be organized in certain ways to create clarity and uniformity. Learning why these things were important, meeting educators that could explain how these pieces came together, was important for a nontraditional student with obligations outside of school.

Thomas

NCCU taught me to write at an advanced level; and while the academic side of writing is a bit dry for my taste, I was still able to insert a bit of who I am into everything I wrote. Every sentence I created helped me learn how to craft a creative voice unique to myself. Whatever writing I do in the future I owe to my experience at Central. It was a significant emotional challenge to be an adult learner in such a youth-centric environment, but that trial became a part of who I am and what I bring to the page.

Conclusion

As Steff listened to these voices come together around her kitchen table, the message was clear. In their diverse reflections on their writing experiences at NCCU, Adrienne, Thomas, Yaseen, and Stuart illustrate the profound impact of age, life responsibilities, and their own unique life trajectories on their writing. Their reflections demonstrate that adulthood brings a richness of perspective and a depth of commitment that have significantly influenced both their approach to learning and their feelings about the value of writing. For Adrienne and Yaseen, returning to formal education was a deliberate choice amidst familial and professional obligations, where writing became a tool to advance, advocate for, and reflect on generational wisdom. Conversely, Thomas and Stuart navigated a longer academic path, integrating their studies with careers and personal growth, and have used writing to explore their passions and evolve creatively.

The classroom interactions between this group of adult learners and their more traditional classmates, as well as their professors, highlight a dynamic exchange of both knowledge and empathy. Adrienne's and Stuart's perspectives underscore the value inherent in cross-generational dialogue in the classroom, enriching the writing and learning experiences of all students. Challenges such as balancing work, family, and academic demands reveal the resilience and determination of these adult learners, who carve out time for writing amid busy lives. They often seek to expand their writing space, to write big and to write expansively, rather than stick to the constraints and requirements of a particular assignment. Although challenging, these outside demands seemed to foster profound personal growth and a deep appreciation for the transformative power of writing.

Looking ahead, it's clear that these academic writing experiences in the classroom have equipped Yaseen, Adrienne, Thomas, and Stuart with perspectives extending far beyond the walls of the university. For Stuart, writing has intertwined with his explorations in local history and music, while Adrienne has found empowerment in advocacy through writing. Yaseen's realization about the permanence of written words speaks to the enduring impact of his educational journey, while Thomas is planning to pursue his MFA. These experiences collectively challenge traditional notions of studenthood and illustrate how age diversity enriches educational communities. This understanding should prompt a reevaluation of the pedagogical practices of writing faculty. These writing narratives uncover the resilience, diversity, and transformative potential of adult undergraduate writers at NCCU. Their stories call for continued recognition of and support for adult learners in higher education, advocating for inclusive writing practices and assignments that honor the varied paths and contributions of all students. As these voices contribute to broader scholarly discourse, they should remind us of the importance of representation and the power of writing to bridge generational divides, inspiring meaningful change in the classroom and beyond.

We hope that the ideas and experiences told here prompt other scholars, teachers, and program leaders to be actively curious about the adult learners in their own institutions and to ask them similar questions—or, better yet, to afford them opportunities to explain what they wish we would ask them. Their stories invite us to enact inclusive writing pedagogies—such as teacher-facilitated, student-led discussion—that honor who they are, why they are in school, and what they have to offer.

References

Barton, D. (2009). Researching adult learners' lives to understand engagement and progression in learning. *Literacy & Numeracy Studies, 17*(1), 51–61. https://doi.org/10.5130/lns.v0i0.1277

Blaauw-Hara, M. (2021). *From military to academy: The writing and learning transitions of student-veterans*. Utah State University Press.

Cruse, L. R., Eckerson, E., & Gault, B. (2018). *Understanding the new college majority: The demographic and financial characteristics of independent students and their postsecondary outcomes*. Institute for Women's Policy Research. https://iwpr.org/wp-content/uploads/2020/10/C462_Understanding-the-New-College-Majority_final.pdf

Doe, S., & Langstraat, L. (Eds.). (2014). *Generation vet: Composition, student veterans, and the post-9/11 university*. Utah State University Press.

Frigo, S., & Fulford, C. (2025). Radical adaptability: Research with adult learners. *Perspectives on Undergraduate Research and Mentoring, 12*(1).

Fulford, C. (2022). Rethinking research in English with nontraditional adult students. *Pedagogy: Critical Approaches to Teaching Literature, Language, Composition, and Culture, 22*(1), 79–98. https://doi.org/10.1215/15314200-9385488

Hart, D. A., & Thompson, R. (2020). *Writing programs, veterans studies, and the post-9/11 university: A field guide*. Conference on College Composition and Communication of the National Council of Teachers of English.

Hassel, H., & Phillips, C. (2022). *Materiality and writing studies: Aligning labor, scholarship, and teaching*. Conference on College Composition and Communication of the National Council of Teachers of English.

Michaud, M. J. (2013). Literacy in the lives of adult students pursuing bachelor's degrees. *Open Words: Access and English Studies, 7*(1), 72–95. https://doi.org/10.37514/OPW-J.2013.7.1.06

National Center for Educational Statistics. (2021a). *North Carolina Central University*. Retrieved June 13, 2020, from https://nces.ed.gov/collegenavigator/?q=North+Carolina+Central+University&s=all

National Center for Educational Statistics. (2021b). *Table 303.50. Total fall enrollment in degree-granting postsecondary institutions, by level of enrollment, control and level of institution, attendance status, and age of student: 2019*. https://nces.ed.gov/programs/digest/d20/tables/dt20_303.50.asp

Parrish, S., Whitted, J., & Fulford, C. (2019, July 19). *On their own terms: Learning from adult learners* [Conference session]. Diversity, Equity, and Inclusion Conference, Durham, NC, United States.

Rosenberg, L., Fulford, C., McGowan, G. P., & Long, A. (2024). Co-interpretation in action. In R. J. Dippre & T. Phillips (Eds.), *Improvisations: Methods and methodologies in lifespan writing research* (pp. 103–119). WAC Clearinghouse/University Press of Colorado. https://doi.org/10.37514/PER-B.2024.2289.2.06

Sullivan, P. (Ed.). (2020). *Sixteen teachers teaching: Two-year college perspectives*. Utah State University Press.

Tinberg, H., & Nadeau, J. (2010). *The community college writer: Exceeding expectations*. Southern Illinois University Press.

Wladis, C., Hachey, A. C., & Conway, K. (2022). Time poverty: A hidden factor connecting online enrollment and college outcomes? *The Journal of Higher Education, 94*(5), 609–637. https://doi.org/10.1080/00221546.2022.2138385

Promoting Belonging among Adult Learners through Sharing and Feedback

GABRIELLE ISABEL KELENYI

This article highlights how intentionally equipping adult learners to engage in productive and kind sharing and feedback intersects with writerly self-efficacy and belonging. Using qualitative data gathered from a community-engaged ethnographic study of a community writing group for adult undergraduate students called Our Writing Group (OWG), I ask, how can sharing and feedback practices help build and strengthen a sense of community within the writing group and avoid damage to writers' confidence and senses of safety and belonging in OWG? This is important because a writerly self-efficacy lens provides a helpful framework for sharing and feedback on writing across the curriculum that honors adult learners' academic and life experiences. Thus, it's essential that these practices be intentionally crafted to augment writerly self-efficacy and that writerly self-efficacy be seriously considered in discussions of sharing and feedback more broadly.

Introduction

In January 2020, in a small back room at the Venture classroom space, I facilitated the first meeting of Our Writing Group (OWG)[1] around a circular table with four other writers. I had been volunteering and working with my community partner, Venture—a credit-bearing, humanities-based, university-sponsored program for low-income adults[2]—for over eighteen months as a grant-writing intern and writing center instructor when I proposed starting a writing group for alumni of the program. After the initial two-semester Venture course ends, opportunities for program graduates to continue writerly development and build solidarity are limited. OWG fills this gap by providing consistent time, space, and support for Venture alumni to write with others without necessarily moving toward a degree.

---

 1. All names used in this article are pseudonyms, including Our Writing Group (OWG). Participants of the writing group chose their own pseudonyms, while I chose the pseudonyms for the group and adjacent partner program.
 2. To apply for admission to the credit-bearing, university-sponsored program, a prospective student must be at least eighteen years old, have a high school diploma or GED/HSED, and demonstrate financial need (income at or near the federal poverty level).

OWG operates adjacently to Venture: it is a community writing group facilitated by and for graduates of Venture, and OWG benefits from some of Venture's infrastructure, such as using its Zoom Business account, its physical space for in-person annual community readings, and its funds to print the group's biannual magazine. While it started in person before the COVID-19 pandemic, since the fall of 2020 OWG has met weekly on Zoom, and members of the group, including me, take turns facilitating meetings on topics of our choice. The ten regular members of the writing group who agreed to participate in my research range in age from 23 to 66. They are primarily low-income adults of color, and they are either currently based in the Midwest or originally from the Midwest. Some members of the writing group have earned terminal degrees since graduating from Venture; others are currently taking courses toward terminal degrees; and many are not currently enrolled in any credit-bearing, postsecondary-education coursework. Group members are teachers, parents, students, working professionals, retirees, storytellers, poets, rappers, novelists, short-story writers, kid lit authors, life-writers, community activists, and much more. Each two-hour meeting of OWG includes a check-in, an introduction to the member-facilitator's chosen topic, time to respond to optional prompts connected to the meeting's theme, and time to share and get feedback. Members of OWG have facilitated on topics ranging from meditation and women's suffrage to self-actualization and implicit bias. OWG creates a space for adult writers with economic barriers to feel capable of writing and supported in their work.

This article highlights how intentionally equipping adult learners to engage in productive and kind sharing and feedback intersects with writerly self-efficacy and belonging. After a review of literature showing how sharing and feedback have been theorized to impact writerly self-efficacy, as well as how Peter Elbow's teacherless feedback model supports the development of writerly self-efficacy in adult undergraduate writers,[3] I discuss researcher field notes about OWG meetings, OWG participant interviews, and anonymous contributions by participants from the 2020–2021 academic year to collaborative field texts gathered for an IRB-approved, community-engaged ethnography of the writing group. Specifically, I ask, how can sharing and

---

3. I use the term *adult undergraduates* throughout this piece to refer to a heterogeneous group of students who have followed alternative pathways to and through higher education. The word "adult," whether attached to "learners," "students," or "undergraduates," makes room for histories, constraints, hopes, pressures, ambitions, responsibilities, pasts, and futures that can be productively included and addressed in educational spaces. The comprehensive modifier *adult* doesn't necessarily preclude students in the eighteen-to-twenty-two or over-twenty-three age ranges, while the term more often used, *nontraditional*, usually refers to students over the age of twenty-five without a college degree (U.S. Department of Education) and highlights a lack that reflects larger problems regarding race(ism) and class(ism) in higher education and the field of writing studies.

feedback practices help build and strengthen a sense of community within the writing group, thereby avoiding damage to writers' confidence and their sense of safety and belonging in OWG? This is important because a writerly self-efficacy lens provides a helpful framework for sharing and giving feedback on writing across the curriculum that honors adult learners' varying academic experiences and their substantial life experience. I demonstrate how the group enacts love as an action (hooks) and operates with a rhetoric of respect (Rousculp) in OWG meetings through its sharing and feedback practices. Consequently, I establish that sharing and feedback practices can help or hinder the growth of adult undergraduate writers, like those in OWG and those in writing courses across disciplines. Thus, it's essential that these practices be intentionally crafted to augment writerly self-efficacy, and that writerly self-efficacy be seriously considered in broader discussions of sharing and feedback.

Literature Review

Writerly self-efficacy is crucial for adult undergraduates because they have been historically disenfranchised from literacy (Schrantz; Brown; Lundberg et al.; Graff; Perry et al.). Intentional sharing and feedback practices can help writers—especially adult undergraduate writers, who have a lifetime of experience that guides the writing they produce and the feedback they give—recognize and push back against inequitable, marginalizing systemic conditions that they've experienced in other academic and/or writing contexts. As writing studies scholars have theorized, sharing and feedback impact writerly self-efficacy, or students' understandings of their own writing abilities (Pajares and Valiante). Basically, a writer's success in achieving the purpose of a given writing task deeply depends on effectively reaching their audience; it therefore follows that sharing and feedback practices can help boost a writer's confidence by proving that their writing is accomplishing what they intend.

Scholarship in writing studies has also indicated that writing groups can be a significant wellspring of writerly self-efficacy due to their democratization of writing ("Question of Time," Mathieu et al.; Westbrook; Highberg et al.). This is because self-efficacy in writers doesn't bloom in a vacuum; it is cultivated by "engage[ment] with other humans" because writing is a cognitive *and* a social practice (Adler-Kassner and Wardle 65). Writing groups provide a particularly useful and regular opportunity for sharing and feedback. When writers listen to or read other writers' work, as typically happens in writing groups, they are exposed to new or different writing processes and perspectives, such as diverse decision-making models and an array of writing strategies and tools, that can enhance their writerly self-efficacy. Learning happens organically in collaborative writing groups, where writers form a community with other like-minded individuals looking for support and motivation (Highberg et al.); thus, writing groups possess "considerable potential for strengthening writing self-efficacy" (Bruning and Kauffman 167).

Generally, sharing and feedback practices intersect with writerly self-efficacy in that they combat the notion that "writing is an individual activity," which can induce anxiety in writers of all levels and abilities (Bruning and Kauffman 167). Through sharing and feedback practices, writing groups offer a less competitive learning environment where members can see "peer models make errors, engage in coping behaviors . . . , and verbalize emotive statements reflecting low confidence and achievement" (Pajares and Valiante 167), which can help other members feel like they are not alone; in addition, writing group members can be encouraged by and learn from other members' experiences with overcoming difficulties and achieving success (Bruning and Kauffman 161). Thus, sharing and feedback practices within writing groups present great opportunities for writers to engage in vicarious experiences that enhance their writerly self-efficacy: they are able to identify writers who are similar to them (Pajares and Valiante 167), and they engage in important reflection on their own writing choices as well as act on their own writing aspirations in ways that are both similar to and different from their peers (Adler-Kassner and Wardle 78).

I assert that the sharing and feedback practices that are most appropriate for adult undergraduates, and that engage them in these reflections and aspirations, are those outlined in Peter Elbow's teacherless writing-class model because they have at their foundation a sense of writerly competence: a belief that *all* pieces of writing have an effect on readers (78). Importantly, teacherless feedback helps position writers as having agency, experienced, and competent. In *Writing without Teachers*, Elbow asserts that writers can make substantial improvements in their writing by sharing their work with fellow writers "in a supportive atmosphere, often with no response other than appreciation." They can "get responses from readers based on the readers' efforts to understand the writing and enjoy it and tell the story of what was happening in their minds as they were reading—rather than trying to judge it and figure out how to make it better" (xix–xx). This is natural for community writing groups like OWG, according to Paula Mathieu and colleagues, who write,

> When we have witnessed community writing groups, the participants will often stress the positive and productive elements of a piece—an image that works, a sentence that captures a local moment. In an academic class, the next move might then be to critique the piece of writing as well—the word choice is a bit redundant, there is no satisfactory conclusion. This secondary move, the critique, will often not occur in community writing groups. Instead, there is a sense that positive comments can serve the same function of moving the writer toward their ultimate goal. (*Circulating Communities* 13)

Clearly, writers' self-efficacy can improve when they are "being understood" and "hearing readers' experience of [their] words and trying to have their experience" because "different readings help the writer see [their] text through more lenses" (Elbow xix–xx). Elbow's reader-based and writer-based feedback models served as the foundation for the feedback practices taken up in OWG in order to enhance participants' writerly self-efficacy specifically and the democratization of writing more generally.

The scholarly literature on writerly self-efficacy, sharing, and feedback may lean into the transfer benefits of writing with others, but the writers in OWG and I are more interested in the community-building potential of intentional sharing and feedback practices. Community writing groups help build relationships around writing, demonstrating how writing is a relational action and product. Sharing and feedback practices are one way to realize the relational potential of writing because they can reveal the "mixings of sometimes conflicting and sometimes conjoining beliefs and purposes" that characterize a community (Harris 20). Thus, the relationships between writers that sharing and feedback can help build are an even bigger boon to writerly confidence because, in our experience, they help us *feel* like writers and help us *feel* like we are a part of something larger than ourselves—like we *belong* to a community of writers that may even extend beyond OWG. Participating in the sharing and feedback procedures of OWG helps us feel seen and understood as writers; sharing our writing and giving and receiving feedback during meetings serves as the site for building relationships between members. This is important because OWG was started for exactly that purpose: to continue to build long-term, trusting relationships among writers after graduation from Venture. OWG members' responses to writing don't always have to be about writing craft or producing actionable and specific feedback; instead, their responses can be about the content of a piece, experiences writers share, or what listeners learn about the writer as a fellow human being. The reader- and writer-based feedback models used in OWG help members develop sustained relationships with one another, and building trust between members can not only lead to more informed feedback but also influence how productively feedback is received.

Sharing and Feedback as Love and Respect

Sharing and feedback routines are one way group members practice love and respect for writing and for one another, helping Our Writing Group promote a sense of belonging. This is especially meaningful in the face of previous writing experiences that made the adult undergraduates in OWG feel *less than* or like an outlier. In fact, one piece of feedback in the two collaborative field texts from the fall of 2020 reads as follows: "[Writing is] a hidden talent, and I'm leery of sharing. Being misunderstood in real life, I can only expect to be misunderstood in my writing. It sometimes seems that people aren't willing to give me criticism about my writing." Before getting to know one another very well, we could not realize the *full* positive potential of sharing and feedback in OWG. Love, as theorized by bell hooks, and a rhetoric of respect, as conceptualized by Tiffany Rousculp, needed to be cultivated first.

Love, according to hooks, is a combination of knowledge, care, commitment, responsibility, and trust (195). While bell hooks writes about the practice of love as a move toward liberation from white supremacy (195), the practice of love in OWG involves sharing one's writing as a move toward liberation from low writerly self-efficacy. Seen through the lens of hooks's five factors of love, sharing in OWG is what moves the group beyond just a group of individual writers and promotes belonging: members demonstrate *care* for writing, for one another, and for themselves; demonstrate their *commitment* to causes and to one another; demonstrate their *knowledge* and expertise; take *responsibility* for the group; and build on their shared experiences from the original humanities-based course, the writing group itself, and a shared commitment to the regular practice of writing in a community to develop *trust* in one another. This practice of love is nicely summed up in two contributions to the October 2020 collaborative field text: one member wrote, "I think the biggest thing is that we trust the integrants of our group and we share similar experiences so I feel understood and relate [to them]"; another remarked, "OWG is special because [it] helps us to feel we are one whole family so we can trust each other." As is apparent from these field text contributions from just a couple months into the semester, OWG members trusted one another to listen and engage authentically with good intentions. The sense of respect, comfort, and belonging that ensued helped the writers in OWG experience major sources of writerly self-efficacy, such as a sense of mastery and vicarious experiences.

For example, sharing and feedback are mechanisms of OWG through which members gain knowledge about themselves and about writing. This is really important for members, as one contributor pointed out in the November 2020 collaborative field text: "[This writing group] is more enriching because we listen and discuss. Others I've been involved in, no one else wanted to share. You can't learn by just listening all the time." By listening and discussing, as mentioned by this OWG member, writers in the group are enacting love as theorized by hooks because they are exchanging knowledge: members express how much they value the knowledge they gain from listening to each other's writing, which in turn contributes to a sense of mastery and writerly self-efficacy. In fact, throughout the fall of 2020, members' feedback to one another was largely about validating folks' experiences and responses to prompts, enabling another source of writerly self-efficacy—vicarious experience, or "observing others' performances and assessing one's capabilities in relationship to what is observed" (Bruning and Kauffman 161). Initially, focused on my role as a writing center instructor, I viewed OWG members' affective reactions to one another as less important than actionable suggestions because they weren't about the writing. Members did not typically ask for more details, talk about a line or image that stood out to them, or mention craft, organization, or engagement. Instead, members generally talked about the content of stories and poems and gave positive (albeit vague) feedback, like "I loved it," "that was really good," and "I can't wait to see where it goes." However, by engaging in community listening, or listening that prioritizes a community's values rather than outside narratives (Rowan and Cavallaro), I recognized how these responses were important to building a community in OWG because they demonstrated *care* (another of hooks's factors of love). OWG members' responses didn't always have to be about the writing process but could be a means of connecting with the writer, thereby strengthening personal, loving relationships within the group and promoting belonging.

Furthermore, the responses to OWG writers (as opposed to their writing) were cultivating a "rhetoric of respect," which Tiffany Rousculp, director of a community writing center, says "requires . . . maintain[ing] a solid faith in a potential partner's own capability and in their agency to determine what they needed or wanted" (27). As in bell hooks's theorization of love, trust is central to a rhetoric of respect (80). For Rousculp, a rhetoric of respect allowed the community writing center she directed in Salt Lake City to "be a place of collaborative experimentation, a place to take risks without evaluation, where people from all different backgrounds could come to work on any kind of writing task" (47). A similar description could be used to describe OWG: it is a space where writing is not evaluated but shared and responded to responsibly. That is, OWG writers take responsibility for the writing they share as well as the feedback they give and receive as part of enacting love for and within the group. This is why viewing OWG's sharing and feedback practices through the lens of hooks's five factors of love makes sense—because writers in the group *love* OWG. As one member wrote in the March 2021 collaborative field text, "I love everything about OWG but I [especially] love when people share their writing because many times [they] inspire me to keep writing." This feeling is also expressed in another contribution to the same collaborative field text: "I love hearing the different voices throughout the writing process, and I have gained many different perspectives about writing in general, and about my own as well." In the April 2021 collaborative field text, another contributor wrote, "The OWG also is the healthiest place to get feedback on writing that I've ever been involved with! There are no haters in the OWG so everything that is said to you about your writing is said with love[,] so instead of deflecting critique you internalize criticism so you can come week after week with hotter material." These participants specifically mention how much they love OWG's sharing and feedback practices, which enhance their writerly self-efficacy: not only do these practices give writers diverse examples of authentic voices and perspectives, topics to write about, and audiences to reach, but they also provide them with a greater understanding of their own writing process. In the words of another contributor, "[OWG] has given me confidence in the writing that I have shared with the group."

To reiterate, OWG members, in listening to others' writing, were able to gain a sense of other group members' performances and capabilities in relation to their own, establishing the group as a source of both affinity and aspiration and thereby contributing to members' writerly self-efficacy. Furthermore, feedback that validates writers' experiences and responses to prompts offers an important mastery experience that can yield writerly self-efficacy for members, as those responses communicate that a piece was successful. Thus, OWG writers' instincts that a piece of writing is or is not successful were bolstered by social interactions facilitated by the group's sharing and feedback practices from (nearly) the beginning of the fall semester. Nonetheless, as the fall progressed, it became clear that the adult writers in OWG were unsure of *how* to give and receive *actionable* feedback on various pieces of writing, many of which were written in the moment during group meetings. In this way, the adult undergraduate writers in OWG were not unlike other college-level writers, in first-year writing courses and beyond, who develop over time the skills necessary for giving and incorporating productive feedback as a result of direct instruction and practice.

In hindsight, I recognize how augmenting writerly self-efficacy and promoting belonging through community-building went hand-in-hand from the beginning in OWG. The writers in the group were teaching me that good feedback stems from love and mutual respect: treating each other with love and respect helped members come to trust one another, providing a foundation for giving informed feedback with the best intentions. This is important given OWG members' experiences sharing their writing in other spaces that have had detrimental effects on their writerly self-efficacy. For example, during our interview, Sol, a Mexican woman in her thirties, shared that

> there was another group that somebody invited me to be part of with people that has already published books, and I thought maybe this group will help me, you know, but it's so intimidating. It's so intimidating and it's only, I mean, yeah, it's only in English and, but, most people is white, and I just have this difficulty, like, trusting, is it real? Or is it, it doesn't feel real. It feels kind of like business.

Sol makes clear that vicarious experience as a source of self-efficacy only works when writers are learning from other writers with whom they can strongly identify or whom they aspire to emulate (Bruning and Kauffman 161). The first writing group Sol tried was not a positive experience because those members came from such different backgrounds, which made it hard for her to connect with and trust them. Alternatively, sharing and feedback in OWG help inspire Sol. In the same part of our interview, she said,

> Well, when I share my writing, I like the feedback. I feel like it makes me a better writer, it makes me to reflect on the things that the people point out. It helps me grow definitely. And, but also listening to other writers, because, for example, there is a couple of people in the group that . . . write with a lot of passion, and they use a vocabulary that is different than the one that I use. But it's beautiful. And so it's just like . . . wow, you know, like inspire me, like, I want to keep writing because I want to get to that level. You know, or I want to keep writing because, yeah, I want to share something the same.

Sol's experience in OWG enhances her writerly self-efficacy by inspiring her to keep writing and helping her to (in her own words) "grow." Claudia, an Italian American woman in her forties, shared a similar sentiment:

> [OWG has] helped me with confidence in my writing, like I said . . . I'm not very good at sharing my writing with people just because, I don't know, a lot of people don't know me on that level, I guess. And so it's weird. But I also thought that a lot of people could relate to the stuff that I wrote in [OWG]. So that's why it inspired me to share.

Importantly, Claudia and Sol's comments demonstrate how their writerly self-efficacy—and that of the other low-income adult undergraduate members of OWG—was uniquely augmented by participation in OWG, especially due to the group's sharing and feedback practices. What's possible in OWG because of affinity within the group had not been possible elsewhere for OWG writers. In addition, listening to each other's writing as well as the responses to other members' writing during that first semester helped members of the group feel understood and understand the impact of their words on an authentic audience, even though much of the feedback they were receiving did not necessarily provide them with next steps.

Upon reflecting on the fall semester of OWG, and through conducting interviews with participants like those cited above, I recognized that OWG members might benefit from peer-review training similar to that which writing center tutors receive and which writing instructors give to students in their classes. In the spirit of writing center approaches and values, such training should "meet [the] writers where they are" in order to enhance the already positive effects of feedback and sharing in OWG (Nichols and Williams 95). I conducted such training during our second meeting in the spring of 2021. I began by explaining that the workshop was meant to "challenge us all to offer more critical and constructive feedback to one another." On the initial presentation slide, I wrote that this means continuing to be supportive, challenging one another to always push our writing to the next level, and operating according to the belief that no piece of writing is ever truly finished—it's just put away for a while. To accomplish these goals, we can respond as readers and as writers to each other's work using our emotions and our opinions about what makes writing "good." Aloud, I added, "We each have our own ideas of what is good."

I continued my presentation to OWG by defining peer review as an opportunity for writers to articulate what they are trying to say in their pieces and a chance for attentive readers to tell writers what they're hearing and what isn't coming across clearly. OWG members added that it's a respectful, noncompetitive, and supportive practice, clearly building on the love and rhetoric of respect built throughout our fall 2020 meetings. We discussed how peer review is a chance for writers to engage with one another's ideas, use feedback to implement revisions, pull the curtain back on individual writing processes and the stages of various pieces, and practice openness, collaboration, and constructive critique. This peer-review training workshop for OWG members was meant to provide them with "the tool of awareness, with which they could navigate the unease of not knowing what to do" (Rousculp 77). I aimed to encourage OWG members to understand that "practice in feeling scared about how [their audience] might react," as well as "learning how they do react," can be "liberating" because writers "discover the world doesn't fall apart" (Elbow 83). Importantly, writers in OWG had the benefit of practicing this awareness in a space built upon a shared formative experience (Venture) as well as love and respect—and in a group to which they already felt they *belonged*.

In other words, the knowledge, care, commitment, responsibility, trust, and respect already established in the group helped us share our reactions in a way that demonstrated that "people are actually listening," as Song, a Black woman in her sixties, reflected during our interview. Furthermore, it helped us see the benefit of feedback and feel comfortable asking for what we needed or were ready for as writers. To that end, I provided OWG members with possible questions they could ask to indicate whether they were looking for feedback on a part of their work or only praise for a draft. For example, I encouraged them to consider asking questions about the main idea listeners understood from their piece, how they can make their piece more effective or persuasive, and/or what readers gravitated to and where they felt less engaged. In terms of giving feedback, I encouraged members to take on a reader's perspective, providing the following basic sentence structure: "when you wrote (THIS), I felt (THAT) because (REASON)." In these ways, I aimed to capitalize on the love and rhetoric of respect writers had been demonstrating in OWG since the previous semester, and I intended to frame providing and receiving actionable feedback as an opportunity to model kindness and appreciation for each other as writers and humans.

OWG members took to heart this framing of giving and receiving feedback, inspired by the loving and respectful patterns that characterized their initial responses to one another's writing throughout the fall semester. At the next meeting, Heaven, a Black woman in her forties, shared a piece of writing she wrote for a credit-bearing introductory composition course she was taking that semester. Her piece was about the creativity of many influential Black women singers. Heaven asked for "any feedback," and Dean, Sol, and Song all responded with positive feedback, sharing how the piece made them feel: Dean said that Heaven read her piece with a "conviction" that commanded his attention and appreciation; Sol shared that Heaven's "good choice of words" made her feel "empowered"; and Song pointed to a specific question Heaven asked in her piece ("What if they weren't able to sing?") that made her feel "so grateful." All three responses were grounded in Heaven's writing and were not just about the topic she wrote about; moreover, Dean, Sol, and Song's feedback were acts of social persuasion that effectively convinced Heaven that her writing was achieving its goal. This likely contributed to the courage it reasonably took for Heaven to then ask for "any bad feedback," which I rephrased as "areas of growth." Song responded to Heaven's request by suggesting adding "some of the messages that were in the songs that the slaves used to sing where they were sending messages." Heaven was grateful for Song's specific and actionable suggestion. Heaven came away with a sense of mastery, feeling that she had reached her audience with her writing, as well as a sense of potential improvement thanks to a viable direction for revision—both of which contributed to an enhanced sense of writerly confidence.

During this same sharing and feedback session, Song specifically asked for a glow (praise) and a grow (area for growth/ improvement) after sharing her piece, though everyone who provided feedback only provided glows. When Sol shared her piece about the connection between hands and the arc of an amorous relationship, she asked for "a lot of feedback" and expressed uncertainty about whether her message was clear. Here, I saw Sol asking for specific feedback: did her message come across clearly to her OWG peers? Heaven responded by reiterating Sol's message back to her, adding, "I loved it. It sounds very romantic. How you just go on and with your feelings, how you want things, want to hold hands and you don't want to be alone when you die, you want to be with your husband till your last breath." In this piece of feedback, it's clear that Sol's message was not only received but also enjoyed by Heaven. I also responded affirmatively, sharing that "the progression [of the relationship] came across to me as a listener for sure." When I gave Sol a suggestion to number the hands to express time passing, Sol pushed for more by asking for an example. After I provided one example, Song added to my suggestion and responded directly to Sol's specific feedback request when she said, "I like the way I could visualize everything . . . it was so romantic to me. And I could just see it happening, holding hands. . . And also . . . I thought about naming the hands: the hand of matrimony, the hand of romance, the hand of caress on her face, or his face, and stuff like that. As opposed to, um, numbering." Sol's eyes and smile widened as Song spoke, and she expressed gratitude and excitement in response to our suggestions. Similar to Heaven, she had learned specific ways in which she could move her piece forward. In all of these examples from the meeting after the feedback training, but especially the examples from Heaven and Sol, we see writers in OWG navigating the uneasy process of taking risks, making mistakes, and making improvements in their writing. These stories also demonstrate their understanding of "literacy as a collective activity of rhetorical problem solving" and their trust in the group's ability to do that collective work with them (Rousculp 58). I believe that this would not have been possible (or at least as successful) without the sense of belonging that was built in the OWG community the prior semester.

These examples are representative of a larger trend that appeared in OWG over the course of the spring 2021 semester. The feedback practices of the group served to strengthen OWG's value for members and the bonds between them, as described in five contributions about feedback in the four collaborative field texts from that semester. (As stated earlier, our group's feedback practices were mentioned only *once* in the two collaborative field texts from the fall.) For example, in the March 2021 collaborative field text, one writer wrote that their favorite part of OWG is "when we share our writing and appreciate one another because it makes me feel good." In that same field text, another writer called the feedback in OWG "healthy" and "constructive." I think it's important to highlight these positive associations with feedback for the adult undergraduate writers in OWG because they help explain how the Elbow-inspired sharing and feedback practices of OWG contribute to a sense of confidence and potential that the individual writers feel with regard to both themselves and the pieces they produce.

For example, in another collaborative field text from the spring of 2021, an OWG member wrote about the connection between peer feedback and their writerly self-efficacy: "I like that I can reach the readers in the group, all in their own ways. I also enjoy when they like my language, as I tend to overexplain things in my speech; it seems to be well received within the group, as far as my writing goes." This writer specifically acknowledges, and enjoys learning, how different members of OWG understand and react to the writing they share; they even come to view what they previously saw as a negative writing trait—overexplaining—as a positive one, given how it was received by other group members. Similarly, a contribution to a collaborative field text from April 2021 reads,

> Not long ago I got a compliment from someone in the group she told me . . . that now I put more details in my writings and that she loves my style. Listening to those comments helps me to keep improving and also the feedback that I receive helps me to add more or shape my writing better because I know this community really cares for me so they are very honest and that helps me a lot.

Not only does the compliment this person received demonstrate a recognition of this writer's increasing mastery of, or facility with, an aspect of their writing and thus engage in social persuasion that affirms this writer's prowess—significant sources of writerly self-efficacy—but this writer also recognizes the positive impact that feedback they receive in OWG has on their writing. Furthermore, this writer's contribution to this field text names an important and foundational element of OWG that enhances the value of feedback that writers in the group receive: this "community really cares for me." Feedback in OWG is an act of caring and therefore of love and respect. The training in reader- and writer-based feedback techniques—built upon members' sense of belonging in OWG—helped amplify their love and respect for one another and the group.

Additionally, feedback in OWG brings members not only feelings of being cared for but also confidence in their writerly styles and in their capacity to improve. When OWG writers listen to another member's writing and provide the feedback requested by that person, they are able to comment on the effectiveness of the piece as well as demonstrate their responsibility for and commitment to that writer's self-efficacy and growth. For example, one contributor to the March 2021 collaborative field text wrote, "We are mainly a positive bunch, and there's constructive criticism, which helps us become better writers in general. I've been told I'm too wordy, which isn't frowned down upon in the group, and that helps my writing self esteem, which helps me share more with the group." Throughout the spring 2021 collaborative field texts, feedback is frequently cited as members' favorite part of OWG because, as one person wrote, "it helps me to grow" (March 2021 collaborative field text). Another writer shared in the March 2021 field text, "I don't like to be the center of attention, so I try to lift others to that point, help them be comfortable." This comment makes clear that the sharing and feedback practices in OWG, augmented by the training workshop facilitated early in the spring semester, are opportunities that encourage members to demonstrate their love and respect for one another. As is apparent from these field text contributions, OWG members trust one another to listen and engage authentically with good intentions because they feel that they *belong* in the group— because they love OWG. That sense of belonging—built upon a foundation of love and a rhetoric of respect—helps OWG and the writers in it to flourish.

Conclusion

In conclusion, OWG's sharing and feedback practices help the group operate with love and a rhetoric of respect: they offer opportunities for members to have meaningful mastery experiences and celebrate those with one another; have vicarious experiences through pieces of writing with which they identify and which they can aspire to emulate; share and collaboratively address emotional and physical experiences that writing can bring up; and provide one another with social support (or social persuasion, according to Bruning and Kauffman) that helps members remember that their voices and stories are important. However, a sense of community—of belonging—is at the heart of the success of OWG and the growth of the writers in it.

Writers in OWG began with the shared formative experience of my community partner Venture's humanities-based course; and while not all members took the course at the same time, OWG extends the sense of community the Venture course builds by providing a collaborative writing community for participants after they graduate from Venture. All members have the foundational experience of reading and writing about the same material, participating in similar activities with the same instructors, and completing the two-semester course. But the Venture course also establishes a foundation that OWG extends, a foundation articulated by a contributor to the March 2021 collaborative field text: "I feel OWG is an even playing field for us all, as we all relate to being low income/on the poverty line." These baseline experiences are integral to OWG members feeling that the group is "a safe place for our thoughts, feelings, and ideas to be shared with like minded individuals" (April 2021 collaborative field text). This is the kind of setting necessary for the growth of writerly self-efficacy: writers learn best from other writers with whom they can strongly identify or whom they aspire to emulate (Bruning and Kauffman 161; Elbow xii). Therein lies the strength of Elbow's teacherless writing workshop model for adult undergraduate students. This model helped encourage OWG writers to exercise agency when giving and receiving feedback, as represented by Sol's description of what she's learned from OWG in our one-on-one interview: "I learned how to give feedback. I learned how to receive feedback, which was another thing. How to ask for a feedback, like being specific, what do I want?"

Asking for the feedback a writer wants and/or is ready for requires courage and trust. As demonstrated above, writers in OWG practiced this in a space that was built with love and respect and in which they felt they belonged. This led to positive associations with sharing and feedback that worked against the previous negative experiences with writing in academic and professional settings that many members had previous to encountering Venture and OWG. The sharing and feedback practices in OWG are enactments of love and respect for members of the group; this in turn deepens members' sense of belonging and sets in motion an iterative cycle that strengthens the bonds within OWG and members' appreciation of it.

I'd like to end by sharing three takeaways about adult learners' writerly self-efficacy across the curriculum that were yielded by my experience learning about and building upon sharing and feedback practices with members of OWG: (1) productive and kind sharing and feedback are not only about specific actions and next steps but are also about cultivating a sense of belonging; (2) building community and augmenting writerly self-efficacy often go hand-in-hand; and (3) love and mutual respect provide a strong foundation for giving and receiving good, informed feedback and can help writers remember that we are all humans seeking acceptance and appreciation. These takeaways are especially relevant to adult undergraduate writers because promoting love, respect, and belonging in and through sharing and feedback practices helps acknowledge adult learners' various academic experiences and considerable life experiences, proving that these are important values to recognize and practice in diverse writing classrooms.

Works Cited

Adler-Kassner, Linda, and Elizabeth Wardle, editors. *Naming What We Know: Threshold Concepts of Writing Studies*. Utah State University Press, 2015.

Bruning, Roger H., and Douglas F. Kauffman. "Self-Efficacy Beliefs and Motivation in Writing Development." *Handbook of Writing Research, Second Edition*, edited by Charles A. MacArthur et al., Guilford Press, 2016, pp. 160–173.

Brown, Sherry Miller. "Strategies that Contribute to Nontraditional/Adult Student Development and Persistence." *PAACE Journal of Lifelong Learning*, vol. 11, 2002, pp. 67–76.

"Digest of Education Statistics, 2018." Edited by Thomas D Snyder, *National Center for Education Statistics (NCES)*, U.S. Department of Education, Dec. 2019, nces.ed.gov/programs/digest/d18/.

Elbow, Peter. *Writing without Teachers*. 2nd ed., Oxford University Press, 1998.

Graff, Harvey J. *The Literacy Myth: Literacy and Social Structure in the Nineteenth-Century City*. Academic Press, 1979.

Harris, Joseph. "The Idea of Community in the Study of Writing." *College Composition and Communication*, vol. 40, no. 1, 1989, pp. 11–22. *JSTOR*, https://doi.org/10.2307/358177. Accessed 23 May 2024.

Highberg, Nels P., et al. "Introduction: Writing Groups as Literary Events." *Writing Groups Inside and Outside the Classroom*, edited by Beverly J. Moss et al., Routledge, 2004, pp. 1–13.

hooks, bell. "The Practice of Love." *Writing Beyond Race: Living Theory and Practice*, Routledge, 2013, pp. 191–199.

Lundberg, Carol A., et al. "Sources of Social Support and Self-Efficacy for Adult Students." *Journal of College Counseling*, vol. 11, no. 1, 2008, pp. 58–72.

Mathieu, Paula, et al., editors. *Circulating Communities: The Tactics and Strategies of Community Publishing*. Lexington Books, 2011.

Mathieu, Paula, et al. "Question of Time: Publishing and Group Identity in the *StreetWise* Writers Group." *Writing Groups Inside and Outside the Classroom*, edited by Beverly J. Moss et al., Routledge, 2014, pp. 151–169.

Nichols, Amy McCleese, and Bronwyn T. Williams. "Centering Partnerships: A Case for Writing Centers as Sites of Community Engagement." *Community Literacy Journal*, vol. 13, no. 2, 2019, p. 88–106. Project MUSE, https://doi.org/10.1353/clj.2019.0009. Accessed 23 May 2024.

Pajares, Frank, and Gio Valiante. "Self-Efficacy Beliefs and Motivation in Writing Development." *Handbook of Writing Research, First Edition*, edited by Charles A. MacArthur et al., Guilford Press, 2006, pp. 158-170.

Perry, Kristen H., et al. "The 'Ofcourseness' of Functional Literacy: Ideologies in Adult Literacy." *Journal of Literacy Research*, vol. 50, no. 1, 2018, pp. 74–96.

Rousculp, Tiffany. *Rhetoric of Respect: Recognizing Change at a Community Writing Center*. Conference on College Composition and Communication of the National Council of Teachers of English, 2014.

Rowan, Karen, and Alexandra J. Cavallaro. "Toward a Model for Preparatory Community Listening." *Community Literacy Journal*, vol. 13, no. 1, 2018, p. 23–36.

Schrantz, James Lee. *Teaching Composition to Nontraditional Students: Intertextuality and Textual Development*. 1996. Texas Christian University, PhD dissertation.

Westbrook, Evelyn. "Community, Collaboration, and Conflict: The Community Writing Group as Contact Zone." *Writing Groups Inside and Outside the Classroom*, edited by Beverly J. Moss et al., Routledge, 2014, pp. 229–249.

Contributors

Yaseen Abdul-Malik is a 4th grade elementary school teacher in Durham, North Carolina. He serves on several writing and reading curriculum committees and runs several after-school tutoring sessions for struggling students. He received his CELTA certification from Cambridge University and his bachelor's degree from North Carolina Central University.

Sarah Blackstone is the Assistant Director for Analytics & Research at James Madison University. She has expertise in research methodology, survey research, traditional and advanced quantitative modeling techniques and data science.

Lucy Bryan is a Visiting Assistant Professor of English and Journalism at Denison University. She spent nine years as a faculty member in the James Madison University Writing Center, where she served as the liaison to the College of Health and Behavioral Studies. She is the author of *In Between Places: A Memoir in Essays*. Her scholarship, interviews, and creative writing have appeared in a range of publications, including the *Writing Center Journal*, *EcoTheo Review*, *Burningword Literary Journal*, and *Earth Island Journal*.

Patrick Coleman is on the faculty at St. John's College in Annapolis, Maryland, where he teaches throughout their program of liberal education.

Tara Coleman is a Professor of English at LaGuardia Community College, part of the City University of New York, where she currently serves as co-director of the writing program. She regularly leads professional development for first-year writing and ALP faculty. Her research interests include language justice and critical reading in the composition classroom, with a particular focus on the interrelation between institutional structures and individual pedagogies.

Solaire Finkenstaedt-Quinn is the evaluation specialist for Student Success Initiative at the University of Michigan. Prior to this position she was the MWrite Program and Research Manager at the University of Michigan. Her research in that role focused on how writing-to-learn supports student engagement with disciplinary content and reasoning. She has published broadly across journals including *Assessing Writing*, *Chemistry Education Research and Practice*, and the *International Journal for the Scholarship of Teaching and Learning*.

Stefanie Frigo, PhD is Professor of English Language and Linguistics at North Carolina Central University, where she teaches in the Department of Language and Literature and coordinates the Interdisciplinary Studies degree program. Her research centers on the experiences of minority and adult learner students as they navigate the world of higher education. Her work has appeared in *Leadership Exchange, Perspectives in Undergraduate Research & Mentoring, SAGE Research Methods, Journal of Student Success in Writing* and *Across the Disciplines*, and in books from Utah State University Press and Linus Learning Publishing.

Collie Fulford is an associate professor at the State University of New York at Buffalo, where she serves as the writing program administrator. Her research on writing, writers, research methods, and writing programs has appeared in *Pedagogy, WPA: Writing Program Administration, Across the Disciplines, Journal of Effective Teaching in Higher Education,* and in several edited collections.

Dayna Henry is the assistant director of scholarship programs at the Center for Faculty Innovation and associate professor of health sciences at James Madison University. She has been teaching college courses since 2004 across a variety of programs and institutions. Her research is focused on sexuality education and the scholarship of teaching and learning.

Mary Her is a senior majoring in sociology at California State University, Sacramento, graduating in Fall 2024. She brings a rich perspective to her studies, drawing on her life experience as a returning student with a deep appreciation for cultural narratives and social structures. Currently enrolled in a writing-intensive course in children's literature. Mary explores how stories shape identity and community for young readers, with a focus on inclusive narratives and gender portrayals. She is actively involved in her community through her work at Hearts and Hands Counseling, and her research spans topics like family caregiving in Sacramento and the links between education and career opportunities.

Jamie Hudson is a graduate of Boise State University, where she focused on technical communication. She was an Undergraduate Research and Creative Activities grant recipient and was invited to share her research in multiple undergraduate research poster presentations. She hopes her research will help improve access to experiential education opportunities for adult learners in the university setting. She has worked at a local children's hospital for over seventeen years, where she has recently published over 40 articles for internal and external company communication. Her work has also been published in *Eagle* and *Greenbelt* magazines.

Anna Maria Johnson is a lecturer in the School of Writing, Rhetoric and Technical Communication at James Madison University, located in Virginia's Shenandoah Valley. She has been teaching first-year writing courses since 2014 and, since 2023, advises the student-produced undergraduate journal RHETTECH. Her study on using commonplace books in a first-year writing classroom was published in *Pedagogy* in 2021. Her professional research focuses are on rhetorical reading and writing, collaborative writing, environmental and place-based writing, writing and designing for environmental organizations, and instructional design. She is a faculty fellow with JMU's Ethical Reasoning in Action.

Gabrielle Isabel Kelenyi is an assistant professor of English at Lafayette College, where she teaches about writing and rhetoric. She studies and practices community-engaged writing research about self-efficacy, antiracism and activism in writing, composition pedagogy, and community literacies. In her teaching and research, she centers writers' personal knowledge as a valuable base from which to learn and write. Kelenyi is a co-editor of Coda: Community Writing and Creative Work in *Community Literacy Journal*.

Lacie Knight is a technical writer at Clever Devices, a company providing cloud-based ITS and planning and scheduling solutions for public transport providers of all sizes. She assists in the creation of user manuals, training materials, and instructional e-learning courses.

Kendon Kurzer is a continuing lecturer at the University of California, Davis, where he was the Associate Director of Undergraduate Writing Across the Curriculum for four years and teaches developmental writing (frequently for multilingual students) and upper-division writing courses for engineering, business, food science, education, and future medical students. He is also a part-time lecturer at California State University, Sacramento, where he teaches across all writing courses and English grammar and pedagogy classes for future teachers. His work has appeared in *TESOL Quarterly*, *Assessing Writing*, and the *WAC Journal*, among other journals and edited collections.

Natasha J. Lee is a senior undergraduate at the University of California, Davis, majoring in Cognitive Science and minoring in Education and Professional Writing. Her research interests include curriculum design, writing education, and student mindset. She plans to attend graduate school in Education.

Adrienne Long, is a business analyst and a former adult learner. She earned a bachelor's degree in psychology from North Carolina Central University in 2021. While in school, she participated in adult writing andl literacy research of adult learners. She also founded and led the Adult Learner Student Organization until graduation.

Amy Macias-Stowe works as an Administrative Service Coordinator II with Sacramento State University. She handles the event coordination and communications for the dean's office in the College of Natural Sciences & Mathematics. Amy is an academic resumer who is majoring in communication studies and minoring in Spanish. Her intentions are to continue with her degrees while expanding her career in Events & Communications within Sacramento State University. In her spare time, Amy is also an active member of a writing group and enjoys creating fiction and poetry.

Nieva Manalo is a registered nurse and a student at Sacramento State University, Sacramento, where she is currently completing the nursing portion of her bachelor's degree. She is a participant and contributor to this journal, marking her first contribution to a publication.

Megan Mericle is a Marion L. Brittain Fellow at the Georgia Institute of Technology, where she teaches in the Writing and Communication Program. Her work explores science communication in public contexts as well as writing across the curriculum interventions. She has previously published in *Across the Disciplines* and the *American Society for Engineering Education* proceedings with her Writing Across Engineering and Science research team collaborators.

Stuart Parrish wrote for the Triangle Digital Humanities Institute in 2019. He completed research training at the International Conference on Spirituality and Health, Duke University, 2023. He completed trainings with John Evans in Expressive Writing at Duke Integrative Medicine, including "Writing for Resilience through the COVID Pandemic." He is a once and future caregiver now songwriting, composing poetry and music, and performing live—integrating practice as research.

Alicia Romero is a Lecturer III of statistics at the University of Michigan, where she has been teaching for over ten years. She coordinates and teaches the introduction to statistics course, one of the largest courses at the university, with an enrollment of approximately 1,900 students each semester. In her role, she also manages a team of about eighty graduate and undergraduate students who support the course and enhance the learning experience for students.

Ginger Shultz is an associate professor at the University of Michigan, where she serves as Associate Chair of Education and Development in the Department of Chemistry and co-PI for the MWrite program. Her research on writing to learn in science has appeared in journals including *Written Communication, Science Education*, and *Chemistry Education Research and Practice*.

Isabella Sperry is a third-year student at the University of Michigan, where she is studying biology, health, and society with a focus on medical anthropology. She has been a Writing Fellow for statistics for three years.

Thomas Kelly is a self-employed carpenter. He is flirting with his first novel in Durham, North Carolina.

Lacey Wootton is a Hurst Senior Professorial Lecturer, Emerita, at American University, where she taught first-year writing and composition pedagogy. Her work has appeared in *CCC Forum* and in edited collections on academic labor and contingency.

Julie Zilles is a Research Associate Professor in the Department of Crop Sciences at the University of Illinois Urbana-Champaign. In addition to research at the intersection of microbiology, agriculture, and environmental engineering, she leads the Writing Across Engineering and Science team, which applies a transdisciplinary action research approach to the interfaces between writing studies and STEM classes and curricula.

Dominique Zino is a professor of English at LaGuardia Community College (CUNY), where she teaches composition and co-directs the writing program. Her articles on WAC and writing program development have appeared in *Teaching English in the Two-Year College* and the *WPA Journal*. She is co-editor of the *Journal of Basic Writing*.

the WAC Journal

SUBSCRIPTIONS

The WAC Journal is an open-access, blind, peer-viewed journal published annually by Clemson University, Parlor Press and the WAC Clearinghouse. It is published annually in print by Parlor Press and Clemson University. Digital copies of the journal are simultaneously published at The WAC Clearinghouse in PDF format for free download, http://wac.colostate.edu/journal/. Print subscriptions support the ongoing publication of the journal and make it possible to offer digital copies as open access.

- One year: $25
- Three years: $65
- Five years: $95

You can subscribe to *The WAC Journal* and pay securely by credit card or PayPal online at http://www.parlorpress.com/wacjournal. Or you can send your name, email address, and mailing address along with a check (payable to Parlor Press) to

Parlor Press
3015 Brackenberry Drive
Anderson SC 29621

Subcribe to the
WAC Journal

Clemson University   WAC Clearinghouse

PARLOR PRESS
EQUIPMENT FOR LIVING

Now with Parlor Press!

Studies in Rhetorics and Feminism
    New Series Editors: Jessica Enoch and Sharon Yam

Critical Conversations in Higher Education Leadership
    Series Editor: Victor E. Taylor

New Releases

Writing Proposals and Grants 3e by Richard Johnson-Sheehan and Paul Thompson Hunter

Rhetorics of Evidence: Science – Media – Culture edited by edited by Olaf Kramer and Michael Pelzer

Kenneth Burke's Rhetoric of Identification by Tilly Warnock

The Forever Colony by Victor Villanueva

Keywords in Making edited by Jason Tham

Inclusive Aims: Rhetoric's Role in Reproductive Justice edited by Heather Brook Adams and Nancy Myers

Not Playing Around: Feminist and Queer Rhetorics in Videogames by Rebecca Richards

Design for Composition: Inspiration for Creative Visual and Multimodal Projects by Sohui Lee and Russell Carpenter

Forthcoming in 2025

Rhetorical Reception: One Hundred and Fifty Years of Arguing with Sex in Education by Carolyn Skinner

City Housekeeping: Women's Labor Rhetorics and Spaces for Solidarity, 1886–1911 by Liane Malinowski

Check Out Our Website!

Discounts, blog, open access titles, instant downloads, and more.

www.parlorpress.com

WAC Journal **Discount:** Use WAC30 at checkout to receive a 30% discount on all titles not on sale through August 31, 2025.

www.ingramcontent.com/pod-product-compliance
Lightning Source LLC
Chambersburg PA
CBHW031436160426
43195CB00010BB/754